Lecture Notes
in Business Information Processing   101

Series Editors

Wil van der Aalst
Eindhoven Technical University, The Netherlands
John Mylopoulos
University of Trento, Italy
Michael Rosemann
Queensland University of Technology, Brisbane, Qld, Australia
Michael J. Shaw
University of Illinois, Urbana-Champaign, IL, USA
Clemens Szyperski
Microsoft Research, Redmond, WA, USA

T0213460

Joaquim Filipe
José Cordeiro (Eds.)

Web Information Systems and Technologies

7th International Conference, WEBIST 2011
Noordwijkerhout, The Netherlands, May 6-9, 2011
Revised Selected Papers

 Springer

Volume Editors

Joaquim Filipe
Institute for Systems and Technologies
of Information, Control and Communication (INSTICC)
and
Instituto Politécnico de Setúbal (IPS)
Department of Systems and Informatics
Setúbal, Portugal
E-mail: joaquim.filipe@estsetubal.ips.pt

José Cordeiro
Institute for Systems and Technologies
of Information, Control and Communication (INSTICC)
and
Instituto Politécnico de Setúbal (IPS)
Department of Systems and Informatics
Setúbal, Portugal
E-mail: jcordeir@est.ips.pt

ISSN 1865-1348   e-ISSN 1865-1356
ISBN 978-3-642-28081-8   e-ISBN 978-3-642-28082-5
DOI 10.1007/978-3-642-28082-5
Springer Heidelberg Dordrecht London New York

Library of Congress Control Number: 2011945632

ACM Computing Classification (1998): H.3.5, J.1, K.4.4, H.5, D.2

Typesetting: Camera-ready by author, data conversion by Scientific Publishing Services, Chennai, India

Printed on acid-free paper

Springer is part of Springer Science+Business Media (www.springer.com)

Preface

The present book includes extended and revised versions of a set of selected papers from the WEBIST 2011 (the 7th International Conference on Web Information Systems and Technologies), held in Noordwijkerhout, The Netherlands, in 2011, and organized by the Institute for Systems and Technologies of Information, Control and Communication (INSTICC), in cooperation with and ACM SIGMIS.

The purpose of the WEBIST series of conferences is to bring together researchers, engineers and practitioners interested in the technological advances and business applications of Web-based information systems. The conference has five main tracks, covering different aspects of Web Information Systems, including Internet Technology, Web Interfaces and Applications, Society, e-Business and e-Government, Web Intelligence and Web Security.

WEBIST 2011 received 156 paper submissions from 43 countries on all continents. A double-blind review process was enforced, with the help of more than 116 experts from the International Program Committee; each of them specialized in one of the main conference topic areas. After reviewing, 14 papers were selected to be published and presented as full papers and 38 additional papers, describing work-in-progress, as short papers. Furthermore, 36 papers were presented as posters. The full-paper acceptance ratio was 12%, and the total oral paper acceptance ratio was 45%.

The papers included in this book were selected from those with the best reviews taking also into account the quality of their presentation at the conference, assessed by the Session Chairs. Therefore, we hope that you find the papers included in this book interesting, and we trust they may represent a helpful reference for all those who need to address any of the research areas mentioned above.

We wish to thank all those who supported and helped to organize the conference. On behalf of the conference Organizing Committee, we would like to thank the authors, whose work mostly contributed to a very successful conference, and to the members of the Program Committee, whose expertise and diligence were instrumental in ensuring the quality of final contributions. We also wish to thank all the members of the Organizing Committee whose work and commitment was invaluable. Last but not least, we would like to thank Springer for their collaboration in getting this book to print.

October 2011

Joaquim Filipe
José Cordeiro

Organization

Conference Chair

Joaquim Filipe   Polytechnic Institute of Setúbal / INSTICC, Portugal

Program Chair

José Cordeiro   Polytechnic Institute of Setúbal / INSTICC, Portugal

Organizing Committee

Sérgio Brissos	INSTICC, Portugal
Helder Coelhas	INSTICC, Portugal
Andreia Costa	INSTICC, Portugal
Patrícia Duarte	INSTICC, Portugal
Liliana Medina	INSTICC, Portugal
Carla Mota	INSTICC, Portugal
Raquel Pedrosa	INSTICC, Portugal
Vitor Pedrosa	INSTICC, Portugal
Daniel Pereira	INSTICC, Portugal
João Teixeira	INSTICC, Portugal
José Varela	INSTICC, Portugal
Pedro Varela	INSTICC, Portugal

Program Committee

Silvia Abrahão, Spain
Ron Addie, Australia
Margherita Antona, Greece
Valeria De Antonellis, Italy
Liliana Ardissono, Italy
Ismailcem Budak Arpinar, USA
Elarbi Badidi, UAE
Matteo Baldoni, Italy
Panagiotis D. Bamidis, Greece
Denilson Barbosa, Canada
Cristina Baroglio, Italy
Orlando Belo, Portugal
Maria Bielikova, Slovak Republic
Yevgen Borodin, USA

François Bry, Germany
Sonja Buchegger, Sweden
Maria Claudia Buzzi, Italy
Elena Calude, New Zealand
John Carroll, USA
Nunzio Casalino, Italy
Michel Chaudron, The Netherlands
Shiping Chen, Australia
Weiqin Chen, Norway
Evangelos Christou, Greece
Weiqin Chen, Norway
Evangelos Christou, Greece
Chin-Wan Chung, Korea, Republic of
Christophe Claramunt, France

Auxiliary Reviewers

Maxim Davidovsky, Ukraine
Elton Domnori, Italy
Adrián Fernández, Spain
Patricia Fish, Brazil
Zhaochen Guo, Canada
Alexander Hoole, Canada
Slinger Jansen, The Netherlands
Filipe Mesquita, Canada

Silvia Rota, Italy
Federica Sarro, Italy
Alexander Semenov, Finland
Diego Serrano, Canada
Cleyton Slaviero, Brazil
Maurizio Tesconi, Italy
Patricia Victor, Belgium

Invited Speakers

Ivan Ivanov   SUNY Empire State College, USA
Tony Shan   Keane Inc., USA
Donald Ferguson   CA Technologies, USA
Marten Van Sinderen   University of Twente, The Netherlands
Barry Smyth   CLARITY Centre for Sensor Web
                           Technologies/University College Dublin,
                           Ireland
Eric van Heck   Erasmus University Rotterdam,
                           The Netherlands

Table of Contents

Invited Speakers

Cloud Computing in Education: The Intersection of Challenges and Opportunities

Ivan I. Ivanov

State University of New York, Empire State College, Long Island Center, NY 11788, U.S.A.
Ivan.Ivanov@esc.edu

Abstract. In the last few years, in spite of concerns about the hype, cloud computing has expanded steadily both horizontally – across industries, and vertically – in organizations' technology stacks. Most technologies that enable cloud services existed prior to cloud computing's existence, although these days they rejuvenate, evolve and stimulate the computational ecosystem transformations. Actually the radical change for organizations is in rethinking and reengineering their traditional IT resources advancing them with cloud architectures and implementing services based on cloud computing delivery models. The change is underway on a large scale: from vendors and developers to providers and customers, and the key-issues of "cloudiness" are not only in economics and management, but in provisioning, interoperability and security of the integrated services.

The Cloud Computing phenomenon likewise creates exciting challenges and opportunities for the entire educational system. For faculty, students, administration, and IT professionals it is a thrilling journey driven by many agendas—cost cutting, delivering dynamic mobile and interactive computational services, utilizing and leveraging integrated IT infrastructures and systems. This talk will explore the impact of cloud computing on the educational socio-technical system and will provide the author's experience in strategizing and utilizing cloud-based applications and services.

Keywords: Cloud computing, Virtualization, On-demand services, Cloud-based services, On-line learning systems.

1   Introduction

In the last few years, cloud computing has expanded steadily both horizontally – across industries, and vertically– in organizations' information technology stack such as raw computing and storage, databases and system's utilities, e-collaborative tools and enterprise applications. Insightful businesses and organizations grasp the "cloud" ideas discerning what the cloud computing services and models are and how they can utilize them as vendors, providers, or users to create a competitive advantage.

Naturally, as it is with any imaginative idea, the "cloud" and its technologies suffer from confusion and hype. In the latest Gartner's Hype Cycle for Emerging Technologies from 2010, the cloud computing and cloud/web platforms overall just topped the peak of inflated expectations, while private cloud computing is still in rising curve [1].

J. Filipe and J. Cordeiro (Eds.): WEBIST 2011, LNBIP 101, pp. 3–16, 2012.

Although there is substantial interest in the scalability and cost efficiency of cloud computing services, most organizations are still approaching this development cautiously until they have a more complete picture of the risks involved. Competing vendors and lack of standardization, various security threats and undefined risks evolving new business and delivering models, and ambiguous "cloudness" services are slowing down overall the adoption. In spite of present concerns, the most recent Gartner's worldwide survey of executives reveals an increasingly faster than originaly expected, implementation of cloud services. While recently only 3 percent of CIOs reported running their IT services in the cloud, over the next four years the expectations are this number will rise up to 43 percent [2].

The Cloud Computing phenomenon likewise creates exciting challenges and opportunities for the entire educational system. For faculty, students, administration, and IT professionals it is a thrilling journey driven by many agendas – cost cutting, delivering dynamic mobile and interactive computational services, utilizing and leveraging integrated IT infrastructures and systems. The immense economic demands in the last several years, in conjunction with the immediate reduction of upfront capital and operational costs when cloud-based services are employed, increase the speed and the scale of cloud computing adoption at educational institutions.

In the next sections, the IT Scale of Changes and the Impact of Cloud Computing development on the educational socio-technical system are explored in greater details. The findings are based on interviews with IT leading professionals from the US Higher Education system, and the author's experience in strategizing and utilizing cloud-based applications and services for teaching, learning, research and creative inquiry.

2   The Scale of IT Changes

The radical change for organizations is in rethinking and reengineering their traditional IT resources. The process of change starts with answering questions such as: *"Where, and How does the IT Adds Value in the Higher Education Institution (HEI)?" "What IT academic community needs to meet the growing requirements within shrinking budgets?" "Would IT advance with cloud architectures and integrated cloud-based services, and When?"*

This range of questions could be broader; however, answering to these considerations can help us to define and understand the scale of changes already in progress: from vendors and developers to providers and customers. The critical challenges, and, in the same time imperative opportunities for HEI are how to keep the pace with the rapid proliferation of emerging technologies, portable information resources and tools, and to balance the effects and magnitude of changes within the unadventurous educational ecosystem.

2.1   IT in the Organizational Context of HEI

To explore the complexity of the questions and to evade overoptimistic expectations and benefits when employing new technologies and service models, a formal approach of evaluating IT in the organizational context can be applied. In the "Information Systems for Managers" text, the author Gabriele Piccoli emphasizes IT as a critical component of a formal, sociotechnical information system designed to collect, process, store and, distribute information [3].

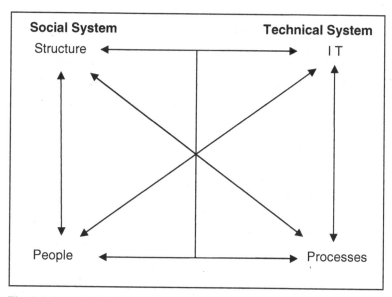

Fig. 1. Information Systems primary components as a Sociotechnical System [3]

The notion of this definition is based on the Sociotechnical theory work developed by Tavistock Institute in London in mid 50-ties and 60-ties. The IT Sociotechnical approach not only visualizes the concept, but reveals the impact of new technologies and processes on the entire work system, and the dependencies and interactions between all other facets and components of the sociotechnical system.

According to Piccoli we can represent any organizational Information System as a Sociotechnical system which comprises four primary components that must be balanced and work together to deliver the information processing functionalities required by the organization to fulfill its information needs. (Figure 1) The IS Sociotechnical model validates the most important driving forces within organizations. However, the model should evolve from micro to macro level to reflect crucial influences of the external environment, especially when we analyze the role of IT in the educational domain.

The specifics of educational organizations' sociotechnical system can be understood better through analyzing the main mission of the HEIs. While missions are diverse in many ways for different HEIs, all they include three major sets of activities: Educate, Research, and Support Processes (Academic and Administrative).

Every educational organization emphasizes one or another primary set of activities or keeps them in a fair balance based on their type, status and / or market positioning. Nevertheless, all HEIs need to run and support a good variety of IT systems, applications and resources to satisfy the constantly growing stakeholders' requirements. In addition, IT systems and resources in HEIs typically exceed the required range of services, as it is anticipated they provide supplementary capacities for local communities, partnering institutions, or creative initiatives (Figure 2).

The strategic IT development discussions should reflect not only on individualized HEI constrains based on the mentioned above sets of activities, and the sociotechnical

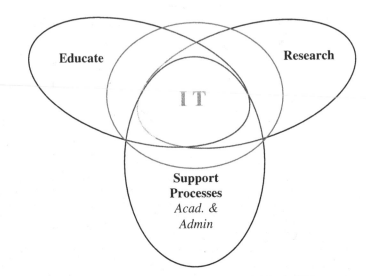

Fig. 2. IT coverage on primary sets of activities in HEI

critical components. In the managerial process of new technology adoption decision, HEI must furthermore consider current trends, important constraints and challenges "that are common to institutions and the educational community as a whole" [4]. In the latest 2011 edition of the Horizon Report, the Advisory Board members defined four common key technology trends as follows:

- The abundance of resources and relationships made accessible via the Internet is increasingly challenging the teaching community, and there is a need to revisit the roles of educators in sense-making, coaching and credentialing.
- With immense broader and vast online communications and content development, people expect to be able to work, learn, and study whenever and wherever they want.
- The world of work is increasingly mobile and collaborative, giving rise to reflection about the way student projects are structured.
- The technologies we use are increasingly cloud-based, and our notions of IT support are decentralized.

Additionally, in report indicates several more critical challenges, three of which directly relate to new technology implementations in the educational domain:

- Digital media literacy is a key skill in every discipline and profession. However the progress is slow and aggravates by the fact that technologies morph and change more quickly at a rate outpacing professional and curriculum development.
- Economic pressures and adoption of new models of education, mainly based on technology advancements, are presenting unprecedented competition to traditional university models. In the distance education survey results from March 2010, U.S. based colleges reported a 22 percent increase for distance education enrollments, substantially higher than the average 2 percent for overall national campus enrolments [5].

- Keeping pace with the rapid proliferation of information, software tools, and devices is challenging for students, faculty and professionals alike.

The listed key trends and critical challenges reveal many new dimensions in addition to the internal constrains, IT professionals and strategists must consider when plan and design their IT services and resources.

2.2   Deliberate IT Transformations

In the last three years all we have experienced the turmoil of a vicious recession while witnessing dramatic technology advances. The educational system has been continuously under pressure not only to cut budgets, but to keep and utilize obsolete systems while having no options in their IT financial plans for new system developments and innovations with emerging technologies. According to IT executives from HEI in the last few years there were practically no CapEx, as the OpEx, mostly staffing and the costs of updates, exhausted entire budgets.

In order to know where and how to begin with IT transformations, a complete analysis of the existing HEI's IT landscape needs to be performed. Additionally, a comprehensive dialog between HEI's stakeholders should examine and lead to answering the previously mentioned three questions.

Along with exploring the first question *"Where and How does IT adds value in the HEI?"* depending on the type and scale of the HEI we may need to examine:

- how the on-premises IT meets the growing needs of services and diverse systems' functionalities;
- could IT efficiency be improved by virtualization and consolidation of on-premises environment;
- what the gain and troublesome effects would be if shared or outsourced services are employed, and how to:
  - measure the risk;
  - control the quality;
  - commence *"Exit strategy"* upon disappointment outcomes.

While investigating the multidimensional aspects of the second question *"What IT academic community needs to meet the growing requirements within shrinking budgets?"* the following critical expectations and requirements should be addressed:

- how to enhance the mobile and to adapt portable applications;
- how significantly the speed of access and the storage volumes should be increased;
- how to provide on-demand capacity for variety of applications;
- What system and / or model would provide cost elasticity leveraging consumption changes?

Specific attention should be focus on the driving forces of emerging mobile technologies and portable applications in the educational realm. The greater demand for these trendy technologies and services are coming primarily from the external environment: current and prospective students, partnering institutions, research grants, and incentive programs.

A comprehensive analysis of the first two questions will thoroughly translate the HEI's strategy and vision and will define the requirements and expectations from the institutional IT domain. The process will result in clarifying and facilitating the third inquiry *"Would the IT advance with cloud architectures and cloud-based services, When, and How?"* Evaluating the third question should not only identify the Technology, but will help specify which Technology and Services should be delivered on-premises and which of them can be obtained off-premises.

The latest 2011 State of Cloud Survey by Information Week [6] shows across industries "… 67% increase in the number of organizations using cloud computing services, from 18% in February 2009 to 30% in October 2010; an additional 13% say they plan to use cloud services in 12 months." One of the key technology trends according to the Horizon Report from 2011 confirms the fact that current technologies in the educational system are increasingly cloud-based, and the notions of IT support are decentralized. While the most forceful driving factors towards cloud-based decisions are initial cost savings, speed to market, speed of innovation, and scalability [4], the truth is that there are many more barriers and concerns the HEI should analyze and consider such as :

- How and when cloud services would deliver strategic value not just incremental cost-savings;
- How to ward off escalating security threats and avoid multitenant data intimidation;
- How to address growing integration complexities and potential channel and interoperability clashes as cloud-based services would be delivered mostly by different on-premises and off-premises providers, and third-party integrators.

A possible approach to analyze any existing and new systems and services, including their relevance to the core sets of HEI activities, is to employ an IT Strategy Map - Figure 3. Every specific or integrated IT application, system or service should be evaluated and positioning on the map according its **strategic importance** to the *Educate*, *Research* and *Support* core activities in the institution. Some of the systems or applications could be intergreted and their strategic importance to improve efficiency and productivity will be greater.

Subsequent to completing the IT Strategy Map phase in the process should be calculating and evaluating the Return on Investments (ROI) and/or Return on Assets (ROA) when new technology and service models are employed. Cloud computing potential to deliver a superior ROA to the institution than the ROA of an organization that owns and operates its own data centers. As ROA indicates how profitable an institution is relative to its total assets, organizations that require large initial investments in physical assets would generally have lower return on assets [7]. However simply comparing ingredient costs of pay-per-use services vs. capital expenditures and operational overheads could create an unrealistic approximation in a long term.

The ROI / ROA phase is very institutional specific and it will require an honest and true costs assessment within a five- to six- year baseline of comparison. A scorecard approach with customizable spreadsheet calculations will provide an accurate representation of the true value of on-premises and off-premises IT solutions.

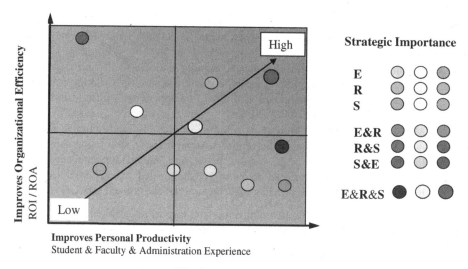

Fig. 3. IT Strategy Map

Developing a new IT strategy and governance model following the above deliberate process will raise both the profile and efficiency of IT within the HEI, and will validate the role of IT in the institution as truly being a mission enabler and driver.

3   Gaining Value of the Cloud

IT architecture evolves over time. In the 1960s, the expensive and labor-intensive monolithic resources were pooled and heavy use was made of virtualization to ensure the very best utilization of them. Today's Cloud is based on foundational concepts that addressed an early need to best leverage computing resources over 40 years ago, taking the concepts of commodity grid computing and virtualization further by allowing self-services, metered usage and more automated dynamic resource and workload management practices.

To design and deliver a future state architecture that captures the promises and the benefits of Cloud Computing, the five core characteristics defined by National Institute of Standards and Technology must be considered [8]:

- **On-demand Self-service:** a consumer can unilaterally provision computing capabilities, such as server time and network storage, as needed automatically without requiring human interaction with service's provider
- **Ubiquitous Network Access:** access to resources in the cloud is available over the network using standard methods in a manner that provides platform-independent access to clients of all types
- **Location Independent Resource Pooling:** the provider's computing resources are pooled to serve all consumers using a multi-tenant model, with different physical and virtual resources dynamically assigned and reassigned according to consumer demand. The customer generally has no control or knowledge over the exact location of the provided resources but may be able to specify location

at a higher level of abstraction (e.g., country, state, or datacenter). Examples of resources include storage, processing, memory, network bandwidth, and virtual machines

- **Rapid Elasticity:** capabilities can be rapidly and elastically provisioned to quickly scale up and rapidly released to quickly scale down. To the consumer, the capabilities available for provisioning often appear to be infinite and can be purchased in any quantity at any time
- **Measured Service:** cloud systems automatically control and optimize resource use by leveraging a metering capability at some level of abstraction appropriate to the type of service (e.g., storage, processing, bandwidth, and active user accounts). Resource usage can be monitored, controlled, and reported providing transparency for both the provider and consumer of the utilized service.

Besides the five core features there are business and logical favorable advances which are a focus for further strategic thoughts toward adopting cloud-based services [9]:

- *Lower Cost.* Consolidated cloud resources operate at higher efficiencies and with greater utilization, often resulting in significant cost reduction. Albeit cloud vendors charge premium for their services, the customers would save money by not paying for services that they aren't using. Additionally some cloud computing deployments lets someone else manage the cloud infrastructure, while the institution will focus on managing their core activities, achieving considerable reductions in IT staffing costs;
- *Ease of Utilizations.* Depending upon the type of services there would be none or minimal hardware and software requirements, upfront costs or adoption time;
- *Quality of Services.* The higher cloud QoS compare to on-premises IT can be obtain under the contract or SLA from the vendor;
- *Reliability.* The scale of cloud resources and their ability to provide load balancing and failover makes them highly reliable, often much more consistent than IT service in a single organization;
- *Simplified Maintenance and Upgrade.* Naturally for centralized systems all patches and upgrades are easily performed and the users always have access to the latest versions;
- *Low Barrier to Entry.* In particular, as upfront CapEx are dramatically reduced no matters of the institutional size, *anyone in* and *because of* cloud computing can be a *giant* at any time.

When exploring the three domains of cloud services model, institutions need to consider not only the capabilities and the economic efficiency of the scale-oriented delivery, but the institutional *comfort with* and possible *resistance to* the idea of third party service provisioning. Cloud initiatives offer promise in the minds of executives and IT professionals alike, but the new delivery models take time to gain acceptance, and there are often technological and organizational inhibitors to adoption reflecting specifics in the socio-technical institutional context.

According to a web-based study comprised over 400 professionals from large companies (1000+) across North America and Europe published by Management Insight Technology, economic factors, and to a lesser extent, better services and

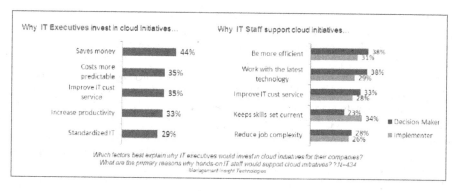

Fig. 4. Why IT Professionals Support Cloud Initiatives [10]

increased productivity are leading executive interests in the cloud. At the same time IT professionals, decision makers, and implementers are enthusiastic to work in the latest technology environment where better technology will lead to greater efficiency, improved services and gaining current skills set [10].

The largest cloud category to date and expecting to keep the lead in the next decade is *Software as a Service* (SaaS). Customers use software applications, such as Learning Management Systems (LMS), CRM or ERP, hosted by a cloud provider and are available over the Internet. The consumer does not manage or control the underlying cloud infrastructure, network, servers, operating systems, storage, or even individual application capabilities. According to Forrester Report "Sizing the Cloud" from 2011, the SaaS revenue will reach in 2011 $21.2 billion from total public cloud share of $25.5 billion. As a result of a strong demand from companies and organizations, Forrester predicts SaaS revenues to elevate up to $92.8 billion by 2016, which would be 26% of the total software market [11]. Leading vendors in this domain are Google (GoogleApps), Salesforce (CRM), Oracle CRM On Demand, Microsoft (Office 365, Dynamics), Workday, Cisco, and Citrix Systems.

While many HEIs are using successfully Google Gmail as an email service for their students, more institutions lean on more sophisticated systems for planning and conducting some of their core educational and business activities. Bryant & Stratton College, a pioneer in career education, utilize Oracle CRM On Demand to create more efficient marketing campaigns [12]. The Oracle cloud-based CRM tracked advertising to perspective students and determined accurate costs for each lead, admission application, and registered attending student. The college benefits from more precise evaluation of marketing programs and from detailed analysis of past campaigns for tech-savvy recent high school graduates as well older returning to schools students. The rapid and steady growth of SaaS will stimulate the growth of PaaS and IaaS services as majority of the SaaS vendors rely on or tie them with their platforms or infrastructures services as well.

Platform as a Service (PaaS) is the third largest cloud delivery model with a market size of $820 million in 2011, with a predicting growth from 2012 on. PaaS is the middleware of the cloud, and customers use infrastructure and programming tools hosted by the service provider to develop their own applications. The customer does not manage or control the underlying cloud infrastructure, but has control over the deployed applications and possibly application hosting environment configurations. Leading PaaS providers are Microsoft (Windows Azure), IBM (Small Business Application Development & Test), Salesforce's Force.com, Google Apps Engine, Tibco, WorkExpress.

The second largest cloud category with a $2.9 billion market size in 2011 is *Infrastructure as a Service* (IaaS). The IaaS provides computing power, storage, archiving, and other fundamental computing resources to an organization with a utility pricing and delivery model. The consumer does not manage or control the underlying cloud infrastructure, however has control over operating systems, storage, deployed applications, and possibly select networking components. The largest vendors in this category are: Amazon Web Services (EC2), Rockspace Cloud, Eucalyptus, GoGrid.

For many institutions the primary question is not related to the delivery models, it is most directed to the purpose of the cloud and the nature of how the cloud is located, in other words - the deployment model. The NIST definition of the four cloud deployment models is as follows [8]:

- *Private Cloud.* The cloud infrastructure is owned or leased by a single organization and is operated solely for that organization. It may be either on- or off-premises;
- *Community Cloud.* The cloud infrastructure is shared by several organizations and supports a specific community that has shared concerns;
- *Public Cloud.* The cloud infrastructure is owned by an organization selling cloud services to the general public or to a large industry group;
- *Hybrid Cloud.* The cloud infrastructure is a composition of two or more clouds (private, community, or public) that remain unique entities but are bound together by standardized or proprietary technology that enables data and application portability.

IT professionals in institutions with a well established and up-to-date data centers are inclined more towards private cloud solutions than to public or other varieties of off-premises cloud services. In Indiana University for example, with their about 1300 virtual servers and dynamic storage capabilities the private cloud architecture is a powerful and efficient data strategy [13]. By deploying internal cloud services on the newly refresh servers at their two data centers, without critical disruption of the institutional sociotechnical system, the university achieved long-term savings, immediate high performance and energy gains, substantial savings related to licensing and staff recruitment and training.

However most executives and financial managers advocate for public clouds as more initial cost-efficient, flexible, and scalable with a global access solution. Not only the cost factor confounds cloud adoption, there are many other internal forces and organizational specifics as it is visible from Figure 5 in favor or against cloud's implementation.

Strategizing the institutional IT solution primarily depends on the type, scale and the targeting market segment. For many educational organizations it might be most appropriate to build a specific hybrid model incorporating internal private cloud for the most sensitive data and critical applications and to off-premises into public or community clouds some less decisive systems and routine applications [14]. Evolving the internal IT infrastructure toward a cloud-like model for supporting the most sensitive and critical business operation at lower risk and higher security will enhance

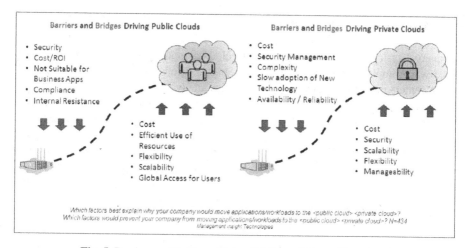

Fig. 5. Barriers and Bridges driving Public vs. Private Cloud [10]

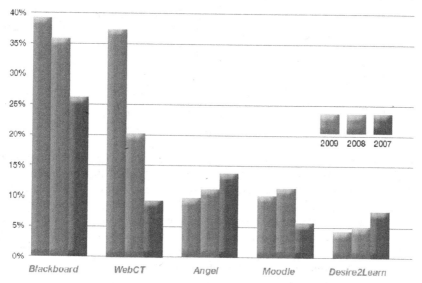

Fig. 6. Learning Management Systems Usage [5]

and facilitate the integration with outside applications running into external clouds. In many HEIs such approach would decrease the risk of disruptive technology and processes changes and the organization will better control its information assets.

Most of the HEIs keep and control in their own data centers students' records and financial systems while widely utilized educational services from external providers such as: on-line course delivering environment – LMS, such as – Blackboard, WebCT, Angel, Moodle, Desire2Learn (Figure 6); student consulting and supporting services such as Smarthinking, E-tutor, Tutorvista; e-collaborative tools such as Elluminate, Wimba, GoToMeeting; customized email services from Google or Microsoft, and back up and archive services from Amazon (S3) or other vendors.

4   Conclusions - Utilizing the Cloud, Deal with Challenges

For many decision makers and professionals, cloud computing represents "a sea change in the way computing will be performed by organizations as computing shifts out of private centers into cloud services." Technologies are available and many best practices are widely shared; the institutions could have unlimited computing resources, elastic infrastructure and more opportunities for new applications. However, how best to tackle the associated challenges in the very traditional educational system?

The optimistic Trends in E-Learning, published by ITC in 2010, highlight not only on the growing demand for distance education and e-learning supporting technologies utilized by HEIs, but also show some major personnel challenges facing faculty, professionals, administrators, and decision makers – Figure 7.

Range for responses 1 = greatest challenge - 7 = least challenging

Challenge	Rank 2009	Rank 2008	Rank 2007	Rank 2006	Rank 2005	Rank 2004
Workload issues	1	1	1	1	1	1
Training	2	2	2	2	3	4
Compensation	5	3	3	3	5	2
Technical support	6	4	5	5	6	5
Buy-in to online instruction	4	5	4	4	4	3
Recruitment	3	6	6	6	2	6
Intellectual property/ownership issues	7	7	7	7	7	7

Fig. 7. Personnel Challenges for Higher Education Institutions [5]

Managing the growth of demanding variety online resources would be possible by providing a balance of on-premises and off-premises supported systems depending on the institutional budgets. Recent critical challenges, illustrated by the survey results, are related to the new institutional processes and the academic and professional personnel. The augmented variety of e-learning supporting technologies and diverse modes of access and delivery leads to a massive faculty load growth, endless training, and demanding recruitment. In many cases emerging technologies, increased options and features creates confusions, destructions and resistance in the institutions – Figure 8. Such projects require a meticulous planning and extensive support not only from the management but from the academic and professional personal in particular.

The new cloud services implications lead to asymmetric competition, speed of innovation and learning, speed to the target audience, and speed of institutional model evolution. The cloud economics cause many institutions and providers to reconsider how they invest and manage large-scale computing resources. While the vast majority of institutions are adopting cloud services and models, especially related to collaborative computing environments, still many adopters consider the highest risks of such projects and they keep their network security ducks in a row in order to leverage the cloud [15]. The organizational commitment would be to use the technology innovation to stretch the institutional core activities and make the educational resources openly accessible at reasonable costs.

Range for responses 1 = greatest challenge 8 = least challenging

Challenge	Rank 2009	Rank 2008	Rank 2007	Rank 2006	Rank 2005	Rank 2004
Support staff needed for training and technical assistance	1	1	1	1	1	1
Adequate student services for distance education students	2	2	2	3	5	2
Adequate assessment of distance education classes (new question)	3					
Operating and equipment budgets	4	3	3	2	2	3
Adequate administrative authority	5	4	5	4	4	5
Faculty acceptance	6	5	4	5	3	4
Adequate space for training and technical assistance	7	6	6	6	7	7
Organizational acceptance	8	7	7	7	6	6
Compliance with HEOA requirements for distance education (new question)	9					
Student acceptance	10	8	8	8	8	8

Fig. 8. Strategic challenges for new learning environment [5]

Ultimately, cloud computing is hovering to make a real impact on educational system, and the society at large. It gives to innovative and smaller institutions a chance to utilize resources and services previously only large and wealthy educational organizations could afford. With the increasing government support and incentive programs, including for education, the cloud computing projections made by Vivek Kundra, Federal CIO are even more important: "The cloud will do for government what the Internet did in the '90s ... I believe it's the future ... It's a fundamental change to the way our government operates by moving to the cloud. Rather than owning the infrastructure, we can save millions ... It's moving technology leaders away from just owning assets, deploying assets and maintaining assets to fundamentally changing the way services are delivered."

As many changes this new mega IT trend and services delivery model may take a while for building institutions' confidence, however like any major concept, it always starts off slowly, but once organizations and society realize the advantages of cloud computing, it will pick up pace rapidly.

References

1. Fenn, J., Gammage, B., Raskino, M.: Gartner's Hype Cycle Special Report for 2010, Gartner, Inc., ID Number: G00205839 (August 2010)
2. Pettey, C.: Gartner Executive Programs Worldwide Survey of More Than 2,000 CIOs Identifies Cloud Computing as a Top Technology Priority for CIOs in 2011, Gartner, Inc., Stamford, Conn. USA (January 2011),
   http://www.gartner.com/it/page.jsp?id=1526414
3. Picolli, G.: Information Systems for Managers: Text and Cases. John Wiley and Sons, Inc., Hoboken (2008)
4. EDUCAUSE and New Media Consortium: The Horizon Report 2011 Edition, The New Media Consortium, Austin, TX , U.S.A (2011)

5. Distance Education Survey Results: Trends in E-Learning: Tracking the Impact of eLearning at Community Colleges. Instructional Technology Council, Washington D.C., U.S.A. (2010)
6. Analytics Report: State of Cloud 2011: Time for Process Maturation. InformationWeek Analytics, Report ID: R1610111 (January 2011)
7. Marks, E., Lozano, R.: Executive's Guide to Cloud Computing. John Wiley and Sons, Inc., Hoboken (2010)
8. Mell, P., Grance, T.: Draft NIST Working Definition of Cloud Computing. National Institute of Standards and Technology, U.S.A (2009),
   http://csrc.nist.gov/groups/SNS/cloud-computing/index.html
9. Sosinsky, B.: Cloud Computing Bible. John Wiley and Sons, Inc., Hoboken (2010)
10. Black, L., Mandelbaum, J., Grover, I., Marvi, Y.: The Arrival of "Cloud Thinking." White Paper, Management Insight Technologies, U.S.A (2010)
11. O'Neill, S.: Forrester: Public Cloud Growth to Surge, Especially SaaS. CIO Magazine (April 26, 2011), http://www.cio.com/article/print/680673
12. Laudon, K., Laudon, J.: Management Information Systems: Managing the Digital Firm. Pearson Education, Inc., Upper Saddle River (2011)
13. Biddick, M.: The Why And How of Private Clouds. InformationWeek (June 05, 2010),
   http://www.informationweek.com/news/hardware/
   data_centers/225300316
14. Ivanov, I.: Emerging Utility and Cloud Computing Models. In: I-WEST 2009. Insticc Press, Portugal (2009)
15. Simon, P.: The Next Wave of Technologies: Opportunities in Chaos. John Wiley and Sons, Inc., Hoboken (2010)

Making Mainstream Web Search Engines More Collaborative

Barry Smyth

CLARITY - Centre for Sensor Web Technologies, School of Computer Science and Informatics
University College Dublin, Dublin, Ireland
firstname.lastname@ucd.ie
http://www.clarity-centre.org

Abstract. Web search engines are perhaps the *killer app* of the modern internet age by providing users with near instant access to the world's information. The success of modern web search engines is due in large part to the ability to handle web-scale information retrieval and also by the sophistication of their algorithmic ranking systems, which combine a variety of measures in order to determine page relevance when it comes to a specific search query. And by and large the heart of web search has remained stable over the past 10 years. However, today researchers are exploring a new approach to supporting web search, once the complements algorithmic ranking techniques by harnessing social signals and supporting a more collaborative view of web search. In this paper we motivate and review recent work in this line of research, including an in-depth case-study of the HeyStaks collaborative search platform.

1 Introduction

Over the course of its first decade the world of the web was one where search engines rule supreme as the primary tools by which users located information online. As conventional information retrieval tools and techniques were adapted to handle the scale and diversity of web content the modern search engine began to crystalize. A key insight in the development of modern web search engines was the realization that conventional term-based techniques, which had worked so well in information retrieval systems, were no longer sufficient to identify relevant content in the web. Simply put, because of the sheer scale and diversity of web content, the words in a page and in a search query, no longer provided a sufficiently clear relevancy signal. The breakthrough came when researchers began to consider the patterns of connectivity between pages and their potential role as a way to identify authoritative pages [4,14]. In short, the combination of term-based methods for page selection and link-based techniques for page ranking proved to be a potent solution to web search and led directly to the mainstream search engines we see today. However, although web search has remained relatively stable over the past decade, this looks set to change as researchers attempt to seek out new techniques to handling some of the many challenges that continue to face web search engines, challenges such as the continued growth of the web, the vague queries that continue to dominate web search, and the ongoing battle between search engines and search engine optimization practices.

J. Filipe and J. Cordeiro (Eds.): WEBIST 2011, LNBIP 101, pp. 17–31, 2012.
© Springer-Verlag Berlin Heidelberg 2012

The quantity and diversity of the information content that is now available online is without precedent and its relentless growth is set to continue as the web continues to evolve to accommodate new forms of content, including the user-generated content [13] of the *social web* and the machine-generated content of the so-called *sensor web* [32]. The popularity of the social web further escalates this issue by making it easy to create and share information at a pace which places strain search engines to locate and index such a fast changing space. The sheer scale and increasing heterogeneity of the modern web introduces for further significant challenges when it comes to providing individual users and communities with access to the right information at the right time. Despite all of the recent developments in search engine technologies, modern search engines continue to struggle when it comes to providing users with fast and efficient access to information. For example, recent studies have highlighted how even today's leading search engines fail to satisfy 50% of user queries [33]. Part of the problem rests with the searchers themselves: with an average of only 2-3 terms [15,38], the typical web search query is often vague with respect to the searcher's true intentions or information needs [37]. Moreover, searchers sometimes choose query terms that are not well represented in the page that they are seeking and so simply increasing the length of queries will not necessarily improve search performance.

In addition to these query-related issues, another challenge that is facing all mainstream search engines is the continuing battle with search engine spam via so-called *black-hat* search engine optimization (SEO) techniques and the rise of the *content farms*. The former involve the manipulation of search engine rankings in order to promote target pages. Indeed so-called content farms have taken SEO strategies to an entirely new level by funding the mass production of content in response to contemporary query trends and then boosting this content in mainstream search rankings via aggressive SEO techniques. The end result of these type of activities for the searcher is that we are increasingly faced with less relevant, lower quality, research results that are boosted by services that seek to manipulate the ranking functions of mainstream search engines. And while search engines can, and do, frequently change their ranking metrics in response to aggressive SEO tactics, this is an arms race that cannot be easily won.

2   On Collaboration in Web Search

Recently two important ideas in web search have emerged as potential solutions to many of these challenges — *personalization* and *collaboration*. These approaches question the core assumptions of mainstream web search engines and suggest important adaptations to conventional web search techniques. The first assumption concerns the *one-size-fits-all* nature of mainstream web search. Simply put, two different users with the same query will, more or less, receive the very same result-list, despite their different preferences — and argues that web search needs to become more *personalized* so that the implicit needs and preferences of searchers can be accommodated [5,7,12,3,16,17,6,24,29,10].

The second assumption concerns the *solitary nature* of web search. Traditionally most web based activities involved isolated interactions between a web user and the online system. However there is the potential for web search to evolve to become a more *social* activity [22,11,9,8], whereby the search efforts of a user might be influenced by the searches of others, potentially leading to a more *collaborative* model of search. This potential for collaboration is made all the more potent by the rise of social networks and the maturation of our online social graphs. These social graphs can be leveraged directly to introduce new forms of collaboration into many different types of web services, including web search. In fact we have already seen how a wide range of systems now exploiting our social graphs for more effective and inclusive applications which harness explicit and implicit connections between individuals; see for example, Last.fm[1], Flickr[2], Wikipedia[3] all of which harness collaboration and sharing to disrupt a range of media markets.

Unsurprisingly then, researchers have recently begun to look towards a new era of *social search* in attempt to unify two distinctive information discovery worlds: the traditional world of web search and the information sharing world of social networks. Only a few years ago, by and large, the majority of people located information of interest through their favourite mainstream search engine. However, recently there has been a very noticeable change in how many web users satisfy their information needs. In addition to web search, many of us are fining relevant information online through our social networks. This is not only a matter of keeping up with the daily lives of our friends and colleagues but also an important way for individuals to locate highly targeted content that is relevant to their long and short-term needs. For example, for many Twitter users, the service is as much about consumed twitter content as it is about generating their own tweets, and many (up to 25% according to a recent survey[4]) of the tweets we read contain links to pages of interest. In this way, our Twitter network plays the role of a social filter that is capable of recommending highly relevant and targeted pages based on our needs and preferences, as reflected by the users we follow. Indeed recent statistics from Twitter claim that its users are explicitly searching tweet content 24 billion times per month[5] as compared to approximately 88 billion queries per month for Google, and less than 10 billion queries per month for Yahoo. Similarly, at the time of writing, Face-Book's own statistics highlight how its users are sharing upwards of 30 billion items of content every month.[6] Many of these items of content would have previously been located through mainstream search engines. Instead, today, they are being accessed via our social networks and, in terms of raw volume of information seeking activity, the social networks are now beginning to compete with mainstream search engines.

The concept of social search has become somewhat muddled in the world of the web. On the one hand there are those approaches that seek to extend search beyond the web of pages and into the world of social networks. In this case social search refers to the indexing and searching our social content (e.g. blog posts, tweets, Facebook status updates, Flickr photos, Quora questions etc.). This is largely a matter for traditional

---

[1] www.last.fm

[2] www.Flickr.com

[3] www.wikipedia.org

[4] http://techcrunch.com/2010/09/14/twitter-seeing-90-million-tweets-per-day/

[5] http://www.boygeniusreport.com/2010/07/07/twitter-handling-24-billion-search-queries-per-month/

[6] http://www.facebook.com/press/info.php?statistics

information retrieval technologies, adapted to the real-time nature of the social web. Recently mainstream search engines like Bing and Google have started to include user-generated content from our social graph within their mainstream search results.

We focus in this work on a particular type of social search, to help people during routine search tasks — that is, when they are using mainstream search engines — by harnessing the recent search experiences of their friends and colleagues via their social networks. The emphasis then is on making the solitary world of web search more collaborative. This relates to recent work in the area of *collaborative information retrieval*, which attempts to capitalize on the potential for collaboration during a variety of information seeking tasks. [34,19,21,36,1]. As part of this we will review the HeyStaks search service (www.heystaks.com) as an example case-study in social search. HeyStaks is designed to add collaborative/social search on top of mainstream search engines, allowing users to search as normal, using their search engine of choice, while benefiting from the past search experiences of their social networks. We will describe how HeyStaks generates result recommendations at search time and present a number of examples of the system in action.

3   Dimensions of Collaborative Web Search

Recent research has found considerable evidence to support the idea that search can be an inherently collaborative process; see for example the work of [25,26,28,27] for examples of collaborative search in specialized information retrieval contexts such as military or medical search tasks. And within a more mainstream search context, recent work by [20] highlights the collaborative nature of general purpose web search. For example, in a survey of just over 200 respondents, clear evidence for collaborative search behaviour emerged. More than 90% of respondents indicated that they frequently engaged in collaboration at the level of the *search process*. 87% of respondents exhibited "back-seat searching" behaviours, where they watched over the shoulder of the searcher to suggest alternative queries. A further 30% of respondents engaged in search coordination activities, by using instant messaging to coordinate searches. Moreover, 96% of users exhibited collaboration at the level of *search products*, that is, the results of searches. For example, 86% of respondents shared the results they had found during searches with others by email. Clearly, even though mainstream search engines, by and large, lack the tools and features to facilitate collaboration during search, there is clear evidence that users implicitly engage in many different forms of collaboration as they search, although. These collaboration "work-arounds" are often frustrating and inefficient by they are are used nonetheless; see [20], . Naturally, this has motivated researchers to consider how different types of collaboration might be supported by future editions of search engines to provide a more natural and supportive environment for collaboration.

It is useful to consider approaches to *collaborative information retrieval* in terms of two important dimensions, *time* — that is, *synchronous* versus *asynchronous* search — and *place* — that is, *co-located* versus *remote* searchers. Co-located systems offer a collaborative search experience for multiple searchers at a single location, typically a single PC (e.g. [1,30]) whereas remote approaches allow searchers to perform their searches at different locations across multiple devices; see e.g. [19,36]. The former enjoy the obvious benefit of an increased facility for direct collaboration that is enabled by the face-to-face nature of co-located search, while the latter offer a greater opportunity for collaborative search. Alternatively, synchronous approaches are characterised by systems that broadcast a "call to search" in which specific participants are requested to engage in a well-defined search task for a well defined period of time; see e.g. [30]. In contrast, asynchronous approaches are characterised by less well-defined, ad-hoc search tasks and provide for a more open-ended approach to collaboration in which different searchers contribute to an evolving search session over an extended period of time; see e.g. [19].

One example of the co-located, synchronous approach to collaborative web search is given by the work of [1]. Their CoSearch system is designed to improve the search experience for co-located users where computing resources are limited; for example, a group of school children having access to a single PC. CoSearch is specifically designed to leverage peripheral devices that may be available (e.g. mobile phones, extra mice etc.) to facilitate distributed control and division of effort, while maintaining group awareness and communication. For example, in the scenario of a group of users collaborating though a single PC, but with access to multiple mice, CoSearch supports a *lead searcher* or *driver* (who has access to the keyboard) with other users playing the role of search *observers*. The former performs the basic search task but all users can then begin to explore the results returned by independently selecting links so that pages of interest are added to a page queue for further review. The CoSearch interface also provides various opportunities for users to associate notes with pages. Interesting pages can be saved and as users collaborate a *search summary* can be created from the URLs and notes of saved pages. In the case where observers have access to mobile phones, CoSearch supports a range of extended interface functionality to provide observers with a richer set of independent functionality via a bluetooth connection. In this way observers can download search content to their mobile phone, access the page queue, add pages to the page queue and share new pages with the group.

The purpose of CoSearch is to demonstrate the potential for productive collaborative web search in resource-limited environments; see Fig. 1. The aim of CoSearch is very much on dividing the search labour while maintaining communication between searchers, and live user studies speak to the success of CoSearch in this regard [1]. The work of [31] is related but focuses on image search tasks using a table-top computing environment, which is well suited to supporting collaboration between co-located users who are searching together. Once again, preliminary studies speak to the potential for such an approach to improve overall search productivity and collaboration, at least in specific types of information access tasks, such as image search, for example. A variation on these forms of synchronous search activities is presented in [30], where the use of mobile devices as the primary search device allows for a remote form of synchronous collaborative search. The iBingo system allows a group of users to collaborate on an image search task with each user using a ipod touch device as their primary search/feedback device (although conventional PCs appear to be just as applicable). Interestingly, where the focus on CoSearch is largely on the division of search labour and communication support, iBingo offers the potential to use relevance feedback from any

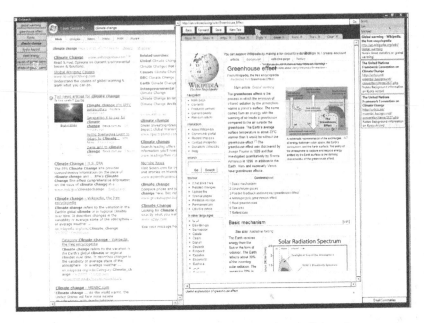

Fig. 1. An example of the SearchTogether interface shows how collaborating users can work together on open-ended search tasks

individual searcher to the benefit of others. Specifically, the iBingo collaboration engine uses information about the activities of each user in order to encourage other users to explore different information trails and different facets of the information space. In this way, the ongoing activities of users can have an impact on future searches by the group and, in a sense, the search process is being "personalized" according to the group's search behaviour.

The aim of SearchTogether is remote search collaboration (whether asynchronous or synchronous), which allows groups of searchers to participate in extended shared search sessions as they search to locate information on particular topics; see also [19] and Fig. 2. SearchTogether system allows users to create shared search sessions and invite other users to join these sessions. Each searcher can independently search for information on a particular topic, but the system provides features to allow individual searchers to share what they find with other session members by recommending and commenting on specific results. In turn, SearchTogether supports synchronous collaborative search by allowing cooperating searchers to synchronously view the results of each others' searches via a split-screen style results interface. As with CoSearch above, one of the key design goals in SearchTogether is to support a division of labour in complex, open-ended search tasks. In addition, a key feature of the work is the ability to create a shared awareness among group members by reducing the overhead of search collaboration at the interface level. SearchTogether does this by including various features, from integrated messaging, query histories, and recommendations arising out of recent searches.

In the main, the collaborative information retrieval systems we have so far examined have been largely focused on supporting collaboration from a division of labour

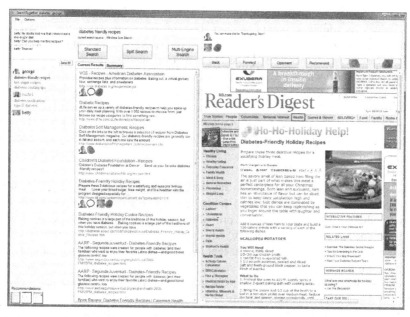

Fig. 2. An example of the SearchTogether interface shows how collaborating users can work together on open-ended search tasks

and shared awareness standpoint, separate from the underlying search process. In short, these systems have assumed the availability of an underlying search engine and provided a collaboration interface that effectively *imports* search results directly, allowing users to share these results. As noted by [23], one of the major limitations of these approaches is that collaboration is restricted to the interface in the sense that while individual searchers are notified about the activities of collaborators, they must individually examine and interpret these activities in order to reconcile their own activities with their co-searchers. Consequently, the work of [23] describes an approach to collaborative search that is more tightly integrated with the underlying search engine resource so that the operation of the search engine is itself influenced by the activities of collaborating searchers in a number of ways. For example, mediation techniques are used to prioritise, as yet, unseen documents, while query recommendation techniques are used to suggest alternative avenues for further search exploration.

4 Bringing Collaboration to Mainstream Web Search

So far in this paper we have motivated the potential for a more collaborative form of web search and described a number of instantiations of this idea. By and large these systems have exemplified different styles of collaborative web search while adopting a common strategy of building a standalone collaborative web search service. The problem with this strategy is that web users today are loathe to leave their trusted search engines of choice, making it extremely difficult for these collaborative search engines to attract significant usage.

Our research has been guided by the desire to bring collaboration to mainstream search engines, by adding a layer of collaboration infrastructure so that users could still use their favorite search engine of choice while at the same time enjoying a more collaborative approach to web search. This has led to a novel search service called HeyStaks (www.heystaks.com), which we shall discuss in the remained of this paper. HeyStaks has been designed to support collaborative web search tasks that are asynchronous and remote but by a tight integration with mainstream search engines via a browser plugin. HeyStaks is designed to operate in parallel with search engines such as Google, Yahoo, and Bing so the searcher can search as normal, using their preferred search engine, while still benefiting from the inherent collaboration potential of their friends and colleagues.

HeyStaks adds two basic features to any mainstream search engine. First, it allows users to create *search staks*, a type of folder for search experiences, at search time and invite others to join the staks by providing their email addresses. Staks can be configured to be *public* (anyone can join) or *private* (invitation only). Second, HeyStaks uses staks to generate recommendations that are added to the underlying search results that come from the mainstream search engine. These recommendations are results that stak members have previously found to be relevant for similar queries and help the searcher to discover results that friends or colleagues have found interesting, results that may otherwise be buried deep within Google's default result-list.

In the following sections we showcase the functionality of HeyStaks in a worked example before reviewing the HeyStaks architecture and detailing how HeyStaks captures search activities within search staks and how this search knowledge is used to generate and filter result recommendations at search time; more detailed technical details can be found in [35,36].

4.1   HeyStaks in Action

In this section we present a concrete example of HeyStaks in action. Imagine a small group of web developer colleagues working on a javascript project together. They know that up until now, they have been spending a lot of search time re-finding pages that they have found in the past or searching from scratch for solutions, tools or hacks that one of their colleagues has already found recently. Recognising the potential for HeyStaks to help with this type of wasted search effort, one of the group creates a new *javascript stak* as shown in Fig. 3(a). The user provides a stak title, a brief description, and the email addresses of fellow javascript developers to invite them to use this new stak.

After the stak has been created and shared it will start to appear in the *stak-list* of the HeyStaks toolbar for each of these users. And as they each search for Javascript-related information, their search actions will add new content to the stak and they will start to receive recommendations about content others have found to complement their mainstream search results. For example, in Fig. 3(b) a search for *javascript DOM help* by one user results in a set of recommendations from HeyStaks based on similar searches by other members. Some of these recommendations originate from Google but others come from Yahoo and Bing, meaning that other stak members found these results on Yahoo or Bing; note the search engine icons after each recommendation to indicate the origin of the result. In this way HeyStaks also provides a form of collaborative *meta-search*.

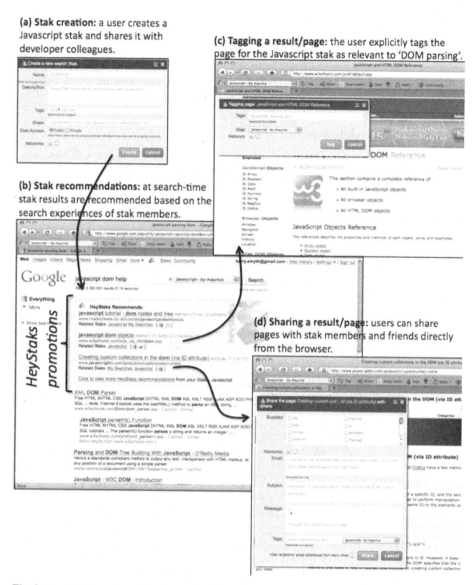

Fig. 3. HeyStaks in action: a) stak creation; b) result recommendations; c) tagging a web page; d) sharing a page directly with others

In Fig. 3(c) our searcher chooses to explicitly tag a given result with the tags *javascript parsing DOM* thereby adding to the stak index for this particular page and helping to re-inforce the relevance of this page across these tag/query terms. In turn, in Fig. 3(d) we can see our searcher opting to share a different recommendation directly with other users, right from the browser; they can share the page via email or through social networks such as Twitter or Facebook. Just like tagging, this explicit sharing of pages provides another strong indicator to HeyStaks regarding the relevance of this page for future similar queries. Over time, these javascript developers will find that their stak becomes an important repository of Javascript knowledge that is integrated directly with their everyday search tools (in this case, Google, Bing and Yahoo). Indeed by making the stak public it can be recommended to other HeyStaks users who are also looking for Javascript information and so promote the rapid growth of stak membership and content.

4.2   The System Architecture

Fig. 4 presents the overall HeyStaks architecture, which takes the form of two key components: a client-side *browser toolbar/plugin* and a back-end *server*. The toolbar has a dual purpose. On the one hand it provides users with direct access to the HeyStaks functions allowing them to create and share staks, tag or vote for pages etc. Importantly the toolbar also provides for the type of deep integration that HeyStaks requires with an underlying search engine. For example, the toolbar captures the routine search activities of the user (query submissions and result click-thrus). Moreover, the toolbar also makes it possible for HeyStaks to augment the mainstream search engine interface so that, for example, HeyStaks' recommendations can be integrated directly into a search engine's results page. The toolbar also manages the communication with the back-end HeyStaks server. Search activities (queries, click-thrus, tags, votes, shares etc) are used by the server to update the HeyStaks stak indexes. These stak indexes provide the primary source of recommendations so that when a user submits a query to a mainstream search engine, in a given stak context, this query is fed to the HeyStaks server in order to generate a set of recommendations based on the target stak and, possibly, other staks that the user has joined.

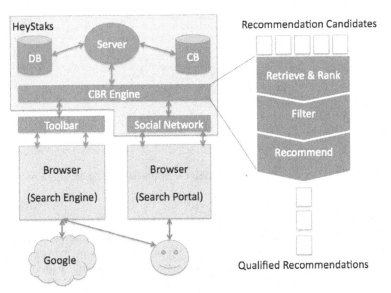

Fig. 4. The HeyStaks system architecture and outline of the recommendation model

4.3   Profiling Stak Pages

In HeyStaks each search stak (S) serves as a profile of the search activities of the stak members. Each stak is made up of a set of result pages ($S = \{r_1, ..., r_k\}$) and each result is anonymously associated with a number of implicit and explicit interest indicators, based on the type of actions that users can perform on these pages. A number of primary actions are facilitated, for example:

- *Selections (or Click-thrus)* – that is, a user selects a search result (whether *organic* or *recommended*). Similarly, HeyStaks allows a user to *preview* a page by opening it in a frame (rather than a window), and *popout* a page from a preview frame into a browser window;
- *Voting* – that is, a user positively votes on a given search result or the current web page;
- *Sharing* – that is, a user chooses to share a specific search result or web page with another user (via email or by posting to their Facebook Wall etc.);
- *Tagging/Commenting* – that is, the user chooses to tag and/or comment on a particular result or web page.

Result selections are an example of an *implicit* action in the sense that this type of action is part and parcel of normal routine search activity. It is also a weak indicator of relevance because users will frequently select pages that turn out to be irrelevant to their current needs. Nevertheless, the frequent selection of a specific page in a specific stak, in response to a particular type of query, suggests relevance. The 3 other forms of actions (voting, sharing, tagging) we refer to as *explicit* actions in the sense that they are not part of the normal search process, but rather they are HeyStaks specific actions that the user must chose to carry out. This type of deliberation suggests a stronger indicator of relevance and as such these actions are considered to be more reliable that simple result selections when it comes to evaluating the relevance of a page at recommendation time. Each result page r_i^S from stak S then, is associated with these indicators of relevance, including the total number of times a result has been selected (sel), the query terms ($q_1, ..., q_n$) that led to its selection, the number of times a result has been tagged (tag), the terms used to tag it ($t_1, ..., t_m$), the votes it has received (v^+, v^-), and the number of people it has been shared with ($share$) as indicated by Equation 1. This idea is related to earlier work by [2] and [34] which involve storing pages indexed by query terms. However, the present technology extends this to include other indicators such as snippets, tags and votes.

$$r_i^S = \{q_1, ..., q_n, t_1, ..., t_m, v^+, v^-, sel, tag, share\} . \tag{1}$$

In this way, each result page is associated with a set of *term data* (query terms and/or tag terms) and a set of *usage data* (the selection, tag, share, and voting count). The term data is represented as a Lucene (lucene.apache.org) index, with each result indexed under its associated query and tag terms.retrieving and ranking *recommendation candidates*.

4.4   Retrieval and Ranking

At search time, the searcher's query q_T, current stak S_T and other staks in the searchers stak-list are used to generate a list of recommendations to be returned to the searcher.

There are two types of recommendation candidates: *primary recommendations* are results that come from the active stak S_t; whereas *secondary recommendations* come from other staks in the stak-list. There are two key steps when it comes to generating recommendations. First, a set of *recommendation candidates* are retrieved from each stak index, S_i, by querying the corresponding Lucene index with q_T. This effectively produces a list of recommendations based on the overlap between the query terms and the terms used to index each recommendation (query, snippet, and tag terms).

Second, these recommendations are filtered and ranked. Staks are inevitably noisy, in the sense that they will frequently contain results that are not on topic. Thus, the recommendation candidate selection stage may select results that are not strictly relevant to the current query context. To avoid making spurious recommendations HeyStaks employs an *evidence filter*, which uses a variety of threshold models to evaluate the relevance of a particular result, in terms of its usage evidence; tagging evidence is considered more important than voting, which in turn is more important than implicit selection evidence. For example, pages that have only been selected once, by a single stak member, are not automatically considered for recommendation and, all other things being equal, will be filtered out at this stage. In turn, pages that have received a high proportion of negative votes will also be eliminated. The precise details of this model are beyond the scope of this paper but suffice it to say that any results which do not meet the necessary evidence thresholds are eliminated from further consideration; see also [35,36]. The remaining recommendation candidates are then ranked according to two key factors: *relevance* and *reputation*. The relevance of a result r with respect to a query q_T is computed based on Lucene's standard *TF*IDF* metric as per Equation 2. The reputation of a result is a function of the reputation of the stak members who have added the result to the stak. And their reputation in turn is based on the degree to which results that they have added to staks have been subsequently recommended to, and selected, by other users; see [18] for additional information. Essentially each result is evaluated using a weighted score of its relevance and reputation score as per Equation 3; where w is used to adjust the relative influence of relevance and reputation and is usually set to 0.5.

$$rel(q_T, r) = \sum_{t \epsilon q_t} tf(t\epsilon r) \times idf(t)^2 . \tag{2}$$

$$score(r, q_T) = w \times rep(r) + (1 - w) \times rel(q_T, r) \tag{3}$$

Currently HeyStaks has been deployed online as a search service offering. HeyStaks plugins and apps are available across a variety of platforms, including the main browser platforms (Firefox, Chrome, Safari, IE) and mobile platforms (iOS and Android); interested users can download its browser toolbars or mobile apps at www.heystaks.com. During the course of its deployment there have been a number of opportunities to conduct live-user trials and studies to explore how people engage with this new approach to search; see for example [35,36]. In summary these studies highlight a number of interesting points. First and foremost, early users demonstrated a willingness to engage in a more collaborative approach to search: they frequently created and shared search staks and they often joined the staks created by others. Moreover, search collaboration was an inevitable and frequent result of this sharing. Those users who shared staks frequently received stak recommendations and often benefited directly from the searches of others.

5 Conclusions

The world of web search is changing and mainstream search engines seek out new ways to improve their ability to bring the right user to the right information at the right time. With the maturation of the so-called social web it is now clear that there is a significant opportunity to harness social signals to inform their relevancy metrics. Recently this has led to some initial experiments by the mainstream search engines, for example, by integrating Twitter and Facebook information (tweets and status updates) into search engine result pages.

In this paper we have argued for a deeper integration between the world of social networking and web search to capitalize on the potential for web search to become a more collaborative affair, where today it is very much a solitary information discovery process. During the course of this paper we have reviewed a variety of recent research that aims to make web search more collaborative and more social. In particular, we have described in detail the HeyStaks system as a concrete case-study in collaborative search. HeyStaks is unique in the level of integration that it provides with mainstream search engines such as Google and Bing, allowing people to search as normal, while benefiting from recommendations that are derived from the searches of people they trust and on topics that matter to them.

References

1. Amershi, S., Morris, M.R.: CoSearch: a system for co-located collaborative web search. In: CHI 2008: Proceeding of the Twenty-Sixth Annual SIGCHI Conference on Human Factors in Computing Systems, pp. 1647–1656. ACM (2008)
2. Amitay, E., Darlow, A., Konopnicki, D., Weiss, U.: Queries as anchors: selection by association. In: Hypertext, pp. 193–201 (2005)
3. Asnicar, F., Tasso, C.: ifWeb: a prototype of user Model-Based intelligent agent for document filtering and navigation in the world wide web. In: Proc. of 6th International Conference on User Modelling (June 1997)
4. Brin, S., Page, L.: The Anatomy of A Large-Scale Web Search Engine. In: Proceedings of the Seventh International World-Wide Web Conference (1998)
5. Chang, H., Cohn, D., Mccallum, A.K.: Learning to create customized authority lists. In: Proceedings of the 7th International Conference on Machine Learning, ICML 2000, pp. 127–134. Morgan Kaufmann (2000)
6. Chirita, P.-A., Nejdl, W., Paiu, R., Kohlschütter, C.: Using odp metadata to personalize search. In: SIGIR, pp. 178–185 (2005)
7. Chirita, P.-A., Olmedilla, D., Nejdl, W.: PROS: A Personalized Ranking Platform for Web Search. In: De Bra, P.M.E., Nejdl, W. (eds.) AH 2004. LNCS, vol. 3137, pp. 34–43. Springer, Heidelberg (2004)
8. Evans, B.M., Kairam, S., Pirolli, P.: Exploring the cognitive consequences of social search. In: CHI Extended Abstracts, pp. 3377–3382 (2009)

9. Evans, B.M., Kairam, S., Pirolli, P.: Do your friends make you smarter?: An analysis of social strategies in online information seeking. Inf. Process. Manage. 46(6), 679–692 (2010)

10. Finkelstein, L., Gabrilovich, E., Matias, Y., Rivlin, E., Solan, Z., Wolfman, G., Ruppin, E.: Placing search in context: The concept revisited. In: Proceedings of the 10th International Conference on World Wide Web, pp. 406–414. ACM (2001)

11. Golovchinsky, G., Qvarfordt, P., Pickens, J.: Collaborative information seeking. IEEE Computer 42(3), 47–51 (2009)

12. Granka, L.A., Joachims, T., Gay, G.: Eye-tracking analysis of user behavior in www search. In: SIGIR 2004: Proceedings of the 27th Annual International ACM SIGIR Conference on Research and Development in Information Retrieval, pp. 478–479. ACM Press, New York (2004)

13. Gulli, A., Signorini, A.: The indexable web is more than 11.5 billion pages. In: WWW 2005: Special Interest Tracks and Posters of the 14th International Conference on World Wide Web, pp. 902–903. ACM Press (2005)

14. Kleinberg, J.M.: Authoritative sources in a hyperlinked environment. In: Proceedings of the Ninth Annual ACM-SIAM Symposium on Discrete Algorithms, pp. 668–677 (1998)

15. Lawrence, S., Giles, C.L.: Context and page analysis for improved web search. IEEE Internet Computing 2(4), 38–46 (1998)

16. Ma, Z., Pant, G., Sheng, O.R.L.: Interest-based personalized search. ACM Trans. Inf. Syst. 25 (February 2007)

17. Makris, C., Panagis, Y., Sakkopoulos, E., Tsakalidis, A.: Category ranking for personalized search. Data & Knowledge Engineering 60(1), 109–125 (2007)

18. McNally, K., O'Mahony, M.P., Smyth, B., Coyle, M., Briggs, P.: Towards a reputation-based model of social web search. In: Rich, C., Yang, Q., Cavazza, M., Zhou, M.X. (eds.) IUI, pp. 179–188. ACM (2010)

19. Morris, M.R., Horvitz, E.: S^3: Storable, Shareable Search. In: Baranauskas, C., Abascal, J., Barbosa, S.D.J. (eds.) INTERACT 2007, Part I. LNCS, vol. 4662, pp. 120–123. Springer, Heidelberg (2007)

20. Morris, M.R.: A survey of collaborative web search practices. In: Proceedings of the Annual SIGCHI Conference on Human Factors in Computing Systems (CHI), pp. 1657–1660 (2008)

21. Morris, M.R., Horvitz, E.: SearchTogether: an interface for collaborative web search. In: UIST 2007: Proceedings of the 20th Annual ACM Symposium on User Interface Software and Technology, pp. 3–12. ACM, New York (2007)

22. Morris, M.R., Teevan, J., Panovich, K.: What do people ask their social networks, and why?: a survey study of status message q&a behavior. In: CHI 2010: Proceedings of the 28th International Conference on Human Factors in Computing Systems, pp. 1739–1748. ACM (2010)

23. Pickens, J., Golovchinsky, G., Shah, C., Qvarfordt, P., Back, M.: Algorithmic mediation for collaborative exploratory search. In: SIGIR 2008: Proceedings of the 31st Annual International ACM SIGIR Conference on Research and Development in Information Retrieval, pp. 315–322. ACM, New York (2008)

24. Pretschner, A., Gauch, S.: Ontology based personalized search. In: ICTAI, pp. 391–398 (1999)

25. Reddy, M., Dourish, P.: A finger on the pulse: temporal rhythms and information seeking in medical work. In: Proceedings of the 2002 ACM Conference on Computer Supported Cooperative Work, pp. 344–353. ACM (2002)

26. Reddy, M., Dourish, P., Pratt, W.: Coordinating heterogeneous work: information and representation in medical care. In: ECSCW 2001, pp. 239–258. Springer, Heidelberg (2001)

27. Reddy, M., Jansen, B.: A model for understanding collaborative information behavior in context: A study of two healthcare teams. Information Processing & Management 44(1), 256–273 (2008)

28. Reddy, M.C., Spence, P.R.: Collaborative information seeking: A field study of a multidisci-
    plinary patient care team. Inf. Process. Manage. 44(1), 242–255 (2008)
29. Shen, X., Tan, B., Zhai, C.: Implicit user modeling for personalized search. In: Proceedings
    of the 14th ACM International Conference on Information and Knowledge Management, pp.
    824–831. ACM (2005)
30. Smeaton, A.F., Foley, C., Byrne, D., Jones, G.J.F.: Ibingo mobile collaborative search. In:
    CIVR, pp. 547–548 (2008)
31. Smeaton, A.F., Lee, H., Foley, C., McGivney, S.: Collaborative video searching on a tabletop.
    Multimedia Syst. 12(4-5), 375–391 (2007)
32. Smyth, B.: The sensor web: bringing information to life. ERCIM News (2009)
33. Smyth, B., Balfe, E., Boydell, O., Bradley, K., Briggs, P., Coyle, M., Freyne, J.: A live-
    user evaluation of collaborative web search. In: International Joint Conference on Artificial
    Intelligence (IJCAI), pp. 1419–1424 (2005)
34. Smyth, B., Balfe, E., Freyne, J., Briggs, P., Coyle, M., Boydell, O.: Exploiting Query Repe-
    tition and Regularity in an Adaptive Community-Based Web Search Engine. User Modeling
    and User-Adapted Interaction 14(5), 383–423 (2004)
35. Smyth, B., Briggs, P., Coyle, M., O'Mahony, M.P.: A Case-Based Perspective on So-
    cial Web Search. In: McGinty, L., Wilson, D.C. (eds.) ICCBR 2009. LNCS, vol. 5650,
    pp. 494–508. Springer, Heidelberg (2009)
36. Smyth, B., Briggs, P., Coyle, M., O'Mahony, M.P.: Google Shared. A Case-Study in So-
    cial Search. In: Houben, G.-J., McCalla, G., Pianesi, F., Zancanaro, M. (eds.) UMAP 2009.
    LNCS, vol. 5535, pp. 283–294. Springer, Heidelberg (2009)
37. Song, R., Luo, Z., Wen, J.-R., Yu, Y., Hon, H.-W.: Identifying ambiguous queries in web
    search. In: WWW 2007: Proceedings of the 16th International Conference on World Wide
    Web, pp. 1169–1170. ACM, New York (2007)
38. Spink, A., Jansen, B.J.: A study of web search trends. Webology 1(2) (2004)

Challenges for Software Agents Supporting Decision-Makers in Trading Flowers Worldwide

Eric van Heck and Wolfgang Ketter

Department of Decision and Information Sciences
Rotterdam School of Management, Erasmus University
P.O. Box 1738, 3000 DR Rotterdam, The Netherlands
{evanheck,wketter}@rsm.nl

1 Introduction

High performing firms are working in business networks with advanced decision making capabilities. Decision making in business networks is a new research area that provides knowledge and insight about how decision rights are allocated and how decision processes are designed and implemented in evolving business networks [22]. In this article we focus on a particular type of support: software agents. Software agents are software programs that act on behalf of users or other programs. Software agents can be autonomous (capable of modifying the way in which they achieve their objectives), intelligent (capable of learning and reasoning), and distributed (capable to being executed on physically distinct computers). Software agents can act in multi-agent systems (e.g. distributed agents that do not have the capabilities to achieve an objective alone and thus must be able to communicate) and as mobile agents (e.g. these relocate their execution onto different processors). Recent research shows that software agents are able to act as a decision support tool or a training tool for negotiations with people. For example, [16] Lin and Kraus (2010) identified several types of agents in several variations of negotiation settings. These agents differ in the number of negotiators, encounters, and attributes they can handle. The identified agents are: Diplomat, AutONA, Cliff-Edge, Colored-Trails, Guessing Heuristic, QOAgent, and Virtual Human. Although software agents are popular in scientific research programs, the use of software agents in real life business situations is limited. We will explore the use of software agents in the flower industry with its complex logistics, commercial, and financial processes on a global scale.

The central research question in this article: what is the potential role and impact of software agents to support decision making in complex business networks? The objective is to explore crucial components for successful support of decision making in complex business networks by software agents.

Section 2 provides the characteristics in human decision making. Section 3 explains where in the complex flower distribution network software agents are able to support decision makers. In section 4 an overview is provided about research challenges of the use and impact of software agents in complex business networks. Section 5 provides conclusions.

J. Filipe and J. Cordeiro (Eds.): WEBIST 2011, LNBIP 101, pp. 32–39, 2012.

2   Decision Making

In evolving business networks complex decision making is a core feature for the actors involved. There are three levels of decision making in business networks:

- The first level of decision making is decision that designs the decision making in business network. These decisions deal with the allocation of decision rights, the governance mechanisms that the network uses to coordinate decisions and activities of different actors in the network.
- The second level of decision making is decision that deals with the creation of business network resources. These decisions deal with the investment in the resources of the different business network actors.

  Recent research shows the strengths of biologically inspired network design. [21]. suggest that the slime mould *Physarum polycephalum* forms networks with comparable efficiency, fault tolerance, and cost to those of real-world infrastructure networks—in this case, the Tokyo rail system. They built a template with 36 oat flakes (a favored food source) placed to represent the locations of cities in the region around Tokyo. They put *P. polycephalum* on Tokyo itself and watched it go. They found that many of the links the slime mould made bore a striking resemblance to Tokyo's existing rail network. The research results suggest that good and complex solutions can emerge from simple rules, and that this principle might be applied elsewhere. The next thing is to discover and use these rules to enable other networks to self-organise in an "intelligent" fashion without human intervention – for example, to link up a swarm of robots exploring a dangerous environment, so that they can talk to each other and relay information back to base [8].

  The core mechanisms needed for adaptive network formation can be captured in a biologically inspired mathematical model that may be useful to guide network construction in other domains.

- The third level decision making are decision that deal with utilization of business network resources. These decisions deal with the level of utilization of resources by the different business network actors.

3   Complex Flower Business Network

We illustrate the third level with key decisions by each of the actors in the complex flower business network. This network is linking thousands of flower growers via the Dutch flower auctions (FloraHolland) to the flower transporters, wholesalers, retailers, and consumers. The Netherlands is the world's leading producer and distributor of cut flowers and potted plants. This industry consists of about 10,000 growers and nearly 5,500 buyers. Growers typically are family businesses, while buyers represent both large and small wholesalers and retailers. The Dutch dominate the world export markets, with around 59% world market share for cut flowers and 48% world market share for potted plants. The Dutch flower auctions established and owned by grower cooperatives play a vital role in Holland's leadership of this industry by providing efficient centers for price discovery, and the exchange of flowers between buyers and sellers. This sector accounts for 6 percent of total export value and 2% percent of the Dutch labor market. The world's two largest flower auctions are in Aalsmeer and Naaldwijk both located in the Netherlands and operated by FloraHolland. Every day the six Dutch auction centers traded over approx. 44 million flowers and 4.8 million potted plants resulting in 125,000 transactions daily, generating together over 4.1 billion Euro in annual sales of cut flower and potted products from the Netherlands and other producers such as Ethiopia, Israel, Kenya, and Zimbabwe. The main export countries are Germany, United Kingdom and France. Within Europe, the main mode of transportation is by truck. Products meant for export to countries outside Europe is brought to Schiphol Airport and flown to destinations all over the world, where they can be sold within one day.

This research is an important step in harnessing the complexity of combinatorial human decision-making in complex, information-rich and dynamic environments such as the Dutch flower auction and distribution network. Improving the quality of decisions will make the Dutch flower industry more competitive in the world market. The Dutch flower network presents additional challenges of this nature which we plan to address in the future. In Figure 1 we show additional places in the network where learning software agents can empower humans in their decision-making capacities, have a positive impact on economic activity, and strengthen the Dutch position on a global scale.

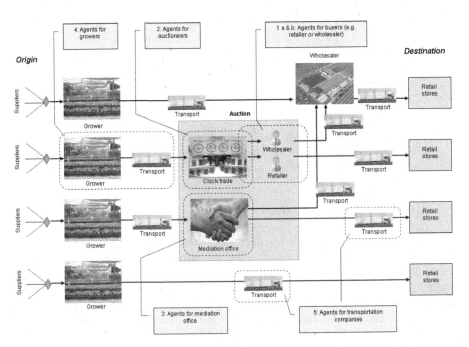

Fig. 1. Applying Learning Software Agents in the Complex Flower Network

We have a long-term relationship with FloraHolland that has not only produced very good research, such as [11], [14], [12] and [15]. It also led to practical insights about the design and implementation of online auctioning and distribution aspects in the Dutch flower industry. For example, FloraHolland used the outcomes of research of [11], [12] such as how to design and implement online auctioning using the developed stakeholder/process framework. The research on screen auctioning [15] resulted in a better understanding of the impact of digital product representation and decoupling from distribution. The results of researching Buying-at-a-Distance auction [14] resulted in a better understanding of online auctioning and its impact on price levels and buying behavior.

Online auctioning was last year growing with 35% in terms of transactions and became an important digital channel for FloraHolland, wholesalers, and retailers. For the coming years the design and implementation of learning agents in online markets and the decoupling from auctioning and logistics and distribution with new forms of distribution will be create new opportunities to create value for stakeholders involved (see Table 1).

The distribution network consists of three sub-networks. The first sub-network deals with the logistical flow of perishable flowers from growers to the final consumers. The second sub-network deals with the financial flow from the final customers to the growers. The third sub-network is information that is flowing among the different actors in the business network. Adaptive network formation is making constantly tradeoffs among the cost, efficiency, and resilience of the expanding network. The network expands towards areas with customers that are able to buy flowers taking into account distributions and communication costs.

Advanced decision support systems and software agents promise to assist businesses by acting rationally on behalf of humans in numerous application domains. Examples include procurement [20], scheduling and resource management [3], Internet shopbot agents [10], and personal information management [18]. We research rapid-fire Dutch flower auctions and distribution systems whereas research so far has dealt only with slow ones taking several days [2]. In this research we plan to enable people to interact with an agent in a collaborative manner. The agents could predict the appropriate next steps, helping to speed up, and improve the quality of a user's overall decision process. Such agents are sometimes referred to as expert or interface agents [17] [19]. There has been significant academic research on personalization and recommendation systems [1] to model user preferences. The most prominent approach is based on collaborative filtering [9].

The proposed research will draw on the fields of computer science, economics, information systems, machine learning, operation research, and supply chain management to develop techniques to analyze human behavior and to evaluate intelligent decision support systems. Our research will proceed by incremental construction and evaluation of a prototype learning agent. First, we will build a model of human preferences based on machine learning research. Second, we will draw on research in recommender systems and operations research to incorporate the model into an agent that will acquire and display information and recommend actions that are in the best interest of users given the learned preferences. We expect to extend the current literature in these areas, since we are creating human preference models which are based on explicit and implicit human-agent interaction. Figure 2 shows the

Table 1. Decision Making Characteristics of Flower Business Network Actors

Business Network Actor	Decision Process	Crucial Information	Software Agent Support
Flower grower	Decision to sell its flowers.	Supply information (own, other growers); Demand information (historical, current); Specific	Comparison of different sales channels (auction, brokerage, direct); Timing support (for example day of the week)
Auctioneer	Decision to auction off flower lots.	Supply information (historical, current day); Demand information (historical; current day); Minimum units to auction; Auction speed;	Support of the starting price for each auctioned lot; Support to determine the auction speed; Support to determine the minimum transaction amount.
Wholesaler	Decision to buy flowers; Decision to bundle and transport to retailers.	Supply information (historical, current day); Demand information (historical; current day); Specific order information;	Support purchase decision (price level, quantity) Support based on preference modeling; Comparison of different procurement channels (auction, brokerage, direct);
Transporter	Decision to bundle orders and provide shortest routes.	Specific transportation details (traffic routes, traffic jams etc)	Support for bundling transports; Support for route optimization;
Retailer	Decision to buy flowers.	Supply driven versus demand driven approach	Support purchase decision (price level, quantity) Comparison of supply versus demand driven supply chain strategy
Consumer	Decision to buy flowers.	Price, quality and delivery time and delivery reliability of retailer.	Comparison different offline and online retail stores Support based on consumer preferences.

preference elicitation methods (dashed lines) and the recommendation models (Feedback).

Below we list, as shown in Figure 2, the novel characteristics we expect to demonstrate in our learning agent:

1. The agent will learn implicit and explicit human preferences over time through:
   a. Observing user behavior through tracking of the interface – we will begin with simulations and historical data and then move toward real-world deployment.
   b. Adapting based on user feedback.
   c. User survey and teaching through examples.
2. The agent will recommend actions based on:
   a. A formal model of human preferences and the business domain.
   b. Order-book as well as other contextual constraints.

We will evaluate our approach through laboratory and field experiments with human subjects, using multi-agent simulation and real world data from the Dutch flower auctions, wholesalers, and transporters.

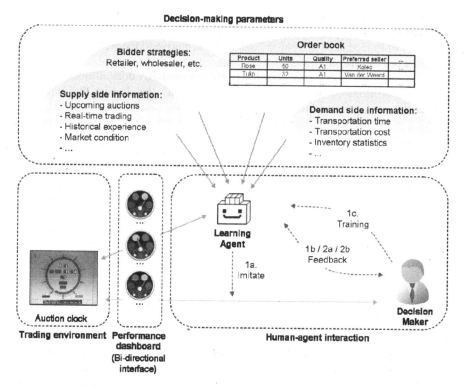

Fig. 2. Human Decision Making Supported by Learning Software Agents

4   Challenges

The proposed research will draw on the fields of computer science, economics, information systems, machine learning, operation research, supply chain management, and software engineering to develop techniques to analyze human behavior and to evaluate intelligent decision support systems [5] [6]. The research may also lead to insights in facilitating human decision making in other complex environments. Concretely, we will contribute to human preference elicitation and representation, to decision recommendations based on human preferences, to human-agent interaction, and to agent architecture.

What is particularly exciting about researching preferences in the context of the DFA is that not only has FloraHolland granted researchers data, but moreover, those data are not anonymous. This means that researchers can not only build models of user preferences, but further, they can test the accuracy of their models by through testing and interviewing users. This research is getting underway in the Netherlands, and involves a team of interdisciplinary researchers that includes both computer scientists and psychologists. This is a great opportunity to facilitate the business science interaction and to speed up the transfer of knowledge into business.

Roughly ten years ago, FloraHolland introduced the remote buying application (RBA), a computer interface that enables buyers to bid in the DFA without being physically present in one of the auction houses. As the name suggests, RBA facilitates remote bidding. RBA opens up a world of opportunities for bidders. A small retailer in the south of France need no longer send a representative to the Netherlands once or twice per week to procure flowers for him, but rather his representative can bid daily in the comfort of his own home. But that is all that the RBA does. It does not make bid recommendations or manage information in a way that lowers the burden of cognitive processing for the bidder.

We are proposing to engineer intelligent agents for the complex business network of the DFA that provide decision support to auctioneers and bidders [4] [7]. To do so, we must overcome technical challenges in preference modeling and elicitation, prediction [13], and optimization. User interface design is a further challenge, but one which is at least partially solved (on the buyer side) by the existing RBA, upon which we plan to build our initial prototypes.

This research is very challenging since it demands a unique end-to-end modeling, i.e. going from empirical models based on real-world data to agent-based simulation, to agent-human lab experiments, and finally real field experiments. This really challenges researchers to obtain this unique skill set and to work in interdisciplinary teams.

5   Conclusions

The goal of our work is to develop and evaluate highly personalized adaptive learning agents to complement the cognitive and computational capacity of humans, while leveraging the experience and contextual knowledge of seasoned DFA decision makers (auctioneers and buyers) to facilitate decision making processes. These agents will collaborate with their users to gather and present information and recommend action. To work effectively and efficiently in a supply chain environment, these agents will learn the interests, habits, and preferences of their users with respect to the decision context.

Research needs an application and the Dutch flower auction network is a complex, challenging, and economically important application domain. This makes it an ideal environment for our learning agent research. The knowledge that will be gained during this research can then be applied to many other supply chain decision-making settings, such as the resource allocation problem of container ships in the Rotterdam harbor.

Acknowledgements. This paper was written in memory of Prof. Dr. Ir. Jo van Nunen (1945 - 2010). Jo had a great personality, was a convinced scientist, a leading figure in logistics, and a passionate believer in his ideals. Jo is greatly missed, especially with his encouragement for young researchers to bring out the best in them through his motivating and joyful manner, and to stimulate many positive developments inside and outside of the Rotterdam School of Management, Erasmus University.

References

1. Adomavicius, G., Tuzhilin, A.: Toward the Next Generation of Recommender Systems: A Survey of the State-of-the-Art and Possible Extensions. IEEE Transactions on Knowledge and Data Engineering 17(6), 734–749 (2005)

2. Carare, O., Rothkopf, M.H.: Slow Dutch Auctions. Management Science 51(3), 365–373 (2005)
3. Collins, J., Ketter, W., Gini, M.: A Multi-Agent Negotiation Testbed for Contracting Tasks with Temporal and Precedence Constraints. International Journal of Electronic Commerce 7(1), 35–57 (2002)
4. Collins, J., Ketter, W., Gini, M.: Flexible decision support in a dynamic business network. In: Vervest, P., van Liere, D., Zheng, L. (eds.) The Network Experience – New Value from Smart Business Networks, pp. 233–246. Springer, Heidelberg (2008)
5. Collins, J., Ketter, W., Gini, M.: Flexible decision support in dynamic interorganizational networks. European Journal of Information Systems 19(4) (September 2010a)
6. Collins, J., Ketter, W., Gini, M.: Flexible decision control in an autonomous trading agent. Electronic Commerce Research and Applications 8(2), 91–105 (2009)
7. Collins, J., Ketter, W., Sadeh, N.: Pushing the limits of rational agents: the trading agent competition for supply chain management. AI Magazine 31(2), 63–80 (2010b)
8. Economist, The, A Life of Slime: Railways and Slime Moulds, p. 71 (January 23, 2010)
9. Goldberg, D., et al.: Using collaborative filtering to weave an information tapestry. Communications of the ACM, 61–70 (1992)
10. Haeubl, G., Trifts, V.: Consumer Decision Making in Online Shopping Environments: The Effects of Interactive Decision Aids. Marketing Science 19(1), 4–21 (2000)
11. Kambil, A., Van Heck, E.: Reengineering the Dutch Flower Auctions: A Framework for Analyzing Exchange Organizations. Information Systems Research 9(1), 1–19 (1998)
12. Kambil, A., van Heck, E.: Making Markets: How firms can design and profit from online auctions and exchanges. Harvard Business School Press (June 2002)
13. Ketter, W., Collins, J., Gini, M., Gupta, A., Schrater, P.: Detecting and Forecasting Economic Regimes in Multi-Agent Automated Exchanges. Decision Support Systems 47(4), 307–318 (2009)
14. Koppius, O.R.: Information Architecture and Electronic Market Performance. 2002: Erasmus Research Institute of Management (ERIM, PhD Dissertation), Erasmus University Rotterdam
15. Koppius, O., van Heck, E., Wolters, M.: The importance of product representation online: Empirical results and implications for electronic markets. Decision Support Systems 38, 161–169 (2004)
16. Lin, R., Kraus, S.: Can automated agents proficiently negotiate with humans? Communications of the ACM 53(1), 78–88 (2010)
17. Maes, P.: Agents that reduce work and information overload. Communications of the ACM 37(7), 30–40 (1994)
18. Myers, K., et al.: An Intelligent Personal Assistant for Task and Time Management. AI Magazine, 47 (2007)
19. Rich, C., Sidner, C.L.: COLLAGEN: A Collaboration Manager for Software Interface Agents. User Modeling and User-Adapted Interaction 8(3), 315–350 (1998)
20. Sandholm, T., et al.: CABOB: A Fast Optimal Algorithm for Winner Determination in Combinatorial Auctions. Management Science 51(3), 374–390 (2005)
21. Tero, A., Takagi, S., Saigusa, T., Ito, K., Bebber, D.P., Fricker, M.D., Yumiki, K., Kobayashi, R., Nakagaki, T.: Rules for Biologically Inspired Adaptive Network Design. Science 327(5964), 439–442 (2010)
22. Van Heck, E., Vervest, P.: Smart business networks: how the network wins. Communications of the ACM 50(6), 29–37 (2007)

Part I
Internet Technology

Web Service Matchmaking by Subgraph Matching

Hamida Seba[1,*], Sofiane Lagraa[2], and Hamamache Kheddouci[3]

[1] GAMA, Université Lyon1, IUT Lyon1, 71, rue Peter Fink, Bourg en Bresse, France
[2] LIG, Université Joseph Fourier, 681 rue de la Passerelle, Saint Martin d'Heres, France
[3] GAMA, Université de Lyon, Université Lyon1
43 bd du 11 Novembre 1918, Villeurbanne, France
hamida.seba@univ-lyon1.fr, sofiane.lagraa@imag.fr
hamamache.kheddouci@univ-lyon1.fr

Abstract. Several approaches have been proposed to deal with the web service matchmaking problem. Unfortunately, most of these solutions are purely syntactic measures based on the input/output interface specifications of web services and consequently lake accuracy. This is a serious drawback in a fast growing Internet that is facing the challenge to deal with an increasing number of published services. The proposed solutions to cope with this limitation consider the process part of a service description as a graph in the similarity measure. This kind of solutions has better accuracy but suffer from high computational complexity because they rely on time consuming graph matching tools. To avoid this heavy time computing overhead, we propose in this paper a solution that decomposes the process graph into smaller subgraphs and construct similarity of web services based on the similarity of their subgraphs. Simulation results show that our solution is both accurate and fast to compute.

Keywords: Web service Matchmaking, OWL-S, Graph matching, Graph edit distance, Graph kernels.

1 Background and Motivation

As service oriented computing becomes a fundamental computing orientation, the need for mechanisms that efficiently discover services over the net get acute. One essential part of web service discovery is web service matchmaking. This implies comparing web service descriptions and selecting the one that corresponds to the demand. The first approaches to web service matchmaking used keyword search. However, a syntactic comparison of keywords turned out to be insufficient. So, new solutions have been proposed recently. These solutions rely on richer descriptions of web services, mainly semantic descriptions. OWL-S (Web Ontology Language for Web Services) provides such description. OWL-S (formerly, DAML-S)[1] describes a web service by a Profile, a Grounding and a Model. The profile describes inputs, outputs, preconditions and effects of the web service. Inputs and outputs in the service profile refer to concepts belonging to a set of ontologies. The grounding provides the details necessary to invoke the service such as message format, transfer protocol, etc. The service model describes

---

* Corresponding author.

J. Filipe and J. Cordeiro (Eds.): WEBIST 2011, LNBIP 101, pp. 43–56, 2012.

a service as a process, either atomic or composite. Composite processes have a set of sub-processes associated with a control structure. The control structures specify the order in which different sub-processes are executed. Examples of control structures are: Sequence, Split, Split+Join, Any-Order, Choice, If-Then-Else, Iterate, Repeat While and Repeat Until. Processes may be modeled by automata, petri nets or graphs. A graph of an OWL-S process is a labeled directed graph $G = (V_A, V_C, E)$ where:

- V_A is the set of vertices that represent the atomic activities of the service.
- V_C is the set of vertices that correspond to control structures such as choice, sequence, if-then-else, etc. These structures can be represented by logic connectors namely XOR and AND. For instance, a choice is represented by a XOR.
- E is the set of edges that bind the different vertices.

Furthermore, a process graph can have a vertex "start" and one or several vertices "end" [22]. Figure 1 gives un example of an OWL-S process and its corresponding graph.

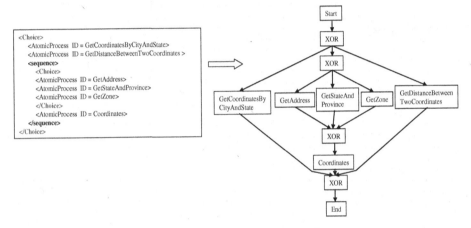

Fig. 1. A graph representation of an OWL-S process

In the case of non cyclic operations, an OWL-S process can also be represented by a tree where the root and the internal nodes are the different control structures (choice, sequence, if-then-else,..., etc.) and the leafs are the atomic services. Figure 2 illustrates an example.

The earlier matching approaches of OWL-S web services [20] rely on the service profile. In fact, several matchmaking algorithms use only inputs and outputs in the similarity measure. One of the pioneers in this context is the work of Paloucciet al. [26]. Then, several extensions of this algorithm have been proposed [4]. In [3], the authors extend the algorithm of [26] by computing a matching in a bipartite graph composed of the concepts of the published service and those of the query. In [5], the authors consider pre-condition matching in addition to inputs and outputs. In [15], the authors present a similarity measure that allows advertisements and requests to be expressed in different ontologies. In [2], the authors present a method for semantic matchmaking which takes into account the preference of concepts provided by the user.

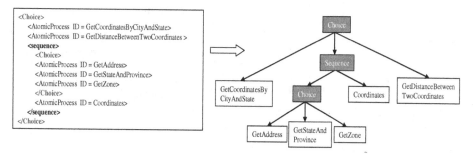

```
<Choice>
    <AtomicProcess ID = GetCoordinatesByCityAndState>
    <AtomicProcess ID = GetDistanceBetweenTwoCoordinates >
    <sequence>
        <Choice>
            <AtomicProcess ID = GetAddress>
            <AtomicProcess ID = GetStateAndProvince>
            <AtomicProcess ID = GetZone>
        </Choice>
        <AtomicProcess ID = Coordinates>
    </sequence>
</Choice>
```

Fig. 2. A tree representation of an OWL-S process

Comparing profiles has been soon pointed out to be insufficient to achieve an acceptable accuracy. To address the challenges involved in searching for web services more information about web service description must be considered. In [31], the authors consider the QoS information through the matching process. For this, the author suppose the existence of an interface where users can submit their feedback on the perceived QoS of consumed services. Wang and Stroulia [32] were the first researchers that introduced the structure of web service operations during web service discovery. Their matching method is based on the hierarchical structure of the XML syntax of WSDL specifications. For this, they adapted a tree edit distance algorithm [13] to the matching of WSDL specifications. In [12], Dong et al. built Woogle, a web service search engine that uses a clustering algorithm to group names of parameters of web-service operations into semantically meaningful concepts. Then these concepts are used to measure similarity of web-service operations. In [30], Shen and Su formally define a behavior model for web service by automata and logic formalisms. In [11], the authors use graphs to represent web service operations. Then, they use a graph matching algorithm proposed in [24] to compare graphs. However, this algorithm is space search based and consequently have an exponential time complexity. In [10], the authors also use graphs to match semantic web services. To match web service graphs, they use an A* based algorithm proposed in [23]. A* is an algorithm that uses a depth first search approach to traverse a tree representing all the possible matching situations of the compared graphs. Hao et al. [16] discover similar web services by matching the XML trees corresponding to data types in WSDL. In [21], authors use Petri nets to represent and compare web service operations. In [25] and [33], authors use finite state machine to represent web service operations.

We can see on Table 1, that summarizes some of the above approaches, that the main drawback of the solutions that rely on structural matching is the high time complexity of the matching process especially for general graphs. So, how to improve the matching accuracy of web services with structural matching while avoiding this computational complexity?

In this paper, we investigate a matching approach where web service graphs are compared based on a decomposition into smaller subgraphs. The contribution of the paper consists in identifying the nature of the subgraphs and their similarity measure.

We have implemented a prototype and conducted several experiments to evaluate the effectiveness and efficiency of our matching approach. The obtained results are promising and confirm the effectiveness of our solution.

Table 1. Web service matchmaking approaches

	Similarity level	Representation	Similarity kind	Complexity
Dijkman et al. [11]	Web service operations	Graphs	Structural : graph edit distance	Exponential
Corrales et al. [10]	Web service operations	Graphs	Structural : graph edit distance	Exponential
Nejati et al. [25] Wombacher [33]	Web service operations	Finite state machine	Structural	-
Mandell and McIlraith [20] Paolucci et al. [26]	Profile (OWLS)	Concepts in an ontology	Semantic	-
Ould Ahmed and Tata[21]	Web service operations	Petri nets	Semantic	-
Hao and Zhang [16]	Web service operations	Trees	Structural	$O(n^6)$

This paper is organized as follows: in Sect. 2, we firstly present a general description of our scheme and its theoretical foundations. Then, we provide the details of our similarity measures. We also describe a semantic similarity for atomic processes. Finally, we present the results of the experiments that evaluate our approach. Section 3 brings our remarks concluding the paper.

2 Matchmaking Web Service Processes by Subgraph Matching

2.1 Preliminaries

When web service operations are represented by graphs the problem of their matching is a graph matching problem [6,8]. The main traditional algorithmic approach to graph matching that is used to extract a list of results corresponding to a query is inexact matching or error-tolerant matching. Inexact matching computes a distance between the compared graphs. This distance measures how much these graphs are similar and is associated to a cost function. Graph edit distance is the most used inexact matching measure. Similarity or edit distance between two graphs is the minimum number of edit operations needed to transform one graph into the other [9,29]. An edit operation is an insertion, a suppression or a relabeling of a vertex or an edge in a graph. Figure 3 shows an example of edit operations that are necessary to get the graph G_2 from G_1 with the suppression of three edges and a vertex and the insertion of a vertex and two edges. To each edit operation e_i is associated a cost $c(e_i)$ and the edit distance between two graphs G_1 and G_2 is then the minimum cost related to the set of operations that transform G_1 into G_2.

$$d(G_1, G_2) = \min_{(e_1,\ldots,e_k) \in \Upsilon(G_1,G_2)} \sum_{i=1}^{k} c(e_i) \tag{1}$$

where $\Upsilon(G_1, G_2)$ is the set of edit operations that transform G_1 into G_2. However, finding the minimal edit distance is NP-hard [7] and it is often difficult to find the appropriate costs for individual edit operations [6].

Another and perhaps most powerful inexact graph matching tool is graph kernels. Graph kernels is one of the most recent approaches to graph matching that is presented as an alternative to existing solutions. Graph kernels belong to a class of kernels on structured data called R-convolution kernels or decomposition kernels [17]. The idea

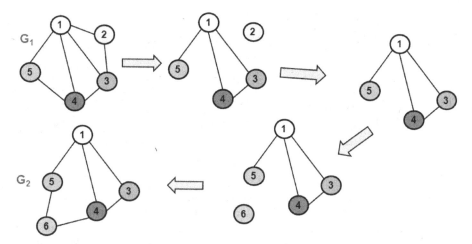

Fig. 3. Example of edit operations in a graph

of graph kernels is constructing similarity of graphs based on the similarity of small parts, i.e. subgraphs, of the compared graphs. The concept of decomposing a discrete compound object x into parts $(x_1, x_2, ..., x_d)$ can be formally modeled by a predicate R that returns true if $(x_1, ..., x_d)$ is a valid decomposition of x. The set of all valid decompositions of x is noted $R^{-1}(x) = \{(x_1, ..., x_d) : R(x_1, ..., x_d)\}$. The kernel function k between two objects x and x' is given by [17]:

$$k(x,x') = \sum_{\substack{(x_1,...,x_d)\in R^{-1}(x) \\ (x'_1,...,x'_d)\in R^{-1}(x')}} \prod_{i=1}^{d} k_i(x_i, x'_i) \tag{2}$$

where k_i is a kernel that gives the similarity between two parts.

For graphs, the natural and most general R-convolution kernel would decompose each of the two compared graphs G and G' into all of their subgraphs and compare them pairwise. This all-subgraphs kernel is defined as follows [6]:

$$k(G,G') = \sum_{\substack{S \subseteq G \\ S' \subseteq G'}} k_i(S, S') \tag{3}$$

where k_i is a function that gives the similarity between two subgraphs. The challenge of kernel based approaches is to find the decomposition that is fast to compute and that gives the required accuracy.

The idea of decomposing the graphs to be matched prior to the matching process has also been used with graph edit distance and the results are promising. In [19,28] the authors use a star decomposition of the graphs and then define graph edit distance onto the obtained substructures. Table 2 gives examples of matching methods that rely on decomposition into small substructures. It shows the kind of substructures used in the matching and the time complexity of the decomposition and the matching tasks.

Table 2. Decomposition-based graph matching approaches

Approach		Kind of graphs	Application domain	Decomposition		Matching complexity
				Type	Complexity	
Graph edit distance	Riesen and Bunke[28]	Non directed labeled	Pattern recognition	Star	$O(n^2)$	$O(n^5)$
	Jouili and Tabbone [19]	Non directed labeled	Pattern recognition	Star	$O(n^2)$	$O(n^5)$
Graph kernels	Borgwardt and Kriegel [6]	Simple graph	Biology	Shortest paths	$O(n^3)$	$O(n^4)$
	Ramon and Gartner [27]	Simple graph	X	Tree	Polynomial	Exponential
	Horvath et al. [18]	Non directed labeled	Biology	Cycle	Exponential	Exponential

2.2 Algorithms

It follows from the above description of graph matching approaches that graph decomposition allows to have more efficient solutions either via graph kernels or graph edit distance. The question here is what is the decomposition to use when matching web services? To attempt to give a satisfactory answer, we propose here two kinds of decomposition of web service graphs through two matching algorithms: Algorithm 1 and Algorithm 2. Both of them focus on the main characteristic of the graphs of web service processes: directed edges. Algorithm 1 uses graph kernels and Algorithm 2 uses graph edit distance. We also attempt to reduce the matching delay by avoiding redundancy in the obtained substructures.

Algorithm 1

In this algorithm, we extend an existing graph decomposition, the star decomposition, to take into account edge-direction. We call this star, where all edges are out-coming edges, a *FaS* for Father and Sons substructure. A *FaS* substructure is composed of a node connected to its sons by out-coming edges. This decomposition is adapted for acyclic graphs. So we apply it for trees of web service operations. Figure 4 shows an example of a decomposition of an OWL-S process tree into *FaS* substructures.

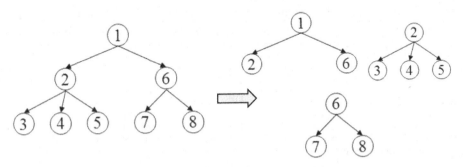

Fig. 4. Decomposition of a service tree into *FaS*s

Principle. To compare two OWL-S processes, we first decompose their corresponding trees into *FaS*s. Then, each *FaS* of the first process is compared to every *FaS* of the second process (see Algorithm 1). Comparing a pair $< FaS_i, FaS_j >$ of *FaS*s consists

---

Algorithm 1. Matching algorithm using a decomposition into *FaS*s and tree kernels

---

Input:Two OWL-S process trees A_1 and A_2

Output: similarity degree between A_1 and A_2 computed as a tree kernel

Begin

Decompose A_1 and A_2 into *FaS*s.

For $i = 1, nA_1$ do /* nA_1 is the number of *FaS*s in A_1 */

    For $j = 1, nA_2$ do nA_2 is the is the number of *FaS*s in A_2*/

        $Sim(i, j) = 0$;

    EndFor

EndFor;

For $i = 1, nA_1$ do

    For $j = 1, nA_2$ do /* compare FaS_i and FaS_j */

$$d_{father}(FaS_i, FaS_j) = \begin{cases} 0 & \text{if } father_{FaS_i} = father_{FaS_j} \\ 1 & \text{otherwise} \end{cases}$$

$$d_{son}(FaS_i, FaS_j)) = max(\|FaS_i\|, \|FaS_j\|) - \|FaS_i \cap FaS_j\|$$

$$d_{edge}(FaS_i, FaS_j) = |\,\|edge(FaS_i)\| - \|edge(FaS_j)\|\,|$$

$$d(FaS_i, FaS_j) = d_{father}(FaS_i, FaS_j) + d_{son}(FaS_i, FaS_j)) + d_{edge}(FaS_i, FaS_j)$$

$$k(FaS_i, FaS_j) = exp^{-d(FaS_i, FaS_j)}$$

        If $k(FaS_i, FaS_j) > Sim(i, j)$ Then $Sim(i, j) = k(FaS_i, FaS_j)$; EndIF

    EndFor

EndFor

$$K(A_1, A_2) = \sum_{i=1, j=1}^{nA_1, nA_2} Sim(i, j) \text{ /*tree kernel of } A_1 \text{ and } A_2 \text{ */}$$

End

---

to compute the kernel function $k(FaS_i, FaS_j) = exp^{-d(FaS_i, FaS_j)}$ which allows us to find for a given FaS_i of the first tree the most similar FaS_j of the second tree given by the best value of $k(FaS_i, FaS_j)$ noted $Sim(i, j)$. The kernel function sums up distances between *FaS*s, each computed looking at the number of edges in the compared *FaS*s, the number of sons, and a comparison between fathers and sons:

$$K(A_1, A_2) = \sum_{i=1, j=1}^{nA_1, nA_2} Sim(i, j) \tag{4}$$

Example. Figure 5 illustrates a matching example of two web service trees A_1 and A_2 with Algorithm 1. The decomposition gives 2 *FaS* substructures for each tree. The best value of the kernel function for $FaS_1(A_1)$ is the one that matches it with $FaS_1(A_2)$ and it is equal to e^{-2}. The best value of the kernel function for $FaS_2(A_1)$ is the one that matches it with $FaS_2(A_2)$ and it is also equal to e^{-2}. So, the final value of the similarity between the two trees is $e^{-2} + e^{-2} = 2e^{-2}$.

Time Complexity. The algorithm has a complexity of $O(\triangle n^3)$ time steps where n is the number of vertices in the largest tree and $\triangle$ is the maximum degree in the tree. In fact the complexity of the decomposition into *FaS* substructures is polynomial. In the worst case it is $O(\triangle n)$. To match the obtained sets of *FaS*s, we need $O(\triangle n^3)$ time steps.

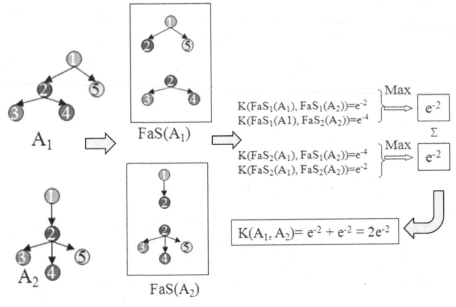

$$K(\text{FaS}_1(A_1), \text{FaS}_1(A_2))=e^{-2}$$
$$K(\text{FaS}_1(A1), \text{FaS}_2(A_2))=e^{-4}$$

$$K(\text{FaS}_2(A_1), \text{FaS}_1(A_2))=e^{-4}$$
$$K(\text{FaS}_2(A_1), \text{FaS}_2(A_2))=e^{-2}$$

$$K(A_1, A_2)= e^{-2} + e^{-2} = 2e^{-2}$$

Fig. 5. A matching example with Algorithm 1

This gives a global complexity of $O(\triangle n^3 + \triangle n = \triangle n^3)$ time steps. As in the worst case $\triangle = n$, we have a complexity of $O(n^4)$.

Algorithm 2

In this algorithm, we propose a new graph decomposition that emphasizes edges and their direction. This decomposition, called *EaS* for (**E**dge **a**nd its endpoint **S**tars) is a graph substructure composed of a directed edge, its endpoint vertices and all the out-coming edges from the two endpoints. Figure 6 shows an example of the decomposition of a graph into *EaS*s.

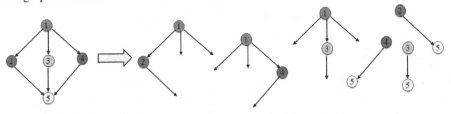

Fig. 6. Example of decomposing a graph into *EaS*s

Principle. To compare two OWL-S processes, we first decompose their corresponding graphs into *EaS*s. Then each *EaS* of the first process is compared to every *EaS* of the second process (see Algorithm 2). Comparing a pair $<EaS_i, EaS_j>$ of *EaS*s consists to compute the edit distance $d(EaS_i, EaS_j)$ between two subgraphs. We use a matrix *Sim* where $Sim(i,j) = d(EaS_i, EaS_j)$ to save the computed distances. *Sim* is a $nG_1 \times nG_2$

Algorithm 2. Matching algorithm based on *EaS.* and Edit distance

---

Input: Two OWL-S process graphs G_1 and G_2

Output: similarity degree between G_1 and G_2 computed as a graph edit distance

Begin

Decompose G_1 and G_2 into *EaSs.*

For $i = 1, nG_1$ do /*nG_1(resp. nG_2) is the number of *EaSs* in G_1(resp. G_2)

    For $j = 1, nG_2$ do

        $Sim(i, j) = 0$;

    EndFor

EndFor

For $i = 1, nG_1$ do

    For $j = 1, nG_2$ do

        /* compare *EaS*$_i$ and *EaS*$_j$ */

        $d(EaS_i, EaS_j) = c(father_i, father_j) + c(son_i, son_j) + |\,\|E(EaS_i)\| - \|E(EaS_j)\|\,|$

        where $c(x, y)$ is the cost of the substituting x by y.

        $Sim(i, j) = d(EaS_i, EaS_j)$

    EndFor

EndFor

$$d(G_1, G_2) = \frac{\sum_{i=1, j=1}^{NG_1, NG_2} min \ Sim(i, j)}{|nG_1 - nG_2|} + |\,\|G_1\| - \|G_2\|\,|$$

End

---

matrix, where nG_1(resp. nG_2) is the number of *EaSs* in G_1(resp. G_2). Then, the distance between the two graphs is the sum of the minimal distances between *EaSs*.

Example. Figure 7 illustrates a matching example of two graphs G_1 and G_2 with Algorithm 2. The decomposition gives 5 *EaS* substructures for G_1 and 3 *EaS* substructures for G_2. The matrix of similarity *Sim* between *EaSs* is 5×3. In Fig. 7, each *EaS* is represented by the directed edge that determines it i.e. a pair of nodes $(father, son)$. Each cell of the matrix contains the edit distance between two *EaSs*. For example $Sim(1, 1) = 2$ because if we consider that all edit operations have the same cost 1, then the distance between $EaS_1(G_1)$ and $EaS_1(G_2)$ is equal to the cost of two re-labeling operations: 2 to 1 and 3 to 2. By summing the minimal distances between all pairs of *EaSs*, we obtain a distance between the two graphs that is equal to 7.

Complexity. The complexity of Algorithm 2 is $O(n^2 \triangle^2)$ where n is the number of vertices in the largest graph and $\triangle$ is its maximum degree. In fact, to decompose a graph of n nodes into *EaSs* we need $O(n^2)$ time steps. To compare two *EaSs*, we need $2\triangle^2$ time steps. So, if we consider that, in the worst case a graph of n nodes has $2n$ *EaSs* then to construct the matrix *Sim* of all comparisons between the *EaSs*, of two graphs, we need $O(4n^2 * 2\triangle^2) = O(n^2 \triangle^2)$ time steps.

To compute the minimum distance between *EaSs*, we need $O((2n)^2) = O(4n^2)$ time steps.

So, the complexity of the algorithm is $O(n^2 \triangle^2)$. As in the worst case $\triangle = n$, we have a complexity of $O(n^4)$.

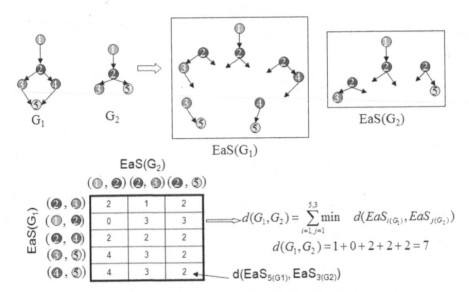

$$d(G_1,G_2) = \sum_{i=1,j=1}^{5,3} \min \ d(EaS_{i(G_1)}, EaS_{j(G_2)})$$

$$d(G_1,G_2) = 1+0+2+2+2 = 7$$

Fig. 7. A matching example with Algorithm 2

2.3 Similarity between Atomic Processes

To obtain an accurate similarity measure, we also consider semantic similarity of inputs and outputs. To do so, we extended the semantic similarity of [26] with Kernels. In fact, we propose a kernel function to evaluate the four degrees of similarity *Exact*, *PlugIn*, *Subsume* and *Fail* introduced in [26]. We affect a weight w to each of the four degrees. This weight is either given by the user or determined according to the application. So, we compare two concepts cx_1 and cx_2 that correspond to the inputs or outputs x_1 and x_2 of the compared services by the following function:

$$k_{Sem}(x_1,x_2) = \begin{cases} w_{Exact} & if \ Exact(cx_1,cx_2) \\ w_{PlugIn} * \frac{1}{d(cx_1,cx_2)} & if \ PlugIn(cx_1,cx_2) \\ w_{Subsumes} * \frac{1}{d(cx_1,cx_2)} & if \ Subsumes(cx_1,cx_2) \\ w_{Fail} & otherwise \end{cases} \tag{5}$$

where $d(cx_1,cx_2)$ is the number of edges that separate the two concepts cx_1 and cx_2 in the ontology.

Thus, the semantic similarity between two services S_1 and S_2 is the sum of the most similar inputs and outputs of the two services as follows:

$$k(S_1,S_2) = \sum_{x_1 \in S_1, x_2 \in S_2}^{nbS_1, nbS_2} max \ k_{Sem}(x_1,x_2) \tag{6}$$

where nbS_1 (resp. nbS_2) is the number of inputs/outputs of S_1 (resp. S_2) and $k_{Sem}(x_1,x_2)$ is the similarity between two concepts.

Example. Let S be a published service with two input parameters: "vehicle" and "parts" and one output "price". Let Q a query with input parameters "Car" and "parts" and one output "price". We suppose that the ontology is the one presented on Fig. 8 and that $w_{Exact} = 1$, $w_{Plug-In} = 0.8$, $w_{Subsumes} = 0.5$, $w_{Fail} = 0$.

The similarity between the inputs of the published service and the query is :

$$\begin{cases} k_{Sem}(car, vehicle) = w_{PlugIn} * \frac{1}{1} = 0.8 \\ \\ k_{Sem}(car, parts) = w_{Fail} = 0 \end{cases} \overset{Max}{\Rightarrow} 0.8 \tag{7}$$

$$\begin{cases} k_{Sem}(parts, vehicle) = w_{Fail} = 0 \\ \\ k_{Sem}(parts, parts) = w_{Exact} = 1 \end{cases} \overset{Max}{\Rightarrow} 1 \tag{8}$$

The similarity between the outputs of the two services is:

$$k_{Sem}(price, price) = w_{Exact} = 1 \overset{Max}{\Rightarrow} 1 \tag{9}$$

This gives the following similarity between the two services:

$$k(S_1, S_2) = 0.8 + 1 + 1 = 2.8 \tag{10}$$

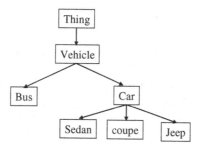

Fig. 8. Vehicle ontology

2.4   Evaluation

In this section, we provide an overview of our experiments and some of the results we obtained. The experiments were conducted on a Windows XP Laptop with a 1.73 GHz Pentium IV CPU and 1Gb main memory. The data set used in our tests is a web service repository collected by [14]. We considered 15 Query graphs and 100 Target graphs. Target graphs are generated by distorting each query graph using adaptive operations such as: changing atomic activity names, changing inputs/outputs of atomic activities, removing atomic activities, changing the execution order of query fragments, etc.

We first evaluated the execution time performance of the two algorithms. The time performance is tested with the increase of the number of nodes of the compared graphs. Figure 9 shows the variation of execution times according to the size of target graphs. The results reported in this graphic represent the average execution times found for

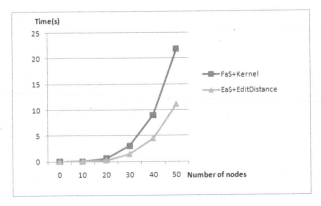

Fig. 9. Execution time vs the size of the graph

each given target graph size. It can be seen that the execution times of Algorithm 1 (FaS+Kernel) and Algorithm 2 (EaS+editDistance) are polynomial w.r.t the number of nodes in the target graph. Moreover, the slope of Algorithm 1 is higher than for Algorithm 2.

We then evaluated the effectiveness of our approach by computing the recall and precision ratios [12]. The precision p and recall r are defined as follows:

$$p = \frac{A}{A+B} \tag{11}$$

$$r = \frac{A}{A+C} \tag{12}$$

where A stands for the number of returned relevant services, B stands for the number of returned irrelevant services, C stands for the number of missing relevant services, $A+C$ stands for the total number of relevant services, and $A+B$ stands for the total number of returned services. As shown on Fig. 10, the precisions of our schemes is 93% for Algorithm 1 and 92% for Algorithm 2 and the recall is 96% for Algorithm 1 and 95% for Algorithm 2. We can see that under the same semantic similarity measure for inputs and outputs, kernels achieve a better accuracy than edit distance but take more time to be computed.

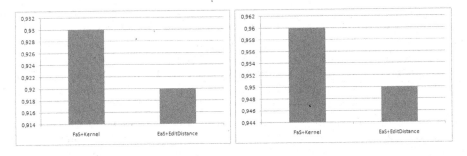

Fig. 10. Precision and Recall

3   Conclusions

In this paper, we presented a web service matchmaking method based on subgraph matching. The main advantage of decomposing the web service graph into subgraphs is to reduce the time complexity of the matching. The proposed algorithms take into account the main characteristic of web service graphs: directed edges and use the most efficient graph matching tools: graph kernels and graph edit distance. We also augmented our structural matching by a semantic similarity measure that enhances the matching precision. Experimental results show that the proposed algorithms are efficient and fast to compute. We are aware that these results are not sufficient to establish the good performance of the proposed method. Further investigations merit attention:

- a more representative data set or benchmark must be considered for future experiments.
- other similarity measures between subgraphs may be considered and tested.
- extend the approach and explore its performance with web service databases.

Acknowledgements. This work was supported by Agence Nationale de la Recherche ANR-08-CORD-009 and CCI de l'AIN.

References

1. Web ontology language for web services, http://www.w3.org/submission/owl-s/
2. Beck, M., Freitag, B.: Semantic matchmaking using ranked instance retrieval. In: SMR 2006: 1st International Workshop on Semantic Matchmaking and Resource Retrieval, Co-located with VLDB (2006)
3. Bellur, U., Kulkarni, R.: Improved matchmaking algorithm for semantic web services based on bipartite graph matching. In: IEEE International Conference on Web Services, ICWS 2007 (2007)
4. Bellur, U., Vadodaria, H.: On extending semantic matchmaking to include precondition and effect matching. In: International Conference on Web Services, Beijing, China (2008)
5. Bellur, U., Vadodaria, H., Gupta, A.: Greedy Algorithms. In: Bednorz, W. (ed.) Semantic Matchmaking Algorithms. InTech, Croatia (2008)
6. Borgwardt, K., Kriegel, H.P.: Shortest-path kernels on graphs. In: 5th Int. Conference on Data Mining, pp. 74–81 (2005)
7. Bunke, H.: Error correcting graph matching: On the influence of the underlying cost function. IEEE Trans. Pattern Anal. Mach. Intell. 21(9), 917–922 (1999)
8. Bunke, H.: Recent developments in graph matching. In: ICPR, pp. 2117–2124 (2000)
9. Bunke, H., Allermann, G.: Inexact graph matching for structural pattern recognition. Pattern Recognition Letters 1, 245–253 (1983)
10. Corrales, J.C., Grigori, D., Bouzeghoub, M.: Behavioral matchmaking for service retrieval: Application to conversation protocols. Inf. Syst. 33(7-8), 681–698 (2008)
11. Dijkman, R., Dumas, M., García-Bañuelos, L.: Graph Matching Algorithms for Business Process Model Similarity Search. In: Dayal, U., Eder, J., Koehler, J., Reijers, H.A. (eds.) BPM 2009. LNCS, vol. 5701, pp. 48–63. Springer, Heidelberg (2009)
12. Dong, X., Halevy, A., Madhavan, J., Nemes, E., Zhang, J.: Simlarity search for web services. In: VLDB 2004, pp. 372–383 (2004)

13. Garofalakis, M., Kumar, A.: Correlating xml data streams using tree-edit distance embeddings. In: ACM PODS 2003, pp. 143–154. ACM Press, San Diego (2003)
14. Gater, A., Grigori, D., Bouzeghoub, M.: Owl-s process model matchmaking. In: IEEE International Conference on Web Services, Miami, Florida, USA, July 5-10 (2010)
15. Guo, J.L.R., Chen, D.: Matching semantic web services across heterogenous ontologies. In: The Fifth International Conference on Computer and Information Technology, CIT 2005 (2005)
16. Hao, Y., Zhang, Y.: Web services discovery based on schema matching. In: The Thirtieth Australasian Conference on Computer Science, vol. 62 (2007)
17. Haussler, D.: Convolution kernels on discrete structures. Tech. Rep. UCSC-CRL-99-10, University of California, Santa Cruz (1999)
18. Horvath, T., Gartner, T., Wrobel, S.: Cyclic pattern kernels for predictive graph mining. In: KDD 2004, pp. 158–167 (2004)
19. Jouili, S., Mili, I., Tabbone, S.: Attributed Graph Matching Using Local Descriptions. In: Blanc-Talon, J., Philips, W., Popescu, D., Scheunders, P. (eds.) ACIVS 2009. LNCS, vol. 5807, pp. 89–99. Springer, Heidelberg (2009)
20. Mandell, D., McIlraith, S.: A bottom-up approach to automating web service discovery, customization, and semantic translation. In: Proceedings of the Twelfth International World Wide Web Conference Workshop on E-Services and the Semantic Web (ESSW),Budapest (2003)
21. M'bareck, N.O.A., Tata, S.: BPEL Behavioral Abstraction and Matching. In: Eder, J., Dustdar, S. (eds.) BPM Workshops 2006. LNCS, vol. 4103, pp. 495–506. Springer, Heidelberg (2006)
22. Mendling, J., Lassen, K., Zdun, U.: Transformation strategies between block-oriented and graph-oriented process modelling languages. In: Lehner, F., Nsekabel, H., Kleinschmidt, P. (eds.) Multikonferenz Wirtschaftsinformatik, pp. 297–312 (2006)
23. Messmer, B.: Efficient Graph Matching Algorithms for Preprocessed Model Graphs. Ph.D. thesis, University of Bern, Switzerland (1995)
24. Messmer, B.T., Bunke, H.: A decision tree approach to graph and subgraph isomorphism detection. Pattern Recognition 32, 1979–1998 (1999)
25. Nejati, S., Sabetzadeh, M., Chechik, M., Easterbrook, S., Zave, P.: Matching and merging of statecharts specifications. In: ICSE 2007, pp. 54–63 (2007)
26. Paolucci, M., Kawamura, T., Payne, T.R., Sycara, K.: Semantic Matching of Web Services Capabilities. In: Horrocks, I., Hendler, J. (eds.) ISWC 2002. LNCS, vol. 2342, pp. 333–347. Springer, Heidelberg (2002)
27. Ramon, J., Gartner, T.: Expressivity versus efficiency of graph kernels. In: First International Workshop on Mining Graphs, Trees and Sequences (2003)
28. Riesen, K., Bunke, H.: Approximate graph edit distance computation by means of bipartite graph matching. Image and Vision Computing 27, 950–959 (2009)
29. Sanfeliu, A., Fu, K.: A distance measure between attributed relational graphs for pattern recognition. IEEE Transactions on Systems, Man, and Cybernetics (Part B) 13(3), 353–363 (1983)
30. Shen, Z., Su, J.: Web service discovery based on behavior signatures. SCC 1, 279–286 (2005)
31. Vu, L.-H., Porto, F., Hauswirth, M., Aberer, K.: A search engine for qosenabled discovery of semantic web services. International Journal of Business Process Integration and Management 1(4), 244–255 (2006)
32. Wang, Y., Stroulia, E.: Flexible interface matching for web-service discovery. In: WISE 2003 (2003)
33. Wombacher, A.: Evaluation of Technical Measures for Workflow Similarity Based on a Pilot Study. In: Meersman, R., Tari, Z. (eds.) OTM 2006, Part I. LNCS, vol. 4275, pp. 255–272. Springer, Heidelberg (2006)

Distributed XML Processing over Various Topologies: Characterizing XML Document Processing Efficiency

Yoshiyuki Uratani[1], Hiroshi Koide[2], Dirceu Cavendish[3], and Yuji Oie[3]

[1] Graduate School of Computer Science and Systems Engineering
Kyushu Institute of Technology, Kawazu 680-4, Iizuka, Fukuoka, 820-8502, Japan
[2] Faculty of Computer Science of Systems Engineering, Kyushu Institute of Technology
Kawazu 680-4, Iizuka, Fukuoka, 820-8502, Japan
[3] Network Design Research Center, Kyushu Institute of Technology
Kawazu 680-4, Iizuka, Fukuoka, 820-8502, Japan
uratani@klab.ai.kyutech.ac.jp, koide@ai.kyutech.ac.jp,
{cavendish,oie}@ndrc.kyutech.ac.jp

Abstract. This study characterizes distributed XML processing on networking nodes. XML documents are sent from a client node to a server node through relay nodes, which process the documents before arriving at the server. When the relay nodes are connected in tandem, the XML documents are processed in a pipelining manner. When the relay nodes are connected in parallel, the XML documents are processed in a parallel fashion. We evaluate distributed XML processing with synthetic and realistic XML documents. Well-formedness and grammar validation pipelining and parallel processing characterization reveals inherent advantages of the parallel processing model.

Keywords: Distributed XML processing, Task scheduling, Pipelining and parallel processing.

1 Introduction

XML technology has become ubiquitous on distributed systems, as it supports loosely coupled interfaces between servers implementing Web Services. Large XML data documents, requiring processing at servers, may soon require distributed processing, for scalability. Recently, distributed XML processing has been proposed and studied from an algorithmic point of view for well-formedness, grammar validation, and filtering [1]. In that work, a Prefix Automata SyStem is described, where (PASS) nodes opportunistically process fragments of an XML document travelling from a client to a server, as a data stream. PASS nodes can be arranged into two basic distributed processing models: pipelining, and parallel model. We have studied task allocation of XML documents over pipeline and parallel distribute models in [2] [3]. We leverage their results into an efficient task allocation method in this current work. Moreover, the problem of scheduling tasks on streaming data that follows parallel paths has been addressed in [4]. In that work, we have also studied the migration of tasks between nodes depending on network congestion.

In this paper, we provide a comprehensive characterization of distributed XML processing. We evaluate two distributed XML processing models - i) pipelining, for XML

J. Filipe and J. Cordeiro (Eds.): WEBIST 2011, LNBIP 101, pp. 57–71, 2012.
© Springer-Verlag Berlin Heidelberg 2012

data stream processing systems; ii) parallel, for XML parallel processing systems - with regard to processing efficiency, correlating performance with XML document structure and type of processing task for well-formedness and grammar validation tasks. The paper is organized as follows. In section 2, we describe generic models of XML processing nodes, to be used in both pipelining and parallel processing. In section 3, we describe various experimental environments that implement the distributed XML processing system, and characterize XML processing performance of the pipeline and parallel computation models. In section 4, we address related work. In section 5, we summarize our findings and address research directions.

2   XML Processing Elements

Distributed XML processing requires some basic functions to be supported: **Document Partition:** The XML document is divided into fragments, to be processed at processing nodes. **Document Annotation:** Each document fragment is annotated with current processing status upon leaving a processing node. **Document Merging:** Document fragments are merged so as to preserve the original document structure. XML processing nodes support some of these tasks, according to their role in the distributed XML system.

2.1   XML Processing Nodes

We abstract the distributed XML processing elements into four types of nodes: StartNode, RelayNode, EndNode, and MergeNode. The distributed XML processing can then be constructed by connecting these nodes in specific topologies, such as pipelining and parallel topologies.

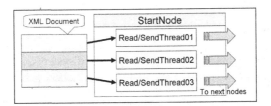

Fig. 1. Components of StartNode (three next nodes case)

StartNode is a source node that executes any pre-processing needed in preparation for piecewise processing of the XML document. This node also starts XML document transfer to relay nodes, for XML processing. We show components of the StartNode in Fig. 1. The StartNode has one or more threads of the type Read/SendThread. In Fig. 1, StartNode has three next nodes. The Read/SendThreads each reads part of an XML document one line at a time, and add checking and processing information. The checking information is used for tag check processing. Processing information describes which RelayNode shall process which parts of the XML document. Each Read/SendThread reads part of the document roughly of the same size. Then, each Read/SendThread sends the processed data to next nodes. Read/SendThreads run concurrently.

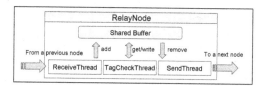

Fig. 2. Components of RelayNode

RelayNode executes XML processing on parts of an XML document. It is placed as an intermediate node in paths between the StartNode and the EndNode. We show components of the RelayNode in Fig. 2. The RelayNode has three types of threads: ReceiveThread, TagCheckThread and SendThread. The ReceiveThread receives data containing lines of an XML document, together with checking and processing information, and stores the data into a shared buffer. The TagCheckThread attempts to process the data, if the data is assigned to be processed at the node. SendThread sequentially sends data to a next node.

EndNode is a destination node, where XML documents must reach, and have their XML processing finished. This node receives data containing the XML document, checking information and processing information, from a particular previous node. If the tag checking has not been finished yet, the EndNode processes all unchecked tags, in order to complete XML processing of the entire document. In addition, the EndNode strips the document from any overhead information, so as to restore the document to its original form. Components of the EndNode are similar to the RelayNode, except that the EndNode has DeleteThread instead of SendThread. The DeleteThread cleans the data from processing and checking information, and deletes the data from the shared buffer.

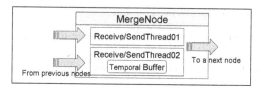

Fig. 3. Components of MergeNode (two previous nodes)

The MergeNode receives data from multiple previous nodes, serializes it, and sends it to a next node, without performing any XML processing. The MergeNode is used only in parallel XML processing topologies. We show a component of the MergeNode in Fig. 3. The MergeNode has more than one thread of the type Receive/SendThread. Each thread receives data from a previous node. The MergeNode further sends the data in order, so some threads may need to wait previous data to be sent before sending its part of data. For instance, in Fig. 3, Receive/SendThread02 waits until Receive/SendThread01 finishes sending its data related to a previous part of the XML document, before sending its own data, related to a subsequent part of the document.

Node Tag Checking Method. XML document processing involves stack data structures for tag processing. When a node reads a start tag, it pushes the tag name into a

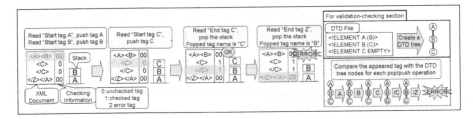

Fig. 4. A Node Tag Checking Example

stack. When a node reads an end tag, it pops a top element from the stack, and compares the end tag name with the popped tag name. If both tag names are the same, the tags match. The XML document is well-formed when all tags match. In case the pushed and popped tags do not match, the XML document is declared ill formed. Checking information is added to the document, for processing status indication: already matched; unmatched; or yet to be processed.

In Fig. 4, we show a simple example for well-formedness and validation checking. When the distributed XML processing system checks well-formedness only, the right box of the figure is not executed. When the distributed XML processing system also executes grammar validation, each node processes validation and well-formedness at the same time. In this case, each processing node has available DTD (Document Type Definition) files for grammar validation, defining the grammar that XML documents must comply with. Each node executing grammar validation reads DTD files, and generates grammar rules for validation checking. We represent these rules as a tree in the figure. Each processing node pops/pushes the tags from/to the stack, as represented in the lower part of Fig. 4. If grammar validation is executed, the node also consults the grammar rules, in order to evaluate whether the tag is allowed to appear at a specific place in the document, according to the grammar.

Node Allocation Patterns. As mentioned earlier, the distributed XML system can execute two types of distributed processing: pipeline and parallel processing. We show pipeline processing in Fig. 5, and parallel processing in Fig. 6.

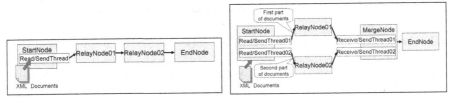

Fig. 5. Pipelining Processing (two stages instance)   **Fig. 6.** Parallel Processing (two path instance)

In Fig. 5, the distributed system has two stages pipeline. All data is transferred from StartNode to EndNode via two RelayNodes. The StartNode reads the XML document one line at a time, adds some information, and sends the resulting document to RelayNode01. RelayNode01 and RelayNode02 process parts of the received data, according to allocation determined by the scheduler. The EndNode receives data from RelayNode02, processes all unchecked data, and produces the final XML processing result. In Fig. 6, the distributed system has two routes from StartNode to EndNode. The route via RelayNode01 relays a first part of documents, and the route via RelayNode02 relays a second part of documents. RelayNode01 and RelayNode02 process parts of the received data, according to the scheduler's allocation. MergeNode receives data from the RelayNodes, merges it, and sequentially sends it to the EndNode. The EndNode receives data from the MergeNode, processes all unchecked data, and produces the final result. Parallel processing models have an extra node, the MergeNode, as compared with the pipeline processing model. Notice that the MergeNode executes only extra processing overhead, needed for merging parts of the document, in the parallel architecture, not executing any XML processing. We could also have integrated such merging capability into the EndNode, an hence obtaining an exact same number of nodes between pipeline and parallel models. We have decided to create a specific MergeNode in order to keep the EndNode the same across both architectures, and the number of nodes executing XML processing the same in both processing models.

3 Distributed XML Characterization

In this section, we characterize distributed XML well-formedness and grammar validation processing.

3.1 Experimental Environment

We use three types of environments, two virtual and a real one. For experiments, we use seven nodes, upon which tasks are allocated to execute distribute XML processing in each environment.

T5440_Env. This environment consists of a Solaris Container on a Sun SPARC Enterprise T5440 Server.The server specification is described in Table 1 and it's environment is shown in Fig. 7. We use the operating system level virtualization technology of Solaris Container to implement distributed XML processing nodes. The Solaris Container treats one operating system as a global zone which is unique in the system. We can dynamically allocate resources to the zones, such as CPU cores and memory space. We have deployed seven nodes in this environment. They execute independently, since the number of CPU cores, 32, is larger than the number of nodes. The operating system running in the global zone is duplicated to non-global zones. So Solaris 10 OS also runs in each node.

PC_Env. This environment consists of two types of PC cluster. One of them has 2 CPU cores (Node 06) and the other 6 PC clusters have each 4 CPU cores. Their specification is described in Table 3 and it's environment is shown in Fig.8.

X4640_Env. This environment is based on PC_Env, and consists of a VMware ESX 4 on a Sun Fire X4640 Server.We use VMware ESX 4, a virtual machine manager, to implement virtual machines for using distributed XML processing nodes. The server specification is described in Table 2 and it's environment is shown in Fig. 9. We allocated two cores to node 06, and four cores to all other nodes, similar to PC_Env.

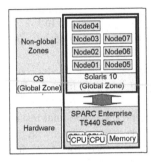
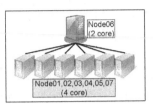
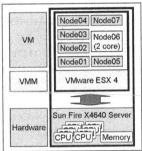

Fig. 7. Zones in T5440 Server   **Fig. 8.** PC Cluster   **Fig. 9.** VMs in X4640 Server

Table 1. T5440 Server Specification

CPU	Sun Ultra SPARC® T2 Plus (1.2GHz) × 4
Memory	128G bytes (FB-DIMM)
OS	Solaris^{TM}10
JVM	Java^{TM}1.5.0_17

Table 2. X4640 Server Specification

CPU	Six-Core AMD Opteron Processor 8435 (2.6GHz) × 8
Memory	256G bytes (DDR2/667 ECC registered DIMM)
VMM	VMware ESX 4
Guest OS	Fedora15_x86_64
JVM	Java^{TM}1.5.0_22

Table 3. PC Cluster Specification

	PC 4core	PC 2core
CPU	Intel Core 2 Quad Q965 (3GHz)	Intel Core 2 Duo E8400(3GHz)
Memory	4G Byte	
NIC	1000 BASE-T Intel 8254PI	1000 BASE-T Intel 82571 4 port × 2
OS	Fedora13_x86_64	
JVM	Java^{TM}1.5.0_22	

3.2   Task Scheduling

Our Task Scheduling System is a platform for parallel distributed processing, implemented in Java^{TM}via several modules, as illustrated in Fig. 10.

Task Controller Module. Task Controller module runs on the scheduler node. This module allocates tasks to Task Manager Modules, which run at worker machines, executing them. The Task Controller implements a scheduler for decision where tasks should be allocated, and when they should be executed.

Task Manager Module. The Task Manager module works on each worker machine. This module executes tasks assigned by the Task Controller module.

Scheduler Class. Scheduler Class implements a scheduling algorithm, which decides allocation of tasks and timing when tasks start. We can install not only static scheduling algorithms such as [5] or [6] but also dynamic scheduling algorithms such as [4] or [7], before starting distributed program execution. However, we use a static

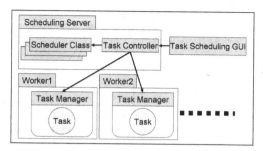

Fig. 10. Task Scheduling System

scheduling algorithm which assigns all tasks beforehand for simplicity. Tasks communicate with each other via streaming connections in the experiments of this paper (Section 3). The tasks are allocated to workers by the scheduler beforehand. Once the tasks start, they will run until the processing or all data is finished. Also the scheduler does not migrate tasks to other workers, even if some worker is idle.

3.3   Node Allocation Patterns

We use several topologies and task allocation patterns for characterizing distributed XML processing, within the parallel and pipelining models. We vary also the number of RelayNodes, within topologies, to evaluate their impact into processing efficiency. In Fig. 11–14, tasks are shown as light shaded boxes, underneath nodes allocated to process them.

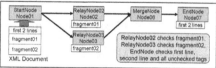

Fig. 11. Two Stages Pipeline   **Fig. 12.** Two Path Parallelism

For two RelayNode case, (Fig. 11 and 12), we divide the XML documents into three parts: first two lines, fragment01 and fragment02. The first two lines contain a meta tag and a root tag. In Fig. 11, we configure two stage pipeline topology. Data flow from StartNode to EndNode via two RelayNodes. RelayNode02 is allocated for processing fragment02, RelayNode03 is allocated for processing fragment01, and the EndNode is allocated for processing the first two lines, as well as processing all left out unchecked data. In Fig. 12, we configure two path parallelism. The first two lines, fragment01 and related data flow from StartNode to EndNode via RelayNode01 and MergeNode. Fragment02 and related data flow from the StartNode to the EndNode via RelayNode02 and the MergeNode. RelayNode02 is allocated for processing fragment01, RelayNode03 is allocated for processing fragment02, whereas the EndNode is allocated for processing the first two lines, as well as processing all left out unchecked data.

In four RelayNode case (Fig. 13 and 14), we divide the XML documents into five parts: first two lines, fragment01, fragment02, fragment03 and fragment04. Fig. 13

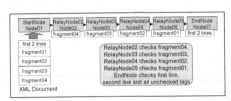

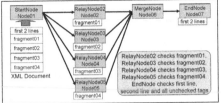

Fig. 13. Four Stages Pipeline   **Fig. 14.** Four Path Parallelism

shows a four stage pipeline topology. Data flow from StartNode to EndNode via four RelayNodes. RelayNodes fragment allocation is as shown in the figure. The EndNode is allocated for processing the first two lines, as well as processing all left out unchecked data. Fig. 14 shows four path parallelism topology. The first two lines, fragment01 and related data flow from StartNode to EndNode via RelayNode02 and MergeNode. Fragment02 and related data flow from the StartNode to the EndNode via RelayNode03 and the MergeNode. Fragment03 and related data flow from the StartNode to the EndNode via RelayNode04 and the MergeNode. Fragment04 and related data flow from the StartNode to the EndNode via RelayNode05 and the MergeNode. RelayNodes fragment allocation is as shown in the figure. The EndNode is allocated for processing the first two lines, as well as processing all left out unchecked data.

Notice that, even though the the parallel model has one extra node, the MergeNode, as compared with corresponding pipeline model, the MergeNode does not perform any XML processing per se. Hence, the number of nodes executing XML processing is still the same in both models.

3.4   Patterns and XML Document Types

The distributed XML processing system can execute two types of processing: well-formedness checking, and grammar validation checking of XML documents. Efficiency of these XML processing tasks may be related to: processing model, pipelining and parallel; topology, number of processing nodes and their connectivity; XML document characteristics. We use different structures of XML documents to investigate which distributed processing model yields the most efficient distributed XML processing. For that purpose, we create seven types of synthetic XML documents by changing the XML document depth from shallow to deep while keeping its size almost the same. We have also used three types of realistic XML documents, doc_kernel, doc_stock and doc_scala. The doc_kernel encodes directory and file hierarchy structure of linux kernel 2.6.39.3 in XML format. The doc_stock is XML formatted data from MySQL data base, containing a total of 10000 entries of dummy stock price data. The doc_scala is based on "The Scala Language Specification Version 2.8" (http://www.scala-lang.org/), which consists of 191 pages, totalling 1.3M bytes. The original document in pdf format was converted it to Libre Office odt format, an from that to XML format. We show the XML document characteristics in Table 4. and doc01–07 structures in Fig. 15.

For T5440_Env, we combine four node allocation patterns, two processing patterns and seven XML document types to produce 56 types of experiments.

Table 4. XML Document Characteristics

	doc01	doc02	doc03	doc04	doc05	doc06	doc07	kernel	stock	scala
Width	10000	5000	2500	100	4	2	1	-	-	-
Depth	1	2	4	100	2500	5000	10000	-	-	-
Tag set count (Empty tags)	10000(0)							2255 (36708)	66717 (146)	26738 (1206)
Line count	10002	15002	17502	19902	19998	20000	20001	41219	78010	72014
File size[Kbytes]	342	347	342	343	342			3891	2389	2959

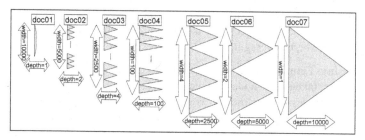

Fig. 15. XML Document Structures

3.5 Performance Indicators

We use two types performance indicators: system performance indicators and node performance indicators. System performance indicators characterize the processing of a given XML document. Node performance indicators characterize XML processing at a given processing node. The following performance indicators are used to characterize distributed XML processing:

Job Execution Time. Job execution time is a system performance indicator that captures the time taken by an instance of XML document to get processed by the distributed XML system in its entirety. As several nodes are involved in the processing, the job execution time results to be the period of time between the last node (typically EndNode) finishes its processing, and the first node (typically the StartNode) starts its processing. The job execution time is measured for each XML document type and processing model.

Node Thread Working Time. Node thread working time is a node performance indicator that captures the amount of time each thread of a node performs work. It does not include thread waiting time when blocked, such as data receiving wait time. It is defined as the total file reading time, data receiving time and data sending time a node incurs. For instance, in the MergeNode, the node thread working time is the sum of receiving time and sending time of each Receive/SendThread. Assume the MergeNode is connected to two previous nodes, with two Receive/SendThreads. Furthermore, one Receive/SendThread spends 200 msec for receiving data and sending data, whereas the other Receive/SendThread spends 300 msec for receiving data and sending data. In this case, the node thread working time is 500 msecs, regardless whether the threads run sequentially on in a parallel manner. We also derive a **System thread Working Time** as a system performance indicator, as the average of node thread working time indicators across all nodes of the system.

Node Active Time. Node active time is a node performance indicator that captures the amount of time each node runs. The node active time is defined from the first ReceiveThread starts receiving first data until the last SendThread finishes sending last data in the RelayNode or finishes document processing in the EndNode. Hence, the node active time may contain waiting time (e.g, wait time for data receiving, thread blocking time). Using the same MergeNode example as previously, assume two threads, one having 200 msec node thread working time, and another having 300 msec node thread waiting time. If one thread runs after the other, in a sequential fashion, the node active time results to be 500 msecs. However, if both threads run in parallel, the node active time results to be 300 msecs. We also define **System Active Time** as a system performance indicator, by averaging the node active time of all nodes across the system.

Node Processing Time. Node processing time is a node performance indicator that captures the time taken by a node to execute XML processing only, excluding communication and processing overheads. We also define **System processing time** as a system performance indicator, by averaging node processing time across all nodes of the system.

Parallelism Efficiency Ratio. Parallelism efficiency ratio is a system performance indicator defined as *"system thread working time / system active time"*.

3.6 Synthetic Data Experimental Results

For each experiment type (scheduling allocation and distributed processing model), we collect performance indicators data over seven types of XML document instances. Fig.s 16 and 17 report job execution time; Fig.s 18 and 19 report system active time; Fig.s 20 and 21 report system processing time; Fig.s 22 and 23 report system parallelism efficiency ratio. On all graphs, X axis describes scheduling and processing models, as well as well-formedness and grammar validation types of XML document processing, as follows: **PIP_wel**:Pipeline and Well-formedness checking, **PAR_wel**:Parallel and Well-formedness checking, **PIP_val**:Pipeline and Validation checking, **PAR_val**:Parallel and Validation checking. Y axis denotes specific performance indicator, averaged over 22 XML document instance processing.

Regarding job execution time (Fig.s 16 and 17), parallel processing is faster than pipeline processing for all docs. Moreover, comparing Figs. 16 with 17, we see that job execution time speeds up faster with increasing the number of relay nodes in parallel processing than in pipeline processing. In parallel processing, StartNode reads concurrently parts of XML documents and sends them to next nodes. Hence, each RelayNode receives/processes/sends only part of the XML document. Likewise, MergeNode receives only part of the XML document at each Receive/SendThread (Fig. 3) and sends them in order to a next node. Each thread in these nodes run concurrently, resulting in reduced system active times for parallel processing in Figs. 18 and 19.

Regarding system active time and document type, the higher the document depth is, the larger the system active time. Useless processing is more pronounced at each RelayNode for documents with higher depth, because the RelayNodes are not able to

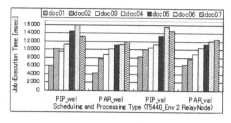

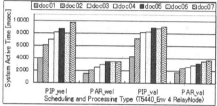

Fig. 16. Job Execution Time (2 RelayNodes in T5440_Env)

Fig. 17. Job Execution Time (4 RelayNodes in T5440_Env)

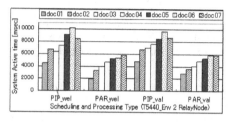

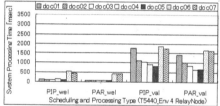

Fig. 18. System Active Time (2 RelayNodes in T5440_Env)

Fig. 19. System Active Time (4 RelayNodes in T5440_Env)

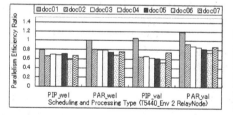

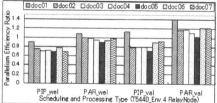

Fig. 20. System Processing Time (2 RelayNodes in T5440_Env)

Fig. 21. System Processing Time (4 RelayNodes in T5440_Env)

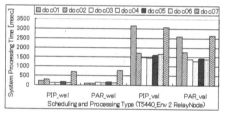

Fig. 22. Parallelism Efficiency Ratio (2 RelayNodes in T5440_Env)

Fig. 23. Parallelism Efficiency Ratio (4 RelayNodes in T5440_Env)

match too many tags within the document part allocated to them. Hence, the EndNode is left with a large amount of processing to be done. We may reduce useless processing if we divide the document conveniently according to the document structure and grammar checking rules. In addition, node activity is more sensitive to the number of

RelayNodes in parallel processing than in pipeline processing. Regarding task complexity, node activity results are similar in pipeline processing regardless of the task performed. Parallel processing induces less node activity if the task is simpler, i.e., for well-formedness checking.

Fig. 24 further shows node active time when processing doc01, for each node in the system (**SN**=StartNode, **RN**=RelayNode, **MN**=MergeNode, **EN**=EndNode). Fig. 24 shows two RelayNode processing case. We can see that the active time of each node is smaller in parallel as compared with pipeline processing.

Processing time is similar for both parallel processing and pipeline processing (Fig. 20 and 21), which shows that the extra activity time in the pipeline processing is due to extra sending/receiving thread times. In addition, well-formedness checking has less processing time than validation checking, which is expected. Also, the average processing time is much affected by whether we can allocate XML data efficiently or not. Efficient scheduling of XML document parts to a given processing model and topology requires further investigation.

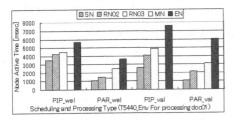 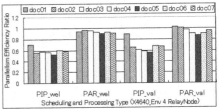

Fig. 24. Node Active Time for Processing doc01 (2 RelayNodes in T5440_Env)

Fig. 25. Parallelism Efficiency Ratio of Processing Synthetic Document doc07 (4 RelayNode in X4640_Env)

Regarding parallelism efficiency ratio (Fig.s 22 and 23), parallel processing is more efficient than pipeline in every case, because in parallel case, more threads are operating concurrently on different parts of the document. In addition, Fig. 25 shows parallelism efficiency ratio for synthetic documents in X4640_Env. T5440_Env parallelism efficiency ratio is about 20 % better than in other environments.

Fig. 26 shows node thread working time when the system processes doc01 for two RelayNodes. In this graph, we can see that there is more XML processing in validation than in well-formedness. Moreover, comparing **PIP_val** with **PAR_val**, there is more processing at the EndNode in case of pipelining processing. So pipelining is less efficient than parallel in distributed processing XML documents of type 01. This is also true for other types of documents, whose results are omitted for space's sake. Fig. 27 shows node thread working time for processing doc07 on parallel processing in both PC_Env and X4640_Env. Comparing Node Thread Working Time of PC_Env and X4640_Env, time spent on communication is less in X4640_Env than in PC_Env in some cases. Virtual machines have the advantage of low communication speed when they are in the same server. Overall, both PC_Env and X4640_Env have similar node thread working time performance. For convenience, we organize our performance characterization results into Table 5.

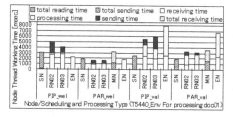
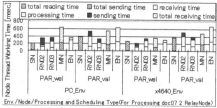

Fig. 26. Node Thread Working Time for Processing doc01 (2 RelayNodes in T5440_Env)

Fig. 27. Node Thread Working Time of Processing Synthetic Document doc07 (2 RelayNode in PC_Env and X4640_Env)

Table 5. Distributed XML Processing Characterization Summary

	Two RelayNodes		Four RelayNodes		Number of RelayNodes	
	Pipeline	Parallel	Pipeline	Parallel	Pipeline	Parallel
Job execution time	Parallel is better				No change	Reduces
System active time	Parallel is better		Similar to two RelayNode	Smaller than two RelayNode	No effect	Reduces
System processing time	Parallel is better				Reduces	
Parallelism efficiency ratio	Parallel is slightly better		Parallel is better		Slightly better	Better

3.7 Realistic Data Experimental Results

We show experimental results of realistic XML documents over PC_Env and X4640_Env environments. Fig. 28 reports job execution time of distributed XML processing for doc01–07 in PC_Env. Comparing Fig. 28 with Fig. 16, T5440_Env job execution time is about 10 times higher than in PC_Env. Further investigation shows that this is directly related to CPU processing time performance, which is ten times faster in PC_Env than in T5440_Env.

In contrast, Fig. 29 shows that job execution time in PC_Env and X4640_Env are similar, for realistic XML documents. System processing time and system node active time, not shown for space constraints, are similar, evidencing that there is little difference between real and virtual machine environments. In addition, processing time for stock document is highest because it has more tags to be processed than the other documents. In every experiment, job execution time, system active time and system processing time are proportional to the amount of processing which is shown as tag processing. Even though Kernel document consists of a larger file than the stock document, its processing time is smaller than stock document. This shows that efficiency of distributed XML processing depends on structure of XML document rather than it's file size.

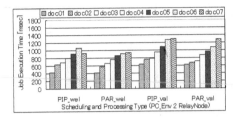 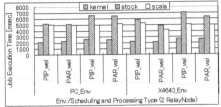

Fig. 28. Job Execution Time of Processing Synthetic Documents (2 RelayNode in PC_Env)

Fig. 29. Job Execution Time of Processing Realistic Documents (PC_Env and X4640_Env)

4   Related Work

XML parallel processing has been recently addressed in several papers. [8] proposes a multi-threaded XML parallel processing model where threads steal work from each other, in order to support load balancing among threads. They exemplify their approach in a parallelized XML serializer. [9] focuses on parallel XML parsing, evaluating multi-threaded parsers performance versus thread communication overhead. [10] introduces a parallel processing library to support parallel processing of large XML data sets. They explore speculative execution parallelism, by decomposing Deterministic Finite Automata (DFA) processing into DFA plus Non-Deterministic Finite Automata (NFA) processing on symmetric multi-processing systems. To our knowledge, our work is the first to evaluate and compare parallel against pipelining XML distributed processing.

5   Conclusions

In this paper, we have studied two models of distributed XML document processing: parallel, and pipelining. In general, pipeline processing is less efficient, because parts of the document that are not to be processed at a specific node needs to be received and relayed to other nodes, increasing processing overhead. Regardless the distributed model, efficiency of distributed processing depends on the structure of the XML document, as well as its partition: a bad partitioning may result in inefficient processing. Optimal partition of XML document for efficient distributed processing is part of ongoing research. So far, we have focused on distributed well-formedness and validation of XML documents. Other XML processing, such as filtering and XML transformations, can be studied. We also experimented in virtual machine and real machine. They are very similar, so we can apply our results to both environment. A future research direction is to process streaming data at relay nodes [11]. In such scenario, many web servers, mobile devices, network appliances, are connected with each other via an intelligent network, which executes streaming data processing on behalf of connected devices.

Acknowledgements. Part of this study was supported by a Grant-in-Aid for Scientific Research (KAKENHI:21500039).

References

1. Cavendish, D., Selcuk Candan, K.: Distributed xml processing: Theory and applications. Journal of Parallel and Distributed Computing 68(8), 1054–1069 (2008)
2. Uratani, Y., Koide, H.: Implementation and evaluation of a parallel application which processes streaming data on relay nodes. IEICE Technical Report 109(228), 133–138 (2009)
3. Uratani, Y., Koide, H., Cavendish, D., Oie, Y.: Characterizing Distributed XML Processing – Moving XML Processing from Servers to Networking Nodes. In: Proc. 7th International Conference on Web Information Systems and Technologies (2011)
4. Yoshinaga, K., Uratani, Y., Koide, H.: Utilizing multi-networks task scheduler for streaming applications. In: International Conference on Parallel Processing - Workshops, pp. 25–30 (2008)
5. Kelley Jr., J.E., Walker, M.R.: Critical-path planning and scheduling. In: IRE-AIEE-ACM 1959 (Eastern), pp. 160–173 (1959)
6. Tarek Hagras, J.J.: A static task scheduling heuristic for homogeneous computing environments. In: 12th Euromicro Conference on Parallel, Distributed and Network-Based Processing (PDP 2004), pp. 192–198 (2004)
7. Manimaran, G., Siva Ram Murthy, C.: An efficient dynamic scheduling algorithm for multiprocessor realtime systems. IEEE Transactions on Parallel Distributed System 9(3), 312–319 (1998)
8. Lu, W., Gannon, D.: Parallel xml processing by work stealing. In: SOCP 2007, pp. 31–37 (2007)
9. Michael, R., Head, M.G.: Approaching a parallelized xml parser optimized for multi-core processors. In: SOCP 2007, pp. 17–22 (2007)
10. Michael, R., Head, M.G.: Performance enhancement with speculative execution based parallelism for processing large-scale xml-based application data. In: HPDC 2009, pp. 21–29 (2009)
11. Shimamura, M., Ikenaga, T., Tsuru, M.: Advanced relay nodes for adaptive network services - concept and prototype experiment. In: International Conference on Broadband, Wireless Computing, Communication and Applications, pp. 701–707 (2010)

Cofocus: REST Framework for Collaborative Endpoint Network in Mobile Environment

Li Li and Wu Chou

Avaya Inc., 233 Mount Airy Road, Basking Ridge, New Jersey, 07920, U.S.A.
{lli5,wuchou}@avaya.com

Abstract. In this paper, we present an approach to enable collaborative endpoint network for mobile phones and devices. In particular, we expose functions on mobile phones as REST web services and make mobile phones as web service providers for rapid integration with communication and collaboration applications. To accommodate the distinct features and constraints in mobile environment, this paper describes a lightweight and efficient protocol, Compact HTTP, which consists of a small subset of HTTP 1.1 to reduce the footprint of REST services. We expand bindings of HTTP to multiple messaging protocols, including XMPP, and make the REST services invariant to network and protocol changes. These expanded bindings introduce asynchrony into REST, a desired property for communication and collaboration services. Furthermore, HTTP over XMPP described in our approach introduces the concept of hyperlink presence in collaboration, and it is used to mitigate the broken link issue which is acute in mobile environments as devices and resources can come and go in an unpredictable pattern. To provide end-to-end message security, a symmetric key based security scheme is described for service authentication and authorization. A prototype system based on the proposed approach is developed that allows both local operators and remote directors to control and monitor resources in a secure manner on Android phones and devices, e.g. camera, camcorder, audio, location, telephony, motion, power, etc. Experimental results indicate that the proposed approach is feasible, lightweight, and has satisfactory performance.

Keywords: REST web service, Mobile device, Compact HTTP, HTTP over XMPP, Android, Security.

1 Introduction

As mobile phones become more and more advanced, they are replacing other devices, such as PDA and notebook computers as the next generation personal digital assistant. Compared to other computing devices, the mobile phones offer a unique combination of telephony functions (making and receiving phone calls), sensory functions (sound, camera, camcorder, location, acceleration, temperature, etc.), and communication networks (3G, WiFi, Bluetooth, Wimax, etc.). More and more applications are designed for mobile phones to take advantage of these capabilities. This is evidenced by the popularity and amount of iPhone and Android applications in their App Stores.

J. Filipe and J. Cordeiro (Eds.): WEBIST 2011, LNBIP 101, pp. 72–87, 2012.

The focus of this paper is to build intelligent collaborative endpoint network with mobile phones by exposing functions on mobile phones as REST web services, such that these functions can be accessed by other endpoints in real-time manner. Collaborative endpoint network is an emerging area with critical applications in different market spaces, including smart home, healthcare, travel services, traffic control, and smart city, etc. There are many motivating use cases to extend the collaborative endpoint network to mobile phones. For example, we can use a mobile phone as a surveillance device to monitor a room or a car. Mobile phones can also be used to monitor and remind patients of their treatments, as well as to find and locate medical professionals to treat them. A travel or a smart city application can use mobile phones as the virtual tour guide and push relevant multimedia content to a visitor as he moves around a tourism site. Mobile phones can also be used as devices to keep track of traffic flows where the speed of many drivers with mobile phones on the road can be obtained and aggregated automatically. All these applications require the ability to monitor, share, and control one or multiple functions on the phone in real time or near real-time fashion, as many functions, such as location, may change frequently and in-time responses are needed.

A main challenge to build collaborative endpoint network in mobile environment is to manage the complexity and dynamics of mobile phone functions. There are many types of mobile phones, each with different functions and ways to access and operate them. Moreover, these phones and functions are not static as new mobile phones are added and existing phones are upgraded constantly. It is difficult, if not impossible, to develop collaborative applications without a proper form of abstraction of these functions. To address this issue, we adopt a web service based approach to turn mobile phones into web service endpoints (web sites). This approach exposes the fundamental functions on the phones as REST web services so that they can be invoked and composed in different ways by different applications. This reduces the complexity in accessing and operating mobile phone functions, because REST services are independent of programming languages and transport protocols. The dynamics of mobile functions can also be accommodated because REST supports a decentralized architecture in which components can evolve independently. REST deals with changes in services by asking the applications (clients) to interact with the services following the hypermedia [11]. For example, if a phone obtains a new sensor function, the new service can be added and exposed through a hyperlink at the home page of that phone. A client can find the new service through the home page and interact with it by following the link.

There are two types of web services: SOAP based [10] and REST based [11]. Many approaches have chosen REST based web services for mobile devices because of its simplicity and close relationship with the architecture of Web. We choose REST in our approach for the similar reason. However, we found that HTTP 1.1 protocol commonly used in current REST web services needs both compaction and expansion in mobile environments. First, we need to compact HTTP 1.1 messages as they can be complex and large while some features are never used in mobile phones. Second, we need to expand HTTP to multiple transport protocol bindings besides TCP/IP to support REST services in heterogenous mobile environments. To address these issues, we propose and define a "Compact HTTP" protocol, consisting of only the essential elements of HTTP 1.1 to enable collaborative endpoint network of mobile phones.

Moreover, we describe how Compact HTTP can be bound to multiple messaging protocols, in particular to XMPP [12]. These protocol bindings introduces asynchrony into REST, a necessary feature for real-time collaboration applications on mobile phones. Furthermore, HTTP over XMPP in our approach introduces hyperlink presence into REST services to mitigate the broken link issue which is accute for mobile phones. A security protocol is also devised to permit flexible and quick setup of security contexts between collaborataive endpoints. Based on this protocol, we develop a lightweight REST web services framework on an Android phone. Within this framework, we implement a few dozen resources, including sound, camera, camcorder, location, power, motion, scheduler, and telephony manager as secured REST web services that are accessible to web browsers. Our collaborative endpoint network framework also supports web storages, including Google Sites, YouTube, Picasa, etc., to upload the captuered media for instant sharing and collaboration.

The rest of this paper is organized as follows. Section 2 surveys some related work in developing REST web services for mobile devices. Section 3 describes the Compact HTTP protocol. Section 4 describes the binding of this protocol to multiple transport protocols especially to XMPP. Section 5 presents a security protocol to address related security issues. Section 6 describes the implementation and experiments of a prototype systems running on a live wirless carrier network (T-Mobile). And we conclude and sumarize this paper in Section 7.

2   Related Work

The principles and architectures of REST web services are extensively discussed in [11] and [14], which are followed by this paper whenever applicable.

WAP [23] is a suite of protocols to connect wireless mobile phones to the Web. The typical WAP architecture consists of Content Server, WAP Gateway and mobile devices. When requested by the Content Server, the WAP Gateway uses a protocol WSP [25], which is a binary version of HTTP, to transfer encoded WML content [24] to the devices. However, modern smart phones rarely support WAP as they can interpret HTML directly.

Constrained REST Environments (Core) [9] is a recent IETF activity to simplify HTTP for low-end devices, such as 8-bit microcontrollers with up to 12 KB of memory. It proposes a binding of HTTP to UDP that deals with asynchronous messages. However, this approach is not suitable for mobile environments, as the phones do not have a reachable IP address, a major issue that has to be addressed properly.

MacFaddin et al. [3] proposed a REST web service framework for mobile commerce spaces. Liu and Conelly [6] proposed to combine REST web service with semantic web technology to support services on mobile computing units. Lozano et al. [7] promoted the use of REST web services to expose IMS capabilities to Web 2.0 applications. In particular, it proposes the use of AtomPub protocol to publish the IMS resources.

Antila et al. [2] discussed the hosting of REST web services on mobile devices to support person-to-person communication and collaborations over Wifi and 3G networks. Aijaz et al. [4] presented a REST web service provisioning system and compared it with its SOAP counterpart. Their experiments showed that REST messages have much lower overhead than SOAP messages.

Pruter et al. [5] described an approach to adopt resource-oriented service framework to automatically control robots for industrial automation tasks. It uses a special mechanism called MIRROR to handle events. Performances of their framework are evaluated under three physical networks: wireless LAN, Bluetooth and ZigBee. The results showed that the REST framework has lower overhead than the SOAP based DPWS.

AlShahwan et al. [1] compared the performances of the same SOAP and REST services implemented on mobile devices. They concluded that REST is more suitable for mobile devices as it requires less processing time and memory. Stirbu [8] presented a REST based architecture to render web interfaces on mobile devices, in which REST protocol is used to synchronize states between applications.

However, the abovementioned prior work does not touch upon the proposed approach of HTTP over XMPP and the concept of hyperlink presence to connect mobile phones in an intelligent collaborative endpoint network.

3   Compact HTTP

HTTP 1.1 has a set of very powerful features, and some of them can be very expensive to implement and support on resource-constrained mobile devices. Even though it is possible to run a HTTP 1.1 server on Android mobile phones, many of HTTP 1.1 features may never be utilized. Therefore, we elect to develop a lightweight compact protocol, Compact HTTP, for mobile phones. It consists of a subset of HTTP 1.1 protocol, but is still capable to enable the endpoint network and collaborative applications of mobile phones. Protocol compaction in our approach is only a process not the final goal – as mobile phones become more powerful, more features can be included. For this reason, we choose to represent HTTP message in plain text, instead of binary, as this compact subset of HTTP 1.1 may grow to support further extensions.

3.1   Message Templates

To reach a compacted subset, we start from an empty feature set and add features to it as necessary until the desired services are covered. In our case, this exercise leads to the following Compact HTTP request and response templates that follow HTTP 1.1 closely:

```
------------------------------------
{operation} {path} {version}
Authorization:{token}
x-tid:{string}

{form}
------------------------------------
{status} {reason} {version}
Authorization:{token}
x-tid:{string}

{form}|{html}
------------------------------------
```

Fig. 1. Message Templates for Compact HTTP request (above) and response (below)

All the variables, including {operation}, {path}, {version}, {status}, and {reason} are defined in HTTP 1.1. For Compact HTTP, the version is HTTP/1.1c. {form} represents form encoded data with media type application/x-www-form-urlencoded and {html} represent HTML with media type text/html. Both are defined by HTML 4 [13]. The differences with HTTP 1.1 are described below.

Authorization contains the access token for the message. In HTTP 1.1, this is a request header to authorize requests. We extend it to responses because they also need to be authorized in asynchronous interactions. For example, a client needs to authorize a response before updating the user interface.

x-tid represents transaction ID introduced in Cofocus REST service framework, an idea borrowed from Core [9]. It is a new header to HTTP 1.1 for clients to correlate asynchronous responses and events to requests. Its value is set in a request and echoed back in the responses.

The templates omit some headers considered important for REST services, such as the ETag response header. The reason is that our resources tend to have small representations that can be updated and transmitted without checking the versions. We also omit content negotiation headers as we focus on two common media types of HTML, i.e. form encoded data and HTML.

3.2   Message Exchange Patterns

Typical HTTP messages follow the request-response pattern. This message exchange pattern can only support atomic services that complete in one step. However, many services on the mobile phones have intermediate states before completion. For example, to control the camera to take a picture involves the following steps: 1) adjust focus; 2) take shot; 3) upload picture to a web site. The completion times of these steps are outside the control of the service. In real-time applications, the service should notify the client these states so it can react accordingly. This type of interactions cannot be modeled as atomic services. Instead, they are modeled as multi-step services.

A multi-step service accepts a request and returns multiple responses, which indicate service progression towards completion. The status for the intermediate responses should be 202 Accepted or 206 Partial Content, while the final response should be 200 OK or 201 Created. Status 206 is used only with response to GET in HTTP 1.1, and here we extend it to any response of a multi-step service. All asynchronous responses are correlated to its request by x-tid for both atomic and multi-step services.

Another important type of message exchange pattern is event subscription and notifications. For example, a client can subscribe to a phone's location tracking service to receive notifications about location changes of the phone. In this pattern, a subscribe request is followed by a response and notifications. As all the subsequent messages have the same x-tid, a client can correlate notifications with subscriptions.

For other more complex message exchange patterns in collaboration and communication systems, such as session, multi-resource and multi-state, we suggest to consult the REST service design patterns [15].

4   Compact HTTP Bindings

In conventional REST web services, there is a basic and implicit assumption that a HTTP server has a IP address reachable by clients. However, this is not possible in mobile environment, as a mobile phone is typically behind its provider's NAT gateway and its IP address is private and not reachable from outside. The enterprise applications that control and monitor phones are also behind corporate firewalls. This creates an issue for many real-time applications where two-way messaging is required. On the other hand, many 3G mobile phones can join different communication networks over different protocols such that messages can be exchanged without IP addresses. For instance, a phone can be addressed by a phone number for SMS messages, an email address for email messages or a JID for XMPP messages.

Therefore, to support REST services in these heterogeneous environments, it is necessary to decouple HTTP from TCP/IP. In addition to TCP/IP, it is both convenient and advantageous to treat these messaging protocols as "transport" for HTTP. This approach makes the REST services invariant to the protocol changes as the mobile phones move to different networks. This allows us to keep the same services while optimizing their performance over available networks and protocols. For example, we may choose to transmit time sensitive messages over TCP/IP or XMPP, and noncritical ones over SMS or SMTP. Furthermore, HTTP over XMPP can bring presence information into REST architecture. In particular, we can track hyperlink presence to address the issue of broken links in distributed hypermedia systems.

The idea of separating protocol messages and transport is not new. It is actually one of the tenets of web service paradigm as web services should be agnostic to transport protocols. SOAP based web services community has embraced this approach by defining SOAP bindings to HTTP [16], to XMPP [17], and to JMS [18]. However, as far as we know, HTTP itself has bindings only to TCP/IP and UDP.

4.1   URI Scheme

When HTTP is bound to TCP/IP, the URI to a resource only needs to specify the HTTP schema and the domain name, which can be resolved to an IP address by DNS lookup. For example http://www.google.com identifies a resource located at IP 71.125.225.17 that accepts HTTP. However, to bind HTTP to different transport protocols, we need to specify the transport protocol over which HTTP messages are sent. This can be achieved by a two-level URI scheme according to [22], where the first level URI identifies the HTTP protocol and the second level URI identifies the transport protocol:

```
uri_1 = http://{uri_2}/...
{uri_2} = transport URI
```

Suppose a resource x is located on a mobile phone which can be reached in several transports, including TCP/IP. To address this resource with HTTP over those protocols, the following two-level URI are used.

To address it with HTTP over XMPP by a JID, we use the following URI which is consistent with RFC5122 [27]:

```
http://xmpp:joe@example.com/x
```

To address it with HTTP over SMS by a phone number, we use:

```
http://sms:5555/x
```

To address it with HTTP over SMTP by an email address, we use:

```
http://smtp:5555@example.com/x
```

To address it with HTTP over TCP by an IP address, we use:

```
http://123.4.5.6/x
```

This two-level URI can be resolved by a client as follows: 1) the client establishes a transport according to `uri_2`; 2) the client transmits HTTP messages over that transport. With this special two-level URI scheme and the resolution algorithm, resources located in disjoint networks can be linked into a global REST service space - an important feature in our Cofocus framework for collaborate endpoint network.

4.2   XMPP

XMPP architecture consists of XMPP servers and clients. Clients are logical peers that can exchange various XMPP messages (stanzas). To exchange messages, clients have to establish a TCP/IP connection to the same or federated XMPP servers.

To connect to a XMPP server, A XMPP client typically needs to know the following information: 1) XMPP host and port (e.g. talk.google.com:5222); and 2) XMPP Service (e.g. gmail.com). This information is not included in URI scheme because different XMPP servers can be used to reach the same XMPP client. Once the user logs into the XMPP server, the established connection is used to transmit all HTTP messages.

To determine if a responding XMPP entity supports HTTP, a requesting entity can send a Service Discovery stanza [26] to the responding entity, asking for the supported protocol and the relevant items:

```
<iq from='{from_jid}' to='{to_jid}' type='get'>
<query xmlns='http://jabber.org/protocol/disco#info'/>
<query xmlns='http://jabber.org/protocol/disco#items'/>
</iq>
```

If the responding XMPP entity supports HTTP, it sends a response stanza including the supported HTTP feature and the entry URI:

```
<iq from='{from_jid}' to='{to_jid}' type='result'>
  <query xmlns='http://jabber.org/protocol/disco#info'>
    <identity category='automation' type='http'/>
    <feature var='http://jabber.org/protocol/http'/>
  </query>
  <query xmlns='http://jabber.org/protocol/disco#items'>
    <item node='/services' name='My REST services' />
  </query>
</iq>
```

HTTP messages can be transmitted in XMPP IQ or Message stanzas. IQ requests are for immediate responses and Message requests can be stored when the target entity is off-line and forwarded when it is on. The following templates illustrate the binding rules:

```
<message from='{from_jid}' to='{to_jid}'
type='chat|groupchat|normal'>
   <body>
     <http>{Compact HTTP message}</http>
   </body>
</message>

<iq from='{from_jid}' to='{to_jid}' type='get|set|result|error'>
   <http>{Compact HTTP message}</http>
</iq>
```

The Message stanzas carry all the HTTP messages in the same way. In contrast, the IQ stanzas carry different HTTP message in different ways as described below:

- HTTP GET is bound to <iq type="get">;
- HTTP PUT, POST and DELETE are bound to <iq type="set">;
- HTTP response codes 1xx - 3xx are bound to <iq type="result">;
- HTTP response codes 4xx-5xx are bound to <iq type="error">;

4.3   Hyperlink Presence

In the Web, there is an annoying issue of broken hyperlinks when the linked resource becomes unavailable. It is difficult for the client to know when the link will be restored unless it polls the server constantly, which creates unnecessary network traffic. A better solution is for the client to monitor the hyperlink and receives the presence information about it. This issue is acute in mobile environment, as mobile devices and collaboration resources resided therein can come and go in an unpredictable pattern, e.g. power shortage, out of signal coverage, etc.

In our approach of HTTP over XMPP, it provides a way of monitoring the hyperlink presence using the presence services provided at the XMPP layer. If a XMPP client listens for presence updates from a JID address, it can receive presence updates about a hyperlink in near real-time. For example, to receive presence updates about a hyperlink: http://xmpp:someone@gmail.com/x, the client subscribes to the presence of JID someone@gmail.com to monitor its availability. By using hyperlink presence, the mobile phones in a collaboration session can synchronize with each other efficiently while managing their own states independently.

5   Security

Security is a critical issue in hosting web services on mobile phones, because if not securely protected, the ability to access resources on other phones and endpoints remotely can be explored by malicious clients. To enhance the security, it is typical to deploy layered security mechanisms from protocol layer up to various applications, such that a breach at lower level can be defended by the layer above. In our approach, security mechanisms are employed from the layers of Compact HTTP and transport protocols to services and applications.

5.1   Secure Messages

Because in mobile environments, a HTTP message may travel through different networks in different protocols, it is necessary to employ end-to-end message level security. Here we outline a symmetric key based security protocol to set up the security contexts between two parties.

The design goal is to allow the user who operates the phone to quickly grant and reject clients and their service requests. For this reason, we chose symmetric key because our applications are aimed at a group of trusted users that can exchange secret keys easily. In some cases, the phone and the client are managed by the same user.

For convenience, the user that configures the phone is referred to as "operator" and the user that configures the application is referred as "director." The protocol consists of the following steps:

1. The operator and director agree upon a secret passphrase P and enter it into the phone and the client respectively.
2. The director creates an access token T1 and tells it to the operator.
3. The operator enters client's URI A and T1 into the phone and creates an access token T2. The token is sent by a "join" message encrypted by P to URI A as follows:

```
PUT operators/{phone} HTTP/1.1c
Authorization: T1
x-tid: {number}

token=T2
```

4. The client decrypts the message with P, store T2 and sends an encrypted response message that indicates acceptance.
5. The phone receives and decrypts the response and activates the security context, which contains (A, P, T1, T2).
6. Any subsequent message from the client to the phone will contain T2 and be encrypted with P. The phone will decrypt any message from A with P and checks it against T2. Any response message to A will contain T1 and be encrypted with P.
7. The operator deactivates the security context by sending a "Delete" message to the client. The corresponding security context becomes invalid on the phone and client, after receiving a Delete message according to the following message template:

```
DELETE operators/{phone} HTTP/1.1c
Authorization: T1
x-tid: {number}
```

Fig. 2 depicts the phone interface for the operator to carry out steps 3-5 and 7.

5.2   Secure Services and Data

Because a mobile phone that hosts REST services is also used for other purposes, the operator can start and stop services, login and out of transport services, as ways to control access to the services. In our system, we further limit message exchange patterns for security reasons:

- The respond messages are always sent back to the requester on the same transport protocol, who has been authenticated and authorized.
- There is only one subscription for each resource and the event listener must be the same as the subscriber, who has been authenticated and authorized.

Our system also secures the access to sensitive data collected by the services, such as captured images, audio, and videos. Instead of returning the content to the authenticated client directly, the system stores it locally or stores it in a web storage site and provides a link to the client, who has to be authorized to retrieve it.

Fig. 2. Screenshot of Join/Leave Director Activity

6   Prototype System

Based on the proposed protocols, we developed a prototype system that hosts a set of REST resources on T-Mobile G1 phones running Android 1.6 in T-Mobile cellular network. The intended relations between various client applications and the phones are illustrated in Fig. 3 where REST services are accessible to clients of different kinds over the heterogeneous networks.

The high-level REST server architecture on an Android phone is illustrated in Fig. 4, where the components in blue color depend on the Android SDK, whereas the components in yellow color depend only on Java SDK. The core REST framework, including the security package, does not import any Android packages and can be run in any Java runtime.

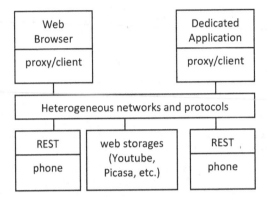

Fig. 3. High level relations between client applications and REST services on the phones

There are three types of Android services in Cofocus framework: transport services, REST services, and storage services.

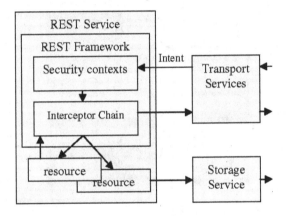

Fig. 4. High level architecture of REST service framework on Android phone

The transport services are responsible to listen and send messages over a transport protocol, such as SMS or XMPP. For XMPP transport, we used a XMPP client library compiled by Srinivas [19] for Android. For SMS, we used Android SmsManager. If an incoming message is intended for the REST Service module, it is forwarded to the REST Service module as an Intent on Android platform.

The REST Service is an Android Service that contains the REST framework. Upon start, the REST Service registers an Intent Listener. Upon receiving a message encapsulated in the Intent, the Intent Listener looks up the security context for the message and invokes the interceptor chain in the REST framework to process the message.

The REST framework contains an incoming interceptor chain, a pivot, and an outgoing interceptor chain. The incoming chain consists of three interceptors to 1)

decrypt; 2) deserializes; and 3) authorize the message. If any of these interceptors fails, the message is discarded and an error message is returned. If the message is a request, the pivot will invoke the corresponding resource; if the message is a response, the pivot forwards it to the Android Notification Service. The outgoing chain consists of four interceptors to 1) endorse; 2) serialize; 3) encrypt; and 4) deliver the responses. The chains can also be invoked by a resource to control another resource. For example, a scheduler resource controls the camera by going through the same incoming chain for security reasons.

For message encryption and token generation, we used Java Crypto packages (`javax.crypto` and `java.security`) with password based encryption algorithm `PBEWithMD5AndDES`. The encrypted messages are encoded as Base64 strings for transmission.

The REST resources in our approach can use web storages provided by Google to upload captured audio (Google Docs), image (Picasa) and video (YouTube) contents, as well as other web storage resources, so that they can be instantly shared for collaboration. The storage service is an abstraction of both local and remote (web) storages, and it consists of three methods: `login(account)`, `logout()`, and `save(uri, content)`. A set of HTTP clients can use these methods to upload multimedia contents to the designated servers and publish the data services at a web proxy (e.g. Google Sites) for collaboration. A phone interface to manage web storage is illustrated in Fig. 5.

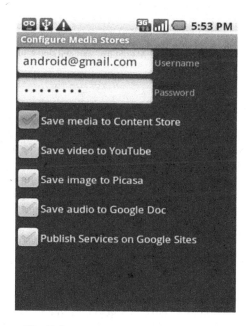

Fig. 5. Screenshot of Web storage Activity

6.1   Implemented Resources

This section lists the major resources developed so far within our collaborative end-point network framework. Each resource is described by one table that defines its path, service, operations and response patterns, where "a" stands for atomic or "m" stands for multi-step (Table 1).

Table 1. Implemented resources

path	/sound/control	
GET	Retrieve current state.	a
PUT	Record or playback sound.	m
path	/camera/control	
GET	Retrieve current state.	a
PUT	Take or display a picture.	m
path	/camcorder/control	
GET	Retrieve current state.	a
PUT	Record or playback video.	m
path	/location, /power	
GET	Get current geo location or battery power status.	a
path	/{source}/monitor, where {source} is one of gyroscope, light, location, magnet, motion, orientation, pressure, proximity, temperature, phone, and power.	
GET	Get current subscription	a
PUT	Subscribe for events from {source}.	a
DELETE	Unsubscribe events.	a
path	/schedule	
POST	Schedule a task in future. For example, start and stop camcorder at given time.	a

6.2   Implemented Clients

Three types of clients were implemented: the Android phone (both client and service), a dedicated Java desktop client, and a web browser. The Android phone client uses the Cofocus stack in Fig. 4. The Java client was based on open source Smack 3.1.0 XMPP library [20], and the Cofocus framework which is independent of Android SDK. The web browser communicates with the phones through a XMPP Javascript library and a HTTP/XMPP gateway. These utilities are from the Kazzing Gateway 9.0.6 from http://kaazing.com/.

6.3   Experimental Results

A main concern was the performance of Cofocus - our REST based collaborative endpoint network framework. On the server side, we measured the total processing time (from entering the incoming chain to leaving the outgoing chain) as well as the processing time of individual interceptors. On the client side, we measured the round-trip latency (which includes the network latency and XMPP library processing time). To obtain the time, we used the XMPP java client on a desktop computer (Dual Core CPU 3.00 GHz with 2GB RAM) connected to the Internet to send 52 HTTP messages over XMPP Message stanzas to each REST service on a T-Mobile HTC G1 phone (Firmware 1.6, Build DMD64) registered in T-Mobile cellular network. The measurements on the phone were collected using Android `TimeLogger` utility and on our Java desktop client using Java `System.nanoTime` function. The performances are summarized in Table 2 and the message sizes are listed in Table 3.

Table 2. Total client time, total server time and individual interceptor times (millisecond)

Process	mean	std	min	max
Client	1400.6	821.7	554.3	3858.3
Server	209.53	86.08	135	590
Encrypt	66.05	25.5	47	153
Decrypt	39.12	19.49	2	84
Deserialize	23.98	25.1	2	196
Serialize	7.4	7.3	4	41
Authorize	1.77	0.53	1	3
Endorse	2.4	3.03	1	24
Pivot	40.33	58.98	4	254
Deliver	28.42	3.8	20	47

Table 3. Message Sizes (byte)

Type	mean	std	min	max
Encrypted	113.36	28.6	88	192
Decrypted	77.93	21.54	56	138

The bar graph in Fig. 6 illustrates the mean times spent in the interceptors. The graph shows that, on average, encryption, decryption and pivot were the top three time consuming components. They took 69% of total server time. Notice that the pivot time is the mean time spent by the resources to execute HTTP methods, which is outside the control of the Cofocus framework. Table 3 shows that the small messages are sufficient to support a variety of basic services.

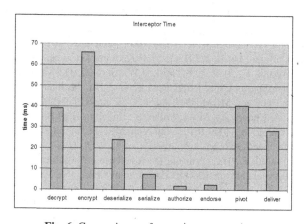

Fig. 6. Comparisons of mean interceptor times

7   Conclusions

The contributions of this paper are summarized as follows:

- We proposed and developed a lightweight protocol, Compact HTTP, consisting of a small subset of HTTP 1.1, to address asynchronous message exchange patterns to enable collaborative endpoint network for mobile phones and related applications.
- We proposed HTTP over XMPP to support real-time collaborative endpoint network where endpoints do not have reachable IP addresses.
- We developed a mechanism for hyperlink presence based on HTTP over XMPP to address the broken link issue in collaboration, which is an acute problem in mobile environment.
- We described a symmetric key based security protocol in collaborative endpoint network that provides end-to-end message level security for service authentication and authorization.
- We developed a REST framework, Cofocus, in Java to support the above mentioned protocols and mechanism, exposing over a dozen REST resources on an Android G1 phone in an ad hoc collaborative endpoint network.
- We developed three types of clients, i.e. Android phone, desktop application and web browser, to control and monitor the mobile phones.

Experimental studies were performed and our results demonstrated the proposed Cofocus collaborative endpoint framework, the approaches, and architecture are feasible, efficient, and extensible. The future work will be focused on lightweight hypertext representations and application development based on the REST services.

References

1. AlShahwan, F., Moessner, K.: Providing SOAP Web Services and REST Web Services from Mobile Hosts. In: 2010 Fifth International Conference on Internet and Web Applications and Services (ICIW), May 9-15, pp. 174–179 (2010)
2. Antila, V., Mantyjarvi, J.: Distributed REST Web Services for Mobile Person-to-Person Collaboration. In: Third International Conference on Next Generation Mobile Applications, Services and Technologies, NGMAST 2009, September 15-18, pp. 119–124 (2009)
3. McFaddin, S., Coffman, D., Han, J.H., Jang, H.K., Kim, J.H., Lee, J.K., Lee, M.C., Moon, Y.S., Narayanaswami, C., Paik, Y.S., Park, J.W., Soroker, D.: Modelling and Managing Mobile Commerce Spaces Using REST Data Services. In: 9th International Conference on Mobile Data Management, MDM 2008, April 27-30, pp. 81–89 (2008)
4. Aijaz, F., Ali, S.Z., Chaudhary, M.A., Walke, B.: Enabling High Performance Mobile Web Services Provisioning. In: 2009 IEEE 70th Vehicular Technology Conference Fall (VTC 2009-Fall), September 20-23, pp. 1–6 (2009)
5. Pruter, S., Golatowski, F., Timmermann, D.: Adaptation of resource-oriented service technologies for industrial informatics. In: 35th Annual Conference of IEEE Industrial Electronics, IECON 2009, November 3-5, pp. 2399–2404 (2009)
6. Yong, L., Connelly, K.: Realizing an Open Ubiquitous Environment in a REST Way. In: IEEE International Conference on Web Services, ICWS 2008, September 23-26, pp. 96–103 (2008)

7. Lozano, D., Galindo, L.A., Garcia, L.: WIMS 2.0: Converging IMS and Web 2.0. Designing REST APIs for the Exposure of Session-Based IMS Capabilities. In: The Second International Conference on Next Generation Mobile Applications, Services and Technologies, NGMAST 2008, September 16-19, pp. 18–24 (2008)
8. Stirbu, V.: A REST architecture for adaptive and multi-device application sharing. In: Proceedings of the First International Workshop on REST Design, pp. 62–66 (2010)
9. Core 2010. Constrained REST Environments, core (2010), https://datatracker.ietf.org/wg/core/
10. SOAP 2007. SOAP Version 1.2 Part 1: Messaging Framework (2 edn.), W3C Recommendation (April 27, 2007)
11. Fielding, R.: Architectural Styles and the Design of Network-based Software Architectures, Ph.D. Dissertation (2000), http://www.ics.uci.edu/~fielding/pubs/dissertation/top.htm
12. XMPP 2004. Extensible Messaging and Presence Protocol (XMPP): Core (2004), http://tools.ietf.org/html/rfc3920
13. HTML 1999. HTML 4.01 Specification, W3C Recommendation (December 24, 1999), http://www.w3.org/TR/REC-html40/
14. Richardson, L., Ruby, S.: REST Web Services. O'Reilly (2007)
15. Li, L., Wu, C.: Design Patterns for REST Communication Web Services. In: ICWS 2010, Miami, July 5-10, pp. 512–519 (2010)
16. WSDL 2001. Web Services Description Language (WSDL) 1.1, W3C Note (March 15, 2001), http://www.w3.org/TR/wsdl
17. SOAP/XMPP 2005. XEP-0072: SOAP Over XMPP (2005), http://xmpp.org/extensions/xep-0072.html
18. SOAP/JMS 2009. SOAP over Java Message Service 1.0, W3C Candidate Recommendation (June 4, 2009), http://www.w3.org/TR/soapjms/
19. Srinivas, D.: (2008), http://davanum.wordpress.com/2008/12/29/updated-xmpp-client-for-android/
20. Smack 3.1.0 API, http://www.igniterealtime.org/projects/smack/
21. SMS 2010. 3GPP TS 23.040 Technical realization of the Short Message Service (SMS) (Release 9) (2010), http://www.3gpp.org/ftp/Specs/archive/23_series/23.040/23040-930.zip
22. RFC 3986. Uniform Resource Identifier (URI): Generic Syntax (January 2005), http://tools.ietf.org/html/rfc3986
23. WAP 2001 Wireless Application Protocol (2001), http://www.openmobilealliance.org/Technical/wapindex.aspx
24. WML 2001. Wireless Markup Language, Version 2.0, (September 11, 2001), http://www.openmobilealliance.org/tech/affiliates/wap/wap-238-wml-20010911-a.pdf
25. WSP 2001. Wireless Session Protocol (July 5, 2001), http://www.openmobilealliance.org/tech/affiliates/wap/wap-230-wsp-20010705-a.pdf
26. XEP-0030: Service Discovery, http://xmpp.org/extensions/xep-0030.html
27. RFC5122, http://tools.ietf.org/html/rfc5122

Modeling and Managing Communities
of Web Service Registries

Olfa Bouchaala, Mohamed Sellami,
Walid Gaaloul, Samir Tata, and Mohamed Jmaiel

TELECOM SudParis, CNRS UMR Samovar, Evry, France
University of Sfax, ReDCAD Laboratory, Sfax, Tunisia
{olfa.bouchaala,mohamed.sellami,
walid.gaaloul,samir.Tata}@it-sudparis.eu,
mohamed.jmaiel@enis.rnu.tn

Abstract. Today, we observe a continuous expansion in the use of Internet technologies, mainly Web services, for electronic B2B transactions. This has triggered an increase in the number of companies' Web services registries. In this context, Web service discovery can be a cumbersome task for a service requester and a costly one for a discovery system. To deal with this issue, one obvious solution is to group Web service registries into communities. Due to the dynamic nature of services oriented environments, such an organization should be managed to maintain its organizational consistency. In this paper, we specify the needed management operations to ensure the communities consistency during a registry/community life-cycle. To test the feasibility of our management approach, we simulate a network of registry communities and develop a community manager.

Keywords: Web service registry, Registry community, Communities management.

1 Introduction

Within a B2B context, we are interested in Web service (WS) discovery in a distributed registry environment, where companies use WSs to achieve transactions with their partners and offer online WSs. The involved companies have to make their WSs accessible on the net and available for consultation through WS registries. As a result, the number of WS registries can be very large. Therefore, WSs discovery will be a cumbersome task. To deal with this problem and to address the large number of WS registries and their poorly organized network, we propose to organize WS registries into communities. We define a WS registry community as a set of registries offering WSs providing similar functionalities. This organization is based on **W**eb **S**ervice **R**egistry **D**escription (WSRD) [1]. WSRD descriptions rely on the descriptions of the WSs belonging to a given registry and "semantically aggregate" the WSs functionalities.

In a distributed registry network, each registry is then described by a WSRD description. According to their descriptions, registries will be virtually structured into communities [2]. This solution reduces the search space for a service requester in the discovery

J. Filipe and J. Cordeiro (Eds.): WEBIST 2011, LNBIP 101, pp. 88–102, 2012.

process. However, it may raise other issues mainly related to community management. Indeed, communities and their members (i.e. WS registries) are dynamic by nature. In fact, a new WS description can be published in a registry and others can be unpublished at any time. In the same way, a registry can join a community or leave it according to its convenience. Therefore, management mechanisms are necessary to monitor these changes and reconcile potential conflicts.

In this context, we propose a graph-based approach for managing communities of WS registries which consists in a set of algorithms and managing operations. The managing operations are pre and post-conditions checking triggers and potential effects for each step of community life-cycle. The algorithms are rather defined for managing the registry life-cycle steps. These algorithms and operations are tested and validated using graph simulation.

This paper is organized as follows: in Section 2, we start by a brief introduction of concepts of the graph theory, we present our registry description model, we provide our definition of registries communities and present our approach for building such communities. The graph based model, that we propose to facilitate the specification of managing operations, is presented in Section 3. In Section 4, we define managing algorithms and operations for registry and community life-cycles. The implementation efforts are shown in Section 5. Finally, we conclude our paper and we foresee some future works.

2 Background

Since we model our WS registry community network based on graph theory, we start by briefly introducing graph prerequisites and some of the special types of graphs playing prominent role in our work. Then, we present the WSRD semantic model used to describe a registry. Finally, we present our community definition and our approach for building communities.

2.1 Background on Graph Theory

We define our distributed registry network based on the notations and concepts offered by graph theory. Indeed, graphs are highly flexible models for analyzing a wide range of practical problems through a collection of nodes and connections between them. A given problem is then mathematically formalized with a graph G, defined as a pair of sets $G = (V, E)$. V is the set of vertices (or nodes) and E is the edge set representing the network connections. The number of vertices $|V|$ of the graph G is its order. When G is not the only graph under consideration, the vertex- and edge-sets are denoted respectively $V(G)$ and $E(G)$.

A graph can be either directed or undirected. In the first case, each edge is an ordered pair of vertices. In the second case, edges represent unordered pairs of vertices. Both directed and undirected graphs may be weighted by a weight function $w : E \longrightarrow \mathbb{R}$ assigning a weight on each edge. A weighted graph is then denoted $G = (V, E, w)$.

Adjacency Matrix. The adjacency matrix A_G of a given graph $G = (V, E)$ of order n is an $n \times n$ matrix $A_G = (a_{i,j})$ where

$$a_{i,j} = \begin{cases} 1 & \text{if} \quad (i,j) \in E \\ 0 & \text{otherwise} \end{cases}$$

In a weighted graph, the adjacency matrix can be used to store the weights of the edges [3]. Hence, the values of the adjacency matrix for G would be defined as follows:

$$a_{i,j} = \begin{cases} w_{i,j} & \text{if} \quad (i,j) \in E \\ 0 & \text{if} \quad i = j \\ \infty & \text{if} \quad (i,j) \notin E \end{cases}$$

Star Graph. Graphs are classified into different types according to the nodes organization as well as the relationship between them. In this work, we use a particular type of graphs, called star graphs. A star graph is a complete bipartite graph $K_{1,k}$ or $K_{k,1}$.

A graph G is called bipartite (or bigraph) [4] if its vertex set can be divided into two subsets X and Y such that every edge joins a vertex in X to another in Y. Such a graph is denoted $G = (X, Y, E)$. A bigraph is complete if every vertex in X is joined to every vertex in Y. This is denoted $K_{n,m}$ with n, m respectively the cardinality of X and Y. If $n = 1$ or $m = 1$, G becomes a star graph.

Operations on Graphs. To simplify the management operations and algorithms that we present in Section 4, we use some operations defined in graph theory. Since graphs are defined as pairs of vertex and edge-sets, we use the set-theoretical terminology to define operations on and between them. Among these operations, we remind the addition/deletion of a vertex or an edge to/from a graph and the complement of a graph.

The addition/deletion of a vertex v (resp. an edge e) to/from a graph $G = (V, E)$ yields to a union/substraction of the vertex set $V(G)$ and $\{v\}$ (resp. the edge set $E(G)$ and $\{e\}$). We remind that the deletion of a vertex v removes not only this vertex but also all edges with this vertex as extremity. The resulting graph is then denoted $G = (V \backslash \{v\}, E \backslash \{(u, v) \in E | u \in V\})$. The complement of a graph $G = (V, E)$ is a graph $\overline{G} = (V, V \times V \backslash E)$ with the same vertices as G but with only those edges that are not in G. $G \cup \overline{G}$ represents a complete graph.

2.2   WSRD: Web Service Registry Description

Our idea to describe a Web service registry consists in aggregating the WSDL descriptions of the Web services it advertises into one description called **W**eb **S**ervice **R**egistry **D**escription (WSRD for short) [1]. Hence a WSRD of a registry gives an abstract description of the mean functionalities offered by the Web services of a registry.

Computing a registry's WSRD description goes through three steps: We first extract the annotating concepts and the number of times they occur from the Web service descriptions of the services published in the registry. Then, we compute a set of potential concepts, taken from the ontology, to annotate the WSRD description. To each concept we associate a value indicating its similarity degree to the whole set of the extracted concepts. Finally, we reduce the computed sets to only keep the concept(s) that will be used to annotate a registry's WSRD description. This is done by selecting the semantically most similar concept(s) (in the created sets) from the one extracted in the first step.

2.3   Communities of WS Registries

The Oxford dictionary defines a community as *"a group of people living together in one place holding certain attitudes and interests in common"*. In the WSs research field, Benatallah et al. [5] define a WS community as *"a collection of Web services with a common functionality although different non-functional properties"*. Zakaria et al. [6] consider a community as *"a means for providing a common description of a desired functionality without explicitly referring to any concrete Web service that will implement this functionality at run-time"*. In the same spirit, we define a WS registry community as a set of registries offering WSs providing similar functionalities. So, a distributed registry network will be virtually structured into communities and each registry belongs to at least one community with a certain extent. We assign for each registry a set of membership degrees indicating its membership to the different communities. In each community we associate to one registry the role of *leader* and to the other members the role of *followers*. The *leader* registry is the most representative registry of the community functionality. Therefore, the *leader* plays a prominent role in managing its community and its members. Obviously, a *leader* for a community c_1 could be a *follower* for another community c_2 and vice versa. The *leader-follower* relationship within a community indicates the level of similarity between the functionalities offered by both of them.

2.4   Building WS Registry Communities

A WS registry community will bring together registries offering similar functionalities. Since a WS registry generally offers services proposing different functionalities, it is difficult to properly define in advance classes categorizing the functionalities of the different registries. To organize WS registries into communities, we used [2] a **clustering** technique (where the different communities will be deduced from the registry descriptions) rather than a classification technique (where the different communities have to be defined in advance). When using a dynamic clustering technique, the different clusters (i.e. the WS registries communities) will be identified from the given input data (i.e. the WSRD descriptions) and each data point (i.e. WS registry) will be assigned to one or many communities.

Since a registry can belong to different communities at the same time (Section 2.3), the use of an exclusive clustering is inadequate for building registry communities.

Therefore, we proposed to use an overlapping clustering method to organize our distributed registries into communities. Using such clustering method, each data point (i.e. registry) represented by its WSRD description may belong to two or more communities with different *degrees of membership*.

Each WSRD description x will be represented as a vector r_x and a distance measure is used to establish the degrees of membership of each WS registry to the different clusters. In this work, we use the cosine similarity measure to establish the similarity between two given vectors r_1 and r_2 (formula (1)).

$$cosine(r_1, r_2) = \frac{r_1 \cdot r_2}{\|r_1\|\|r_2\|} \tag{1}$$

To deduce the distance from the cosine similarity function, we use formula (2).

$$distance(r_1, r_2) = 1 - cosine(r_1, r_2) \tag{2}$$

More details about our WS registries clustering approach can be found in [2].

3   Modeling Communities of Web Service Registries

Communities and WS registries operate within a dynamic environment where changes are mainly initiated by service and registry providers. The service provider can publish or delete a WS. Similarly, the registry provider can register its WS registry or dismantle it at any moment. To keep the consistency of our communities network against these events, management operations are needed. To facilitate the specification of these operations, we model the WS registry community network based on graph theory. In this section, we introduce our model representing a WS registry, a community and a community network.

3.1   Modeling a Web Service Registry

In this work, we refer to each WSRD description of a WS registry by f. A registry can belong to different communities at the same time. Thus, we assign to a registry a set of membership degrees that we call MEM. This set contains its membership degrees to each community in the network. Accordingly, a WS registry is defined as follows:

Definition 1 (Registry). *A registry is defined as a tuple* $r = (id, f, MEM)$ *where:*

- *id is the registry identifier.*
- *f is a vector representing functionalities offered by the advertised WSs within r.*
- *MEM represents the registry membership degrees to the different communities in the network. It is defined as a binary relation on* $C \times [0, 1]$. *We remind that a binary relation is a set of ordered couples.* $MEM = \{(c, d) | c \in C, d \in [0, 1]\}$ *where:*
    - *C is the community set*
    - *d is the membership degree of the registry r to the community c.*

We define the domain and range of $MEM \subseteq C \times [0, 1]$ *as:*
$dom(MEM) = \{c | (c, d) \in MEM$ for some $d \in [0, 1]\}$
$ran(MEM) = \{d | (c, d) \in MEM$ for some $c \in C\}$

3.2   Modeling a Web Service Registry Community

A community in our distributed registry environment is mainly characterized by its mean functionality f which represents the average of community registries functionalities. Registries can enter and leave a community almost at any time. Besides, we fix a threshold th beyond of which a registry could belong to a given community. As reported in section 2.3, we distinguish two kinds of registries (*leader* and *follower*) based on their role inside a community. Therefore, the set of community members (nodes) can be divided into a singleton $L = \{l\}$ representing the *leader* and a set $Fl = \{fl_i | i : 1..n\}$ where n is the number of the community *followers*. Thus, the community nodes are modelled as a star graph G where nodes are registries and each edge represents the functional similarity between the *leader* and a *follower* fl, $fl \in Fl$. The similarity between the functionalities offered by the *leader* and a *follower* can be computed using the cosine function (Section 2.4, formula (1)). Hence, we define a community as follows:

Definition 2 (Community). *A community is a tuple* $c = (id, f, G)$ *with:*

 - id *is the community identifier.*
 - f *is a vector representing the mean functionality of the community c.*
 - $G = (L, Fl, E, w)$ *is an undirected weighted star graph where:*
   - L *is the community* leader*: the registry having the highest membership degree inside c.*
   - Fl *is the set of community* followers
   - $E \subseteq L \times Fl$ *is the set of edges*
   - $w : E \longrightarrow [0, 1]$ *is a weighting function representing the similarity between nodes.*

3.3   Modeling the Community Network

So far, our distributed registry environment which is a set of communities is modelled by a set of star graphs. As the number of registries (nodes) can be very large and a single registry can belong to many communities, the community management is a cumbersome task. To deal with this problem and to have a global view of the network, we define another graph CG, called *Community Graph*, in which nodes represent communities and edges are the relationships between them. If two communities have at least one registry in common, then there is an edge joining them. In this case, we compute the distance between their vectors f representing their mean functionalities. The distance can be computed using formula (2) of Section 2.4. The distance measure will be the weight of the edge relating these two communities. Our distributed registry network is then defined as follows:

Definition 3 (Community Network). *The community network is represented by an undirected weighted graph* $CG = (C, E, w)$

 - C *is a finite set of nodes. Each single node represents a registry community.*
 - $E \subseteq C \times C$ *is the set of edges (representing the relationships between communities).*
 - $w : E \longrightarrow [0, 1]$ *is a weighting function representing the distance between two given nodes.*

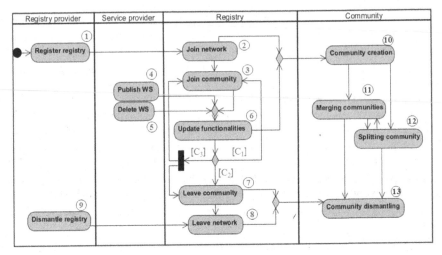

Fig. 1. Communities management process

4   Managing Communities

In the following, we define the necessary management operations to handle WS registries and WS registry communities during their life cycles.

4.1   The Registry Life-Cycle

A registry life-cycle starts when a registry provider decides to **register its WS registry** in the network (Figure 1 (1)). This registry **joins the network** (2) and then **joins
the adequate communities** according to its offered functionalities (3). Since a service
provider can **publish** (4) or **delete** (5) a **WS** within this registry, its WSRD description can change and an **update of the registry functionalities** (6) is needed. In such
scenario, a suitability check of the registry membership should be done: If the registry
membership degree is lower than a certain threshold th set by the designer, it **leaves
the community** (7) and joins another one. Finally, the registry can **leave the whole
network** (8) if its provider decides to **dismantle** it (9). In the following, we detail the
steps (2), (3) and (6) of the registry life-cycle.

Joining the Network. When a new WS registry r joins our distributed registry environment, its WSRD description should be computed. After that, the registry can be
guided to the adequate communities according to its set of membership degrees MEM.
MEM is computed by the *CommunitySelection* algorithm (Algorithm 1). This algorithm takes as input the current registry's WSRD description and it is essentially based
on the computation of the membership degree as the inverse of the distance between
the community mean functionality $c.f$ and the registry functionalities $r.f$ (line 2). This
distance measure is computed according to formula (2) (Section 2.4). This algorithm

outputs the set of membership MEM containing the membership degrees of the current registry to the different communities in the network. Taking into account that the membership degree must be greater than the threshold th defined above (line 4), the registry will be guided to the adequate communities (line 5). If all membership degrees are lower than th, a new community will be created (Section 4.2).

Algorithm 1. *CommunitySelection*

Require: r :registry
Ensure: $r.MEM$
1: **for each** community $c \in C$ **do**
2:    $m \longleftarrow 1/distance(c.f, r.f)$
3:    $r.MEM \longleftarrow r.MEM \cup \{(c, m)\}$
4:    **if** $m >$ th **then**
5:       $V(c.G) \longleftarrow V(c.G) \cup \{r\}$
6:    **end if**
7: **end for**

Joining a Community. When a registry joins a community, it may have a membership degree greater than the community *leader*. In this case, the *LeaderReselection* algorithm (Algorithm 4) should be applied. It checks either or not the new registry will take the role of *leader* in one of the communities it belongs to (line 1, 5). This is done through a simple comparison between the new registry's membership degree and the community *leader*'s one (line 5). If the *leader*'s membership degree is still the greatest, then we only link the current registry with the community *leader* (line 6, 7). Otherwise, we remove all *followers-leader* links (line 9,10,11), add the *leader* to the *followers* set (line 12), the current registry takes the *leader*'s place (line 13) and the community *followers* will be linked to the new community *leader* (line 14,15,16).

Updating Registry Functionalities. We recall that the WSs advertised within a registry frequently change (new WSs arrive, others leave). Therefore, the registry functionalities have to be regularly updated. When a change occurs, the registry can stay in the same community, leave or move from a community to another. After a functionalities update, a registry acceptance or denial in a community happens according to the *CommunityAcceptance* algorithm algorithm (Algorithm 2). By applying this algorithm on a set of updated registries, the following events can happen:

- $E = E'$, i.e. no changes occur in the set of community members, where E and E' are two sets of members of a given community c, respectively before and after updating registries functionalities.
- $E \subset E'$, i.e. some new registries join the set of community members. (Figure 1.[C1])
- $E' \subset E$, i.e. some registries leave the set of community members. (Figure 1.[C2])
- a minha boca um TUMULO$E \not\subset E'$ and$E' \not\subset E$, i.e. some new registries join the set of community members and some others leave. (Figure 1.[C3])

4.2   The Community Life-Cycle

The main steps of a community life-cycle are: creation, dismantling, merging and splitting. When the membership degrees of a registry became lower than the threshold th

---

Algorithm 2. *CommunityAcceptance*

Require: r:registry, c:community
Ensure: (accept/deny)
  1: Let $d \in [0,1]$ such that $(c,d) \in r.MEM$
  2: $d \longleftarrow 1/distance(c.f, r.f)$
  3: **if** $d >$ th **then**
  4:    *return accept*
  5: **else**
  6:    *return deny*
  7: **end if**

---

for all existing communities, a **new community will be created** (Figure 1(10)). Also, a **community will be dismantled** (13) if it becomes empty. Throughout a registry life-cycle, we check the similarity inside and between communities to ensure the principle goal of clustering: **minimizing** the similarity between clusters while **maximizing** it within each cluster. To guarantee this goal, a community can be **merged** (11) to another one or **split** (12). In the following, we present triggers and effects for each step.

Community Creation. A new community $c_{new} = (id, f, G)$ is established automatically, if the membership degrees of a registry to all the existing communities are lower than the threshold th. This situation necessarily implies that c_{new} provides a new functionality in the network. This can happen when a new registry joins the network (Section 4.1) or after an update of the registry's functionalities (see Section 4.1). So the *Pre-condition* for a community creation is modeled as: $\forall d \in ran(r.MEM), d <$ th.

The registry r that triggered the community creation, will get the role of *leader* for the new community c_{new}. The community mean functionality $c_{new}.f$ will be the same as the functionality $r.f$ proposed by the registry. Afterwards, the *FollowersSelection* algorithm (Algorithm 3) will be executed to recruit *followers* for the new community. In this aim, the membership degrees of existing registries to the new community are computed. These different actions form the *Post-condition* for a community creation and are modeled as follows: $c_{new} \in V(CG) \wedge c_{new}.G.L = \{r\} \wedge c_{new}.f = r.f \wedge c_{new}.G.Fl = FolowersSelection(c_{new})$.

Community Dismantling. A community c is automatically dismantled; when it becomes empty $|V(c.G)| = 0$ (all of its members leave or no longer exist). This is the only condition that triggers the disappearance of a community. This *Pre-condition* is modeled as follows: $c \in V(CG) \wedge |V(c.G)| = 0$.

After deleting a community, we must check the *Post-condition* stating that c is not the extremity of any edge in the community graph CG: $c \notin V(CG) \wedge \forall c_1 \in V(CG), (c, c_1) \notin E(CG)$.

Merging Communities. The natural idea that first comes to mind when deciding which communities to merge is closeness. Based on the graph CG and assuming that $(c_1, c_2) \in E(CG)$ (Definition 3), this issue can be specified as follows: $w(c_1, c_2) < \xi$ such that $\xi \in [0,1]$ a threshold beyond of which two communities can be merged.

Algorithm 3. *FollowersSelection*

Require: c_{new} : community
Ensure: $c_{new}.Fl$: Follower Set
 1: **for all** Communities $c \in C$ **do**
 2:    **for all** Registries $r \in V(c.G)$ **do**
 3:       Let $\{l\} \longleftarrow c_{new}.G.L$
 4:       $m \longleftarrow 1/distance(c_{new}.f, r.f)$
 5:       $r.MEM \longleftarrow r.MEM \cup (c_{new}, m)$
 6:       **if** $m > $ th **then**
 7:          $c_{new}.G.Fl \longleftarrow c_{new}.G.Fl \cup \{r\}$
 8:          $E(c_{new}.G) \longleftarrow E(c_{new}.G) \cup \{(l, r)\}$
 9:       **end if**
10:    **end for**
11: **end for**
12: return $c_{new}.Fl$

Algorithm 4. *LeaderReselection*

Require: r: registry
 1: **for all** Communities $c \in dom(r.MEM)$ **do**
 2:    Let $\{l\} \longleftarrow c.G.L$
 3:    Let $d_r \in [0, 1]$ such that $(c, d_r) \in r.MEM$
 4:    Let $d_l \in [0, 1]$ such that $(c, d_l) \in l.MEM$
 5:    **if** $d_r > $ th and $d_l > d_r$ **then**
 6:       $c.G.Fl \longleftarrow c.G.Fl \cup \{r\}$
 7:       $E(c.G) \longleftarrow E(c.G) \cup \{(r, l)\}$
 8:    **else**
 9:       **for all** $fl \in c.G.Fl$ **do**
10:          $E(c.G) \longleftarrow E(c.G) - \{(l, fl)\}$
11:       **end for**
12:       $c.G.Fl \longleftarrow c.G.Fl \cup \{l\}$
13:       $c.G.L \longleftarrow \{r\}$
14:       **for all** $fl \in c.G.Fl$ **do**
15:          $E(c.G) \longleftarrow E(c.G) \cup \{(r, fl)\}$
16:       **end for**
17:    **end if**
18: **end for**

However, the closeness is computed using a geometrical distance without taking into account the registries dispersion. Thus, an exception can take place when communities centers are close to each other but not dense in the middle way between centers. i.e. few registries in the intersection or communities are completely separated . As a consequence the closeness condition is necessary to check the similarity between communities functionalities but not sufficient.

Thus, we define the communities merging pre-condition by adding another condition to the closeness one. This second condition checks if a community is included in another one. Our resulting ***Pre-condition*** will be: $c_2 \in V(CG), \exists c_1 | w(c_1, c_2) < \xi \wedge V(c_1.G) \subset V(c_2.G)$. When this pre-condition is satisfied for two communities, they will be merged

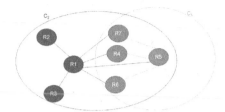

Fig. 2. Merging Pre-condition

into a new one called c_{merg}. The center of c_{merg} is computed as the weighted average of both communities centers $c_1.f$ and $c_2.f$:

$$c_{merg}.f = \frac{c_1.f \times nb_1 + c_2.f \times nb_2}{nb_1 + nb_2} \tag{3}$$

Where:

- $nb_1 = \#\{r|(c_1, d_1) \in r.MEM \wedge (c_2, d_2) \in r.MEM \wedge d_1 \geq d_2\}$, the number of registries in the intersection of c_1 and c_2 having a greater membership degree to c_1.
- $nb_2 = \#\{r|(c_1, d_1) \in r.MEM \wedge (c_2, d_2) \in r.MEM \wedge d_2 \geq d_1\}$, the number of registries in the intersection of c_1 and c_2 having a greater membership degree to c_2.

As a consequence of the merging step, the community c_{merg} is added to the graph CG and both communities c_1 and c_2 are deleted. Thereby, all edges whose ends are one of these two communities are removed too. This ***Post-condition*** is modeled as follows: $V(CG) = (V(CG) - \{c_1, c_2\}) \cup \{c_{merg}\}$.

Splitting a Community. A community is automatically divided if it becomes sparse. The community sparsity describes a non density in the center vicinity and a dispersion between members (Figure 3). If this pre-condition is satisfied, this issue can be observed as a graph partitioning problem. Indeed, we consider a community c represented with its undirected weighted star graph $c.G$ which represents the similarity relationship between the *leader* and its *followers*. $\overline{c.G}$ is the complement of $c.G$ (Section 2.1) and is also a weighted graph representing similarity relationships between *followers*. The weighted adjacency matrix of the complete graph $c.G \cup \overline{c.G}$ contains all similarity weights between each pair of community members (Section 2.1). An algorithm which suits well to our needs taking as input a weighted adjacency matrix of an undirected weighted graph is the *Mcut* algorithm [7] which proposes a graph partition method based on min-max clustering principle: the similarity between two subgraphs is minimized while the similarity within each subgraph is maximized. Figure 3 shows how this algorithm is applied on a community c that satisfied the splitting pre-condition.

5   Implementation

To test the feasibility of our approach, we simulate WS registry communities using graphs. Indeed, we implemented a *Community Manager* (Figure 4) based on the *Jgrapht*[1] java library.

---

[1] http://www.jgrapht.org/

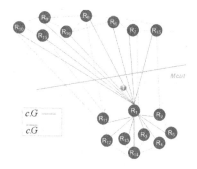

Fig. 3. Splitting a community using *Mcut* algorithm

To validate the proposed algorithms and managing operations, we consider the following scenario: We generate 700 SAWSDL descriptions using the semantic description generator presented in [8]. These descriptions are organized into 7 registries such that each one contains 100 descriptions. We compute the WSRD description of each registry using the *WSRDGen* implemented in [1]. Each description is modeled with a vector $f = [w_1, w_2, ...w_5]$ computed as shown in section 2.4.

These vectors represent the input of the clustering method [2] which outputs the mean functionality vectors $\{c.f|c \in C\}$ and the membership degrees of each registry to different communities $\{r.MEM|r \in R\}$, with R the set of registries in the network.

The vectors $r.f$, $c.f$ and $r.MEM$, such that $r \in R$ and $c \in C$, are saved in an XML file representing initialization data for our *Community Manager* in order to build the graphs modeling the communities and the registries (Figure 4). In Frame 1, we present the graph composed by the set of graphs $c.G$ representing communities. The *leader* of each community is represented by a blue rectangle. In Frame 2, we represent the graph CG representing our community network.

As reported in Section 4, the main triggers of dynamic changes are service and registry providers. In the following, we introduce these changes to test managing algorithms and operations.

Adding a Registry. In order to test *CommunitySelection* and *LeaderReselection* algorithms, we add a new registry in the network represented by its vector f=[0.234 0.314 0.048 0.181 0.534]. The *Community Manager* assigns an identifier to this new registry (r_8) and then compute its membership degrees $r_8.MEM = \{(c_1, 0.1943), (c_2, 0.282), (c_3, 0.2759), (c_4, 0.2479)\}$. MEM is compared with th $= 0.1$. The new registry belongs to all the existing communities. At this level, the *LeaderReselection* algorithm assigns the role of *follower* for r_8 in each community it belongs to. If we change th to 0.3, we notice that all membership degrees of r_8 to the existing communities are lower than th. In this case, the *community Manager* cheks the **community creation** pre-condition and establishes automatically a new community by adding a new vertex to the CG graph. Accordingly, the *FollowersSelection* algorithm is executed selecting *followers* for r_8 which assumes the role of leader in this new community.

Dismantling a Registry. The community c_3 is composed by only two registries: r_3 the *leader* and r_7 its *follower* (Figure 4). By dismantling r_3, the *LeaderReselection*

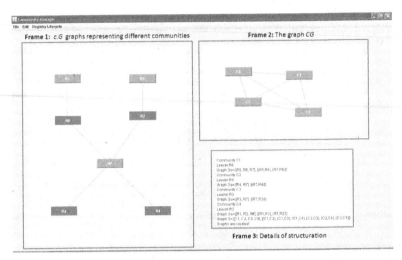

Fig. 4. Community Manager

algorithm is applied assigning r_7 to be the *leader*. By dismantling r_7, the **community c_3 is automaticaly dismantled** since the dismantling pre-condition is satisfied.

Updating Registry Functionalities. The *CommunityAcceptance* algorithm is tested through an update of registry functionalities f. The update is done if a service provider publish, unpublish or modify a WS description advertised within this registry. Using the updated graph of Frame 1 result of the addition of r_8 to the network and assuming that $th = 0.1$, we first update r_3's functionalities. r_3 leaves the community c_3 because its membership to this community is now lower than th. Actually, c_3 is composed of r_7 and r_8. We notice that c_3 is included in c_1, c_2 and c_4. The **merging pre-condition** is partially satisfied. However, we must check that the weights of edges whose ends are c_3 and one of the communities c_1, c_2 and c_4 are lower than $\xi = 0.2$ (Section 3.3). c_2 satisfies this condition. Thereby, c_2 and c_3 are merged into a new community c_5.

These scenarios show the feasibility and validity of our algorithms as well as managing operations used to handle registry and community life cycles. In fact, they execute well and automatically call each other after every change.

6   Related Work

To enhance the WS discovery process in a private registries network, we use a functionality-driven approach to organize them into communities. Such a registry network organization needs to be regularly managed to ensure the consistency of the communities. In this paper, we are interested in the management phase of registry communities. As far as we know, this work is the first attempt to manage communities of WSs registries. Indeed, several WS discovery approaches in distributed registry environments [9,10,11] structure their networks as clusters but did not provide management mechanisms for their clusters. In this section, we overview some related efforts in the field of managing communities that helped us tailor our approach.

In [12], Paik et al. present the WS-catalogNet framework allowing to group e-catalogs having similar domain into communities, build relationships between them and manage them constantly. The system offer monitoring functionalities and managing operations to restructure a community network according to the user interaction. Therefore, authors model the community network and then specify pre-conditions and effects for each operation based on the graph model they defined [13]. However, authors employ a classification technique to organize communities, while we use a dynamic clustering one. Furthermore, we use the functionality criterion to structure communities rather than business domain.

Medjahed and Bouguettaya [14] propose an approach to organize WSs into communities depending on their domain of interest. A community is an instance of an ontology metadata called community ontology and is described by a set of generic operations. In this context, community providers can add, delete or modify some generic operations. Service providers, in turn, can delete a WS from a community or make its operations temporarily unavailable. Thus, authors propose a P2P approach to manage these changes. However, their operations are described informally compared to our management operations.

In [15], Maamar et al. discuss the dynamic nature of WS community and focus on potential conflicts. They propose in [16] an approach to engineer WSs communities in order to reconcile these potential conflicts. This approach is based on the Community development protocol which is interested in managing communities in term of attracting and retaining WSs, creating and dismantling communities. Similarly to our approach, communities are organized according to WSs functionalities. However, this approach did not propose a model and their operation descriptions are rather informal.

7   Conclusions

In this paper, we proposed an approach for managing communities of WSs registries. We first defined a model to facilitate the managing step. Then we identified the main steps of registry and community life-cycles. Afterwards, we specified managing operations and algorithms based on the model that we have proposed. Finally, we implemented a *Community Manager* to test and validte these algorithms and operations. Experiments show that our algorithms and managing operations execute well. The splitting operation has not been tested since its pre-condition is not yet specified. Indeed, we used different methods to detect the sparsity criterion in a given community such as standard deviation of a statical series but each one represents an exception. As part of our short term perspectives, we plan to specify a pertinent pre-condition for splitting operation. Furthermore, we foresee to implement these algorithms on top of the platform P2P *JXTA*[2] in order to test the precision/time ratio of our approach.

---

[2] https://jxta.dev.java.net/

References

1. Sellami, M., Bouchaala, O., Gaaloul, W., Tata, S.: WSRD: A web services registry description. In: NOTERE 2010, Tozeur, Tunisia, May 31-June 2 (2010)
2. Sellami, M., Gaaloul, W., Tata, S.: Functionality-driven clustering of web service registries. In: SCC 2010, Miami, Florida, USA (2010)
3. McConnell, J.J.: Analysis of algorithms: an active learning approach. Jones and Bartlett publishers (2008)
4. Bondy, J.A., Murty, U.S.R.: Graph Theory. Springer, London (2007)
5. Benatallah, B., Sheng, Q.Z., Dumas, M.: The self-serv environment for web services composition. IEEE Internet Computing 7, 40–48 (2003)
6. Maamar, Z., Lahkim, M., Benslimane, D., Thiran, P., Sattanathan, S.: Web services communities - concepts & operations. In: WEBIST 2007 (2007)
7. Ding, C.H.Q., He, X., Zha, H., Gu, M., Simon, H.D.: A min-max cut algorithm for graph partitioning and data clustering. In: ICDM 2001, pp. 107–114. IEEE Computer Society, Washington, DC, USA (2001)
8. Chabeb, Y., Tata, S., Ozanne, A.: Yasa-m: A semantic web service matchmaker. In: AINA 2010, Perth, Australia, April 20-23 (2010)
9. Sellami, M., Gaaloul, W., Tata, S., Jmaiel, M.: Using recommendation to limit search space in web services discovery. In: AINA, pp. 974–981. IEEE Computer Society (2010)
10. Sivashanmugam, K., Verma, K., Sheth, A.P.: Discovery of web services in a federated registry environment. In: ICWS 2004, pp. 270–278. IEEE Computer Society, San Diego (2004)
11. Xu, B., Chen, D.: Semantic web services discovery in p2p environment. In: ICPPW 2007 (2007)
12. Paik, H.Y., Benatallah, B., Toumani, F.: Toward self-organizing service communities. IEEE Transactions on Systems, Man, and Cybernetics, Part A 35, 408–419 (2005)
13. Paik, H.Y., Benatallah, B., Hamadi, R.: Dynamic restructuring of e-catalog communities based on user interaction patterns. World Wide Web 5, 325–366 (2002)
14. Medjahed, B., Bouguettaya, A.: A dynamic foundational architecture for semantic web services. Distributed and Parallel Databases 17, 179–206 (2005)
15. Maamar, Z., Sattanathan, S., Thiran, P., Benslimane, D., Bentahar, J.: An approach to engineer communities of web services - concepts, architecture, operation, and deployment. IJEBR 9 (2009)
16. Subramanian, S., Thiran, P., Maamar, Z., Benslimane, D.: Engineering communities of web services. In: iiWAS 2007, Jakarta, Indonesia, pp. 57–66 (2007)

Towards a Guaranteed (X)HTML Compliant Dynamic Web Application

Paul G. Talaga and Steve J. Chapin

Syracuse University, Syracuse, NY 13244, U.S.A.
pgtalaga@syr.edu, chapin@ecs.syr.edu

Abstract. We report on the embedding of a domain specific language, (X)HTML, into Haskell and demonstrate how this web language can be represented and rendered for strong World Wide Web Consortium (W3C) compliance. Compliance of web content is important for the health of the Internet, accessibility, visibility, and reliable search. While tools exist to verify web content is compliant according to the W3C, few systems guarantee that all dynamically produced content is compliant. We present *CH-(X)HTML*, a library for generating compliant (X)HTML content for all dynamic content by using Haskell to encode the non-trivial syntax of (X)HTML set forth by the W3C. Any compliant document can be represented with this library, while a compilation or run-time error will occur if non-compliant markup is attempted. To demonstrate our library we present examples, performance measurements, and a discussion of library version considerations.

Keywords: W3C Compliance, Web Development, Haskell, HTML, XHTML, XML.

1 Introduction

Conformity of web content to the World Wide Web Consortium's (W3C) standards is a goal every web developer should aspire to meet. Conformity leads to *increased visibility* as more browsers can render the markup consistently, *increased accessibility* for disabled users using non-typical browsing styles[31], *more reliable Internet search* by presenting search engines with consistent page structures[14], and in some cases *compliance with legal requirements* [9,22,33,3].

Unfortunately the majority of web content is non-compliant, with one study finding 95% of pages online are not valid[12]. Not surprisingly, the majority of web frameworks do not guarantee generated content is compliant. Popular internet browsers perpetuate the problem by creatively parsing and rendering invalid code in an attempt to retain users.

While tools exist to check validity of static content, few systems exist that claim strong validity of *all* produced content. With dynamic web applications, it is harder to guarantee validity due to the dynamic nature of their outputs. Assuring compliance for specific inputs is possible, but proving compliance for all inputs is analogous to proof by example. Web frameworks using Model-View-Controller design practices provide some assurances based on compliant templates, but it remains easy for an unknowing developer or user input to break this compliance. Such deficiencies in frameworks can

J. Filipe and J. Cordeiro (Eds.): WEBIST 2011, LNBIP 101, pp. 103–115, 2012.

have security consequences as well[17]. Rather than make it easy for developers to produce invalid content, frameworks should make it impossible to be non-compliant.

1.1 Contributions

We present *CH-(X)HTML*, a Haskell library for building (X)HTML content with strong W3C compliance for all outputs. By using Haskell's recursive types, multiple parameter and functional dependency of type classes, web content is built by separating structure from content in a typed tree data structure way, much like the underlying (X)HTML. The resulting structure can be stored, manipulated, or serialized to a standard W3C compliant textual representation. *CH-(X)HTML* currently supports HTML 4.01 Strict, Loose, and Frameset as well as XHTML 1.0 Strict, Transitional, and Frameset.

We identify five traits common to all W3C (X)HTML specifications which must be met for a document to be compliant and show how *CH-(X)HTML* enforces four of these at compile-time, with the fifth optionally at run-time.

The remainder of the paper is structured as follows. We analyze and categorize commonalities between different W3C (X)HTML specifications in Section 2, identifying requirements a W3C compliant producing system must possess. Section 3 provides an overview of *CH-(X)HTML* and discusses how it is able to enforce the W3C specifications while being easy to use. Sample code is provided showing the use of the library, followed by a performance evaluation in Section 4. Related work and our conclusion are in Sections 5 and 6 respectively.

2   W3C Compliance

The W3C has set forth numerous variants of specifications of HTML and XHTML, with more on the way in the form of HTML5. Examples include HTML 3.2, HTML 4.01 Strict, and XHTML 1.00 Transitional. While conformance to a specific document type definition (DTD) is our goal, identifying commonalities will assure easy conversion to any HTML DTD. For example, the difference between HTML 4.01 Strict and HTML 4.01 Transitional is merely the allowance of certain elements (tags). Likewise, HTML 4.01 Frameset and XHTML 1.00 Frameset differ in their document type: SGML and XML respectively[16] in addition to some element differences.

We have identified five classes of common requirements between different (X)HTML DTDs based on Thiemann's work[27]. A system capable of supporting all requirement classes should be able to include support for all requirements in any of the W3C specifications. These classes include the following:

Well-Formed. An (X)HTML document is well-formed if all elements have appropriate starting and ending characters, as well as an ending tag when needed. All attributes have the form `attribute="value"` inside the tag. All characters should be in the correct context. For example, all markup characters should only be used for markup including `<,>,&,"`.

Element-Conforming. An (X)HTML document is element-conforming if all elements are defined and valid within that DTD. No browser specific elements should be used.

Attribute-Conforming. An (X)HTML document is attribute-conforming if all attributes names are allowed for that specific element. For example, the p element can not contain an href attribute. Similarly, the value type of every attribute matches its DTD description. Required attributes are also provided.

Inclusion and Exclusion. An (X)HTML document obeys inclusion & exclusion if the nesting of all elements follow the specific DTD. For example, in HTML 4.01 no a element can be a descendant of another a element. Similarly, the tr element requires a td element to be its child. While SGML, of which HTML is a member, allows deep nesting rules, XML does not[16]. XML can specify what children are allowed, but not grandchildren or beyond. Thus, the XHTML 1.0 specification recommends the inclusion & exclusion of elements, but can not require it. We feel that since XHTML is fully based on HTML this requirement is important and should be enforced. In support, the W3C online validator marks inclusion & exclusion problems in XHTML as errors. The draft HTML5 specification broadens nesting rules by restricting *groups* of elements to be children[5]. For example, an a element in HTML5 must not contain any *interactive content*, of which 15 elements are members.

Element Ordering. An (X)HTML document obeys element ordering if sibling elements are ordered as described in their DTD. As an example, the head element must precede the body element as children of the html element.

3   CH-(X)HTML

Our system is built as an embedded domain-specific language, implemented in Haskell, capable of embodying the requirements set forth by the W3C. The use of a strongly typed language guarantees strong compliance of the application at *compile* time, while allowing easy representation of the embedded language. Any strongly typed language could be used for such a system, but Haskell's multiple parameter and functional dependency type classes cleans up the syntax for the developer.

CH-(X)HTML is available for download[1] or on Hackage[2]. HTML 4.01 Strict, Transitional, and Frameset, as well as XHtml 1.0 Strict[16], Transitional, and Frameset are currently supported in Version 0.2.0 at this time.

3.1   Implementation Overview

CH-(X)HTML's design is outlined through a series of refinements guaranteeing each of the five W3C specification classes described above. Code examples are meant to convey design methods, not produce fully correct HTML.

Well-Formed and Element Conformance
At its core, *CH-(X)HTML* uses ordinary Haskell types to implement a recursively defined tree data structure representing the (X)HTML document. Each node in the tree represents an element, with inner elements stored as a list of children. Depending on the

---

[1] http://fuzzpault.com/chxhtml
[2] http://hackage.haskell.org/package/CHXHtml

element, the node may have none, or a variable number of children. Element attributes are stored with each node. Character data is inserted using a `pcdata` constructor. An example of this scheme is given:

```
data Ent = Html Attributes [Ent]  |
           Body Attributes [Ent]  |
            P Attributes [Ent]  |
            A Attributes [Ent]  |
            Br Attributes  |
            Cdata String  | ...
data Attributes = [String]
render :: Ent -> String
```

Only defined elements for a specific DTD exist as constructors, thus forcing element-conformance. When the data structure has been constructed and is ready to be serialized, a recursive function `render` traverses the structure, returning a string containing elements and properly formatted attributes and values. All character data (CDATA) is HTML escaped before rendering preventing embedding of HTML markup. Separating content from structure, along with HTML escaping, forces all produced content to be well-formed and element-conforming.

Attribute Conformance

To limit allowed attributes and their types, each element is given a custom attribute type allowing only valid attributes to be used. If an attribute is set more than once the `render` function will use only the last, guaranteeing a unique value for each attribute. Required attributes are automatically inserted with empty values at run-time to guarantee compliance while the `pageErrors` function can be used to report inserted empy attributes for later repair. This run-time compliance issue is discussed in Section 3.2.

The example below implements attribute conformance described above.

```
data Ent = Html [Att_html] [Ent]  |
           Body [Att_body] [Ent]  |
            P [Att_p] [Ent]  |
            A [Att_a] [Ent]  |
            Br [Att_b]  |
            Cdata String  | ...
--
data Att_html = Lang_html String  |
                Dir_html String   | ...
data Att_body = Lang_body String  |
                Dir_body String   |
                Onload_body String | ...
...
render :: Ent -> String
```

Inclusion and Exclusion Conformance

Thus far any element can be a child of any other. For inclusion & exclusion conformance we use new data types representing the context of those elements. Each DTD describes allowed children for each element, required elements, as well as limits on all

Table 1. Inclusion & Exclusion Examples in HTML 4.01

Element	Required Children	Allowed Children	Disallowed Descendants
html	head,body	head,body	
body	+	p,div,...	
p		a,br,cdata,...	
a		br,cdata,...	a
tr	+	th,td	
form	+	p,div,...	form
...			

descendants. For example, Table 1 describes the inclusion & exclusion rules for some elements in HTML 4.01 Strict. A + in the required children column signifies at least one child must exist.

By using unique types for each element only allowed children elements can be inserted. To enforce descendant rules, a new set of types are used which lack the forbidden element. Thus, rather than one constructor specifying an element, a set of constructors may, each valid in a different context. For example the following code correctly prohibits nesting of the a element by effectively duplicating the Ent3 type but lacking the a.

```
data Ent = Html Att_html [Ent2]
data Ent2 = Body Att_body [Ent3]
data Ent3 = A3 Att_p [Ent_no_a] |
            P3 Att_p [Ent3] |
            Br3 Att_b |
            Cdata3 String | ...
data Ent_no_a = P_no_a Att_p [Ent_no_a] |
                Br_no_a Att_b |
                Cdata_no_a String | ...
- Attributes same as above
render :: Ent -> String
```

In practice, preventing a deep descendant results in duplication of nearly all types. Had Ent3 allowed some other child other than itself, then it too must be duplicated with a _no_a version, and so on. A combinatorial explosion could prove this approach unfeasible, but our analysis has shown otherwise. For example, by enumerating all possible valid nesting situations in HTML 4.0 Strict, a total of 45 groups of elements were needed to properly limit allowed children while preventing invalid descendant situations.

Assuring the required children elements exist is checked at run-time which is discussed in Section 3.2.

Element Order Conformance

To validate or warn against element-order conformance errors, a run-time checker pageErrors can be used. Section 3.2 discusses the issues and trade offs involved with such a run-time system.

3.2   Complete Compile-Time Compliance vs. Usability

A trade-off exists between complete compile-time compliance and usability with regard to element ordering, required children elements, and required attributes. A library's interface should be obvious, allowing existing HTML knowledge to be used easily in a new context. For usability we've decided to have four forms of element constructors: two with children, and two without, detailed in Section 3.4. Children elements are specified as a regular Haskell list for those elements allowing children. Similarly, element attributes are described in list form as well. This allows the developer to easily write markup and apply any list manipulation function to elements or attributes. Unfortunately there is no way to restrict the list elements or their order at compile-time. A run-time checker pageErrors can scan the completed document for element ordering, required children, or required attribute errors if needed.

The alternative would be to specify children or attributes as a tuple. Tuples allow different type elements, but all must be provided. List manipulation would not be possible, nor would all elements have a standard interface. Some elements may take a 3-tuple, while others may take a list, or some other combination thereof. Burdening the developer with such complexities and limitations was deemed too harsh given the complete compile-time guarantee benefit. The HaXml project contains a DtdToHaskell utility which enforces ordering in this manner using tuples[32].

3.3   Cleanup

Writing (X)HTML content using complex constructors described in Section 3.1 becomes unwieldy quickly. By using multi-parameter type classes and functional dependencies we can hide this complexity while still retaining the compile-time guarantees. We construct a type class per element such that a function correctly returns a constructor of the correct type based on context. The following example shows the type class for specifying the p element.

```
class C_P a b | a -> b where
    p :: [Att_p] -> [b] -> a
instance C_P Ent3 Ent3 where
    p at r = P_1 at r
instance C_P Ent_no_a Ent_no_a where
    p at r = P_2 at r
```

The class instance used is determined by the context the function is called in, which determines what type children it may have provided by the functional dependency of classes. Thus, as long as the root of the recursive structure has a concrete type all children will be uniquely defined. Nesting errors manifest themselves as compile-time class instance type errors.

Attribute specification is handled in a similar way. Thus, during development, only the element or attribute names must be specified, all complex constructor selection is done by the functional type classes.

3.4 Library Usage

Building an (X)HTML document is done by constructing the recursive data structure and serializing it using the `render` or `render_bs` functions. Content can be served to the web with any number of Haskell web servers such as HAppS[4], Happstack[15], MoHWS[20], turbinado[18], SNAP[13], or via executable with CGI[2][10] or FastCGI[25][11] Haskell bindings. *CH-(X)HTML* can be used anywhere a `String` type containing (X)HTML is needed in Haskell. For speed and efficiency the `render_bs` function returns a lazy ByteString representation suitable for CGI bindings.

All HTML elements are represented in lower case with an underscore _ before or after the element text. Before assigns no attributes, while after allows a list of attributes. Elements which allow children then take a list of children.

Attributes are represented in lower case as well, but suffixed with _att. This assures no namespace conflicts. Assigning an attribute which does not belong results in a compile-time class instance error.

Validating child ordering is done using the `pageErrors` function which takes any node as an argument. A list of errors will be returned, if any, along with the ordering specification in the DTD which failed.

Figure 1 exhibits the obligatory Hello World page where `result` holds the resulting serialized HTML as a string.

For a more through description of the *CH-(X)HTML*'s usage see the `demo.hs` file included with the library source.

```
page name = _html [_head [_title [pcdata "Hello " ++ name]],
              _body [_h1 [pcdata "Hello " ++ name ++ "!"],
                _hr,
                _p [pcdata "Hello " ++ name ++ "!"],
                ]
              ]
result :: String
result = render (page "World")
```

Fig. 1. Hello World implementation in *CH-(X)HTML*

4 Library Performance

To gauge our library's performance against similar dynamic HTML creation systems, we compared it to six other libraries: Text.Html, Text.XHtml, BlazeHtml[21], Hamlet[26], Text.HTML.Light, and PHP. The first five are combinator libraries in Haskell used for building HTML content while PHP is a popular web scripting language. *CH-(X)HTML* was tested twice, once with run-time list checking, and once without and in both cases library version 0.1.4 was used.

Table 2 shows each's W3C compliance guarantees for all produced content with regard to the five W3C areas of compliance. Half-filled circles indicate partial compliance. For example, *CH-(X)HTML*without run-time list checking is not fully inclusion/exclusion compliant due to possible omission of required elements. Other libraries fare even worse by allowing any child element or attribute to be used with any element.

Table 2. W3C Conformance Performance

Library	Well Formed	Element Conforming	Attribute Conforming	Inclusion/ Exclusion	Element Order Conforming
CH-(X)HTML	●	●	●	◐	○
CH-(X)HTML w/runtime	●	●	●	●	●
Text.Html	●	●	◐	○	○
Text.XHtml	●	●	◐	○	○
BlazeHtml	●	●	◐	○	○
Hamlet	●	●	◐	○	○
Text.HTML.Light	●	●	◐	○	○
PHP	○	○	○	○	○

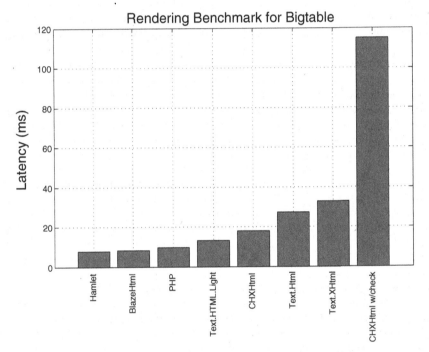

Fig. 2. Rendering times for XHTML libraries for bigtable

It is clear *CH-(X)HTML* without run-time list checking offers stronger compliance than any library tested, with full compliance attainable with run-time checking.

To test rendering performance, an XHTML 1.0 Strict 'bigtable' document was created containing a table with 1000 rows, each with the integers from 1 to 10 in each row's column. `Html`, `head`, `title`, `body` elements were added for W3C compliance with no other content on the page. The table is generated dynamically leading to very short page generating code. The final page consisted of 11,005 elements and about 121kB total size.

To rule out web server performance each library is timed until the content is prepared in memory ready to be sent. The `criterion` library in Haskell is used to benchmark in

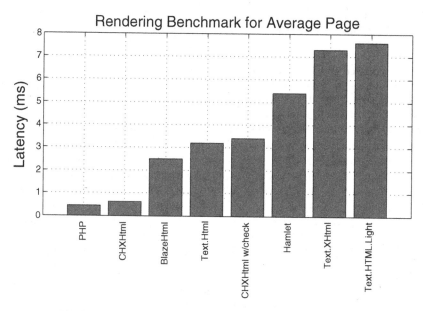

Fig. 3. Rendering times for XHTML libraries for an average page

this way while the cpu time was measured for PHP. Testing was done on a Fedora Core 11 server with an AMD 2.3Ghz Athlon 64 X2 processor with 2GB of RAM.

Speed results are shown in Fig 2. Hamlet was the fastest, with BlazeHtml and PHP slightly slower at 10ms. *CH-(X)HTML* version 0.1.4 without run-time element ordering validation beats out Text.Html and Text.XHtml showing *CH-(X)HTML* is able to compete with generic HTML productions systems while enforcing four of the five compliance classes. Adding element order validation adds significant time, requiring 115(ms) to render bigtable in our current implementation. This is due to an external regular expression library being called for each element; for this case 11,005 times. Further benchmarking with different size tables showed a perfectly linear relation between element count and page rendering time for *CH-(X)HTML* with element ordering validation.

To gauge real-world performance for *CH-(X)HTML* with element order validation, a sample of 31,000 random HTML pages were downloaded from the web and analyzed. The average element count per page was 801, with the 50th percentile having 330 elements. Average page size for the sample was 60kB, with the 50th percentile being 23kB. While bigtable may stress a dynamic web content generator, it does not represent a typical web page with respect to element count or size. A new average page benchmark was constructed by using 30 rows from the bigtable benchmark and adding plain text in a p element resulting in 335 elements and about 60kB total size. Figure 3 shows the vastly different results. PHP now leads, closely followed by *CH-(X)HTML* without element order checking. Even with element order checking *CH-(X)HTML* does quite well beating out three other libraries.

While speed is not our goal, *CH-(X)HTML* preforms on par with similar dynamic HTML production systems for most pages while providing more guarantees on compliant output. For pages containing atypically large amounts of elements, additional speed can be gained by not running run-time list checking.

4.1 Performance and Version Considerations

Recent changes to the Glasgow Haskell Compiler (GHC) has been detremental to *CH-(X)HTML* 's compilation time and should be noted. GHC 6.x compiles all 3 modules in *CH-(X)HTML* in under 15 minutes using library version 0.1.4 (only XHTML in this version). The same version under the newer GHC 7.x errored with an over-memory warning after 60 minutes consuming 2GB of memory. Exchanging the external regular-expression library (pcre-light) for a native implementation (hxt-regex-xmlschema) reduced the compile time in half. *CH-(X)HTML* version 0.2.0 now includes this regular-expression library, compile tweaks, as well as the addition of all three flavors of HTML 4.01. Compilation of this newest version with GHC 7.0.3 now takes 80 minutes but completes on our above system.

Library performance has changed with the new GHC version and library. The 'bigtable' benchmark with GHC 7.0.3 and *CH-(X)HTML* 0.2.0 without run-time element ordering validation took 14ms, a 20% improvement, while with checking it slowed to 167ms. For the average page benchmark without run-time element ordering took 0.4ms, or a 31% improvement, while with validation slowed to 28ms as well, for a 88% slowdown. This shows that the hxt-regex-xmlschema regular-expression library is slower than pcre-light, but reduces library compilation time. Full regular expression evaluation is generally not neccessary for this workload so further work may explore this area for further speed improvements.

GHC 7.x's long compilation time for *CH-(X)HTML* is a concern. The newer 0.2.0 version with GHC 7.x is able to compile and gives a slight speed increase for the non-runtime check situation, but we recommend using GHC 6.x until a better workaround is found.

5 Related Work

There exist two areas related to our work: XML creation and manipulation, and general HTML production. XHTML has now joined these two areas.

Numerous projects have embedded XML into other languages and allowed for its manipulation. Web content creation is not their main goal, but rather generic XML with custom schema.

The mainstream language Java has JAXB[6], which can create a set of Java classes based on an XML schema, as well as the inverse. Data can marshaled in either direction easily allowing dynamic schema to be accessed in Java. If used for XHTML production, inclusion/exclusion errors could still be present as well as possible invalid characters. XMLBeans is a similar tool[8].

The automatic generation of Haskell types from DTD's or schema are covered in the HaXml project: a set of Haskell utilities for parsing, filtering, transforming, and generating XML[32]. Their DtdToHaskell utility produces a Haskell source file containing datatypes conforming to the provided XML DTD. DtdToHaskell's generic XML to Haskell type production system works with XHTML DTDs and even guarantees element-ordering, but at the price of usability. Every element (element) attribute must be specified even if not used due to their record syntax implementation. Elements (elements) requiring an ordered or specific number of children aren't specified using list syntax like most elements, but n-tuples, requiring one to reference either the DTD or datatypes to resolve compilation errors. Our specialized solution of XHTML uses lists for all children, simplifying the syntax. Child ordering can be validated at run-time if needed. XML's lack of element inclusion/exclusion restriction prevents HaXml from enforcing it as well. *CH-(X)HTML* is generated with a similar tool to DtdToHaskell from a raw DTD, but is able to interpret hybrid DTDs containing nesting restrictions.

HSXML is an XML serialization library for functional languages[19]. It is part of a larger effort to parse XML into S-expressions in functional languages such as Scheme and Haskell, with HSXML preforming the reverse. S-expressions are a natural way of representing nested data with its roots in Lisp, thereby guaranteeing a well-formed and element-conforming document. The library's current implementation can handle Inline vs Block context restrictions, but no other inclusion/exclusion or child ordering restrictions are enforced.

Constructing web content by means of a DOM-like data structure isn't new, but libraries guaranteeing near or full HTML validity are scarce. Many HTML libraries use HTML like syntax, unlike the above XML tools, allowing easy construction of pages for the developer, but with little guarantees to the validity of the output. Peter Thiemann's work on W3C compliance is the closest in the Haskell WASH/CGI suite[29,30,27], which includes a HTML & XML content production system using types to enforce some validity. The use of element-transforming style in the library allows Haskell code to look similar to HTML while still being valid Haskell source. The author documents different classifications of validity, which our analysis in Section 2 is based on, followed by a discussion of enforcement of those classifications in his system. The Inclusion & Exclusion issue is raised and discussed briefly in his 2002 work, concluding the type class system is unable to handle inclusion & exclusion in their implementation due to the inability to handle disjunctions of types. As a result, their library does not support inclusion or exclusion with the excuse of extreme code size, difficulty in usability, and a lack of strict guidelines for inclusion & exclusion in the XHTML specification.

Further work by Thiemann explores an alternate way of dealing with the inclusion & exclusion issue in Haskell by way of proposed extensions providing functional logic overloading, anonymous type functions, and rank-2 polymorphism. With these they are able to accurately encode and enforce the inclusion & exclusion properties specified in the DTD[28]. A strong symmetry exists between our work and the suggested extensions. The ability to embed regular expressions on types is analogous to our generous use of recursive types and run-time child validation. While extending the type system further may lead to more enhancements, *CH-(X)HTML* can be used currently without any additional extensions.

The LAML[23] package for Scheme provides a set of functions representing HTML elements and attributes capable of generating HTML programatically. Their goal is bringing abstraction and web authoring to Scheme rather than standards compliance. Their functions are easy to use and provide well-formed, element-conforoming, and some attribute conforming content while not preventing inclusion & exclusion, or element ordering errors.

A common Haskell HTML library is Text.Html[7] and relative Text.XHtml used above, which uses element-transforming style to build pages. Produced content is well-formed and element-conforming due to their structured building method and HTML escaping of text content. Any attribute can be added to any element, thus not being attribute-conforming. All elements are of the same type and can be added in any order leading to element ordering and inclusion/exclusion violations. Blaze-html[21] and Hamlet[26] are similar Haskell libraries, but unfortunately they also suffer from the same lack of compliance guarantees.

XMLC for Java allows an application developer to manipulate a DOM structure obtained from parsing a HTML or XML template file[1]. Manipulation of the DOM is therefore similar to DOM manipulations in JavaScript. When all transformations are complete the DOM is serialized and sent to the user. XMLC does not restrict operations which would result in invalid content being sent to the user.

Separating structure from content in a web setting is advantageous for security as well. Robertson & Vigna[24] explore using a strongly typed system for HTML generation as well as producing SQL queries in the web application. Their goal is to increase security by preventing injection attacks targeting the ad-hoc mixing of content and structure in SQL by representing structure in a typed way and filtering inserted content. Thus, the client or SQL server's parser will not be fooled by the attempted injection attack. Our work similarly mitigates injection attacks but does not address web application vulnerabilities relating to a database.

6 Conclusions

We have shown how (X)HTML W3C compliance can be achieved by Haskell while performing on par with more mature dynamic (X)HTML production systems. We generalize the W3C (X)HTML specifications into five classes of requirements a web production system must be able to enforce to produce compliant output. The inclusion & exclusion nesting requirement of nearly all (X)HTML DTD's has proven difficult to enforce and thus ignored by web production libraries. Our (X)HTML library, *CH-(X)HTML*, is able to partially enforce four of the five classes of requirements at compile-time, including inclusion & exclusion, with full compliance attainable at run-time. Use of the library is straightforward due to multi-parameter type classes and functional dependencies allowing a coding style similar to straight (X)HTML, while guaranteeing strong compliance for all produced content.

References

1. Xmlc, http://xmlc.enhydra.org
2. The common gateway interface, http://hoohoo.ncsa.illinois.edu/cgi/
3. The disability discrimination act (dda),
   http://www.direct.gov.uk/en/DisabledPeople/
   RightsAndObligations/DisabilityRights/DG_4001068
4. Happs, http://happs.org/
5. Html5, http://dev.w3.org/html5/spec/Overview.html

6. jaxb, `https://jaxb.dev.java.net/`
7. Text.html, `http://hackage.haskell.org/package/html`
8. Xmlbeans, `http://xmlbeans.apache.org/`
9. Brewer, J., Henry, S.L.: Policies relating to web accessibility (2006), `http://www.w3.org/WAI/Policy/`
10. Bringert, B.: cgi: A library for writing cgi programs (2010), `http://hackage.haskell.org/package/cgi`
11. Bringert, B., Lemmih: fastcgi: A haskell library for writing fastcgi programs (2010), `http://hackage.haskell.org/package/fastcgi`
12. Chen, S., Hong, D., Shen, V.Y.: An experimental study on validation problems with existing html webpages. In: International Conference on Internet Computing, pp. 373–379 (2005)
13. Collins, G., Beardsley, D., Yu Guo, S., Sanders, J.: Snap: A haskell web framework (2010), `http://snapframework.com/`
14. Davies, D.: W3c compliance and seo (2005), `http://www.evolt.org/w3c-compliance-and-seo`
15. Elder, M., Shaw, J.: Happstack (2010), `http://happstack.com/index.html`
16. Group, W.H.W.: Xhtml 1.0: The extensible hypertext markup language, (2nd edn.) (2002), `http://www.w3.org/TR/xhtml1/`, `http://www.w3.org/TR/xhtml1/`
17. Hansen, R.: Xss (cross site scripting) prevention cheat sheet (2009), `http://ha.ckers.org/xss.html`
18. Kemp, A.: Turbinado (2010), `http://wiki.github.com/alsonkemp/turbinado`
19. Kiselyov, O.: Hsxml: Typed sxml (2010), `http://okmij.org/ftp/Scheme/xml.html#typed-SXML`
20. Marlow, S., Bringert, B.: Mohws: Modular haskell web server (2010), `http://hackage.haskell.org/cgi-bin/hackage-scripts/package/mohws`
21. Meier, S., der Jeugt, J.V.: Blazehtml (2010), `http://jaspervdj.be/blaze/`
22. Moss, T.: Disability discrimination act (dda) & web accessibility (2010), `http://www.webcredible.co.uk/user-friendly-resources/web-accessibility/uk-website-legal-requirements.shtml`
23. Nørmark, K.: Web programming in scheme with laml. J. Funct. Program. 15(1), 53–65 (2005)
24. Robertson, W., Vigna, G.: Static Enforcement of Web Application Integrity Through Strong Typing. In: Proceedings of the USENIX Security Symposium, Montreal, Canada (2009)
25. Saccoccio, R., et al.: Fastcgi (2010), `http://www.fastcgi.com/drupal/`
26. Snoyman, M.: Yesod web framework (2010), `http://docs.yesodweb.com/`
27. Thiemann, P.: A typed representation for html and xml documents in haskell. Journal of Functional Programming 12 (2001/2002)
28. Thiemann, P.: Programmable type systems for domain specific languages (2002a)
29. Thiemann, P.: WASH/CGI: Server-Side Web Scripting with Sessions and Typed, Compositional Forms. In: Adsul, B., Ramakrishnan, C.R. (eds.) PADL 2002. LNCS, vol. 2257, pp. 192–208. Springer, Heidelberg (2002b)
30. Thiemann, P.: An embedded domain-specific language for type-safe server-side webscripting. ACM Transactions on Internet Technology 5, 1533–5399 (2005)
31. Chisholm, W., Vanderheiden, G., Jacobs, I.: Web content accessibility guidelines 1.0 (1999), `http://www.w3.org/TR/WCAG10/`
32. Wallace, M., Runciman, C.: Haskell and xml: Generic combinators or type-based translation?, pp. 148–159. ACM Press (1999)
33. Wittersheim, A.: Why comply? the movement to w3c compliance (2006), `http://ezinearticles.com/?Why-Comply?-The-Movement-to-W3C-Compliance&id=162596`

Reducing Data Transfer by Combining XML-Compression and XML-Caching

Stefan Böttcher, Lars Fernhomberg, and Rita Hartel

University of Paderborn, Computer Science, Fürstenallee 11, 33102, Paderborn, Germany
{stb,lafe,rst}@uni-paderborn.de

Abstract. Whenever a restricted bandwidth is the bottleneck of an application that transfers data from a server hosting a huge XML document to a client with limited resources, there exist mainly two approaches to overcome this problem: caching previously downloaded data on the one hand, and transferring compressed data on the other hand. We present a combined approach that combines both approaches, i.e., that proposes a caching framework working with compressed XML data. Our performance evaluation demonstrates that this combination not only yields a benefit in terms of the data to be transferred, but it also yields a shorter response time for queries to be evaluated on the client. The benefit reached by the combination of caching and compression is even stronger than the sum of the benefits reached by each of these techniques alone.

Keywords: XML databases, Caching, Compression.

1 Introduction

1.1 Motivation

In the last years, more and more standards for data exchange have evolved that are based on the flexible hierarchical data format XML. Examples for such data formats are SEPA (Single European Payment Area) for the financial sector or OTA (Open-Travel Alliance) for the flight sector.

Whereas previously, the clients that participated in internet-based applications got stronger resources, now a reverse development can be observed. More and more small mobile devices (like e.g. tablet PCs and smartphones) that come with restricted internal resources and restricted connection bandwidth participate in web applications.

Therefore, we consider scenarios, in which client applications need to access huge XML documents that are provided on remote web servers, and where the data transfer volume or the data transfer time from the server to the client is a bottleneck.

To overcome this bottleneck, there exist two different technologies: caching previously downloaded data on the one hand and compressing transferred data on the other hand.

A seamless integration of both techniques on the client side is a challenging task as compression combines similar structured data whereas caching isolates data in the cache.

J. Filipe and J. Cordeiro (Eds.): WEBIST 2011, LNBIP 101, pp. 116–130, 2012.

Our approach combines both techniques as follows: we compress the data on the web server and process and transfer them in the compressed format to the client. On the client side, the data is then cached in compressed format, such that it can be used for answering not only identical but also similar queries without access to the web server.

1.2   Contributions

This paper proposes an approach for integrating caching and compression in order to reduce data transfer volume and time and that combines the following properties:

— It compresses the structure and the constant data of the XML document on server side.

— It transfers the data in a compressed way to the client and thereby saves transfer volume and transfer time.

— It transfers to the client only that part of the data that is needed to answer the user query and that is not yet stored within the compressed cached client data.

— The compression technique used for compressing the data can be exchanged. Our approach contains a generic caching framework for compressed data that generalizes the tasks that are common to all compression techniques to be used, such that only a simple interface has to be implemented by each compression technique before it can be used within our approach.

— We provide a technique for integrating compressed fragments on the client side into a single compressed fragment without total decompression of the cached fragments.

We have implemented our system with two different compression techniques and comparatively evaluated our system with querying uncompressed data that is not kept in the cache, querying uncompressed, cached data, and querying compressed data that is not kept in the cache. Our results show that the combination of caching and compression outperforms all the other techniques in terms of transfer volume and in terms of total query evaluation time considering data rates of up to that of UMTS.

1.3   Problem Description

The problem investigated in this paper is how to improve caching of answers to XPath queries in client-server web information systems in the following aspects: first, the overall data exchange volume between the web information source and the client shall be reduced, and second, the time needed by the client to get the results of a query from a remote server shall be reduced.

We follow the principle of compensation queries [1][1], i.e., we calculate compensation queries from a given new query and old queries, the results of which are already contained in the cache. A compensation query of a query Q is a query Q' that, applied to the view V of the database that is represented by the cache, calculates the same query results as Q applied to the data on the server. However, beyond the approach of[1], we consider a much broader subset of XPath including the search or navigation along all the XML forward axes. Thereby, our approach to caching supports a significantly wider field of web applications.

In the current approach, we do not consider, how to handle updates of server data of which a copy is stored in the client cache, but we expect that our current concept does not prevent outdated caches to be managed.

1.4   Paper Organization

This paper is organized as follows: In Section 2, we explain the key ideas of the general solution, including the compression techniques implemented in our caching framework and the mechanisms used for performing query evaluation on the compressed XML representations. Section 3 describes our performance evaluation and the evaluation results. Section 4 describes related work, and Section 5 contains a summary and the conclusions.

2   The Concepts of Our Combined Approach

2.1   Our Example

Fig. 1 shows the example document used in this paper to visualize the concepts of our approach. It shows an XML document containing for each order a customer and the items he purchases. Each item has a name-attribute and a price, which has a currency-attribute and a text node giving the amount.

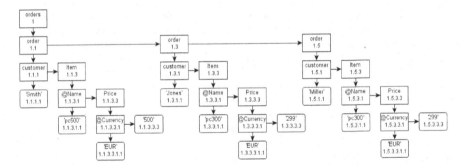

Fig. 1. Example document

Whereas the upper half of the node label is the element name, the attribute name, or the text value, the lower half of each node labels contains the node ID. In our case, we used ORDPATH [2] that allows for two nodes specified by their ORDPATH ID to determine, in which XML axis relation they are to each other, e.g., whether node A is a following-sibling or a descendant of node B.

2.2   The Basic Idea

Our framework for caching compressed XML data consists of a server and a client. The main idea of our caching approach is that the server only sends the data that is needed by the client to answer the query and that is not already contained in the client's cache. The data is transferred to the client and stored on the client in a compressed format. A second requirement is that the server is stateless, i.e., that it does not store the current state of the client's caches, as this would lead to a too large storage overhead on the server side.

In order to transfer only new data that has not yet been cached, the server has to find out whether or not a query requires to access data not already stored in the client's cache. Therefore, the server contains the compressed XML document and a query cache, where it stores results to previously answered queries. When the server receives a query from any client, it assigns an ID to the query (either a new one, or it looks up the ID of the query if it was answered for another client before) and sends the ID of the query together with the answers to the client. As the server is stateless, i.e., it does not maintain any state information on its clients, the client sends in addition to the query to be answered a list of query IDs that describe the queries already stored in its cache. With the help of the query IDs and the global server query cache, the server then can reconstruct the content of the client's cache. Finally, the server computes the result R of the client's query and transfers the difference between the result R and the client's cache's content, i.e., only these nodes of the result that were not already contained in the cache, to the client. In addition, the server stores the client's query, the ID assigned to the query and the result R in its query cache.

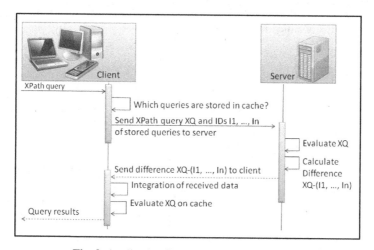

Fig. 2. Application flow of our caching approach

When the client receives the answer to its query, it integrates the compressed XML fragments into its cache. It then can be sure, that applying its query to its cache will yield the same result as applying this query to the server document.

Fig. 2 shows the application flow of the approach presented in this paper.

In order to integrate the transferred data, we use the updateable XML numbering scheme ORDPATH [2][2] that allows for two nodes specified by their ORDPATH ID to determine, in which XML axis relation they are to each other, e.g., whether node A is a following-sibling or a descendant of node B. Depending on the precise requirements, other XML numbering schemes like DLN [3][3], or DDE [4][4] could be chosen.

For example, consider that the first query sent from the client to the server was Q1=//order[Item/@Name='pc300']/customer. After receiving the server's answer, the client's cache contains the orders of the customers 'Jones' and 'Miller' but without the price-sub-tree of the items. The cache is displayed in Fig. 3.

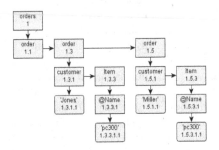

Fig. 3. Cache content after the evaluation of Q1

As a second query, the client sends Q2=//order[customer='Jones']/Item/Price and the ID Q1, which tells the server that the nodes required to answer to the query with ID Q1 are already contained in the clients cache.

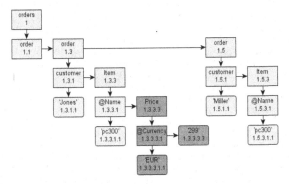

Fig. 4. Cache content after the evaluation of Q1 and Q2

As the answer to the query Q2-Q1, the server sends the sub-tree rooted by the node with ID id2=1.3.3.3 together with this ID to the cache. Starting from the root node, the server compares the ID of the current node with id2 in order to determine, whether id2 is the ID of a descendant or of a following or of a following-sibling of the current node. As soon as this process has reached the node N with ID 1.3.3.1, the client can insert the received fragment as next-sibling of N. Fig. 4 shows the cache content after having integrated the answer to Q2. The nodes inserted into the cache are highlighted by a darker background.

Finally, the client sends the query Q3=//order[customer='Miller']/Item/Price together with the IDs Q1 and Q2 to the server. Fig 5 visualizes the calculation of the result to Q3 – (Q1 + Q2), where Q1 + Q2 is the client's cache content. The white nodes are the nodes which are not needed in order to answer any of the queries Q1 to Q3. The gray nodes are nodes that are needed to answer Q1 or Q2, but not for answering Q3. The nodes filled with a gradient from gray to black are nodes that are needed to answer Q1 or Q2 and to answer Q3, whereas the black nodes are nodes that are parts of the answer of Q3, but are not needed for answering Q1 or Q2. The result of the client's query are the black nodes rooted by the node with ID 1.5.3.3 which are transferred from server to the client and integrated into the client's cache.

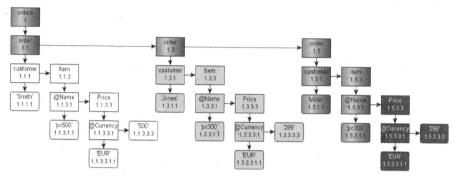

Fig. 5. Calculation of Q3 – (Q1 + Q2)

Although sending differences instead of complete answers saves a lot of transfer costs (e.g. for query Q3, we only have to send 4 out of 13 result nodes), the data transfer costs and the storage costs could be reduced further by using compressed XML instead of uncompressed XML data.

2.3   XML Compression

Our caching approach is designed in such a way that it can work with different XML compression techniques. The requirements to these techniques are that query evaluation and updates are possible on the compressed data directly, i.e., without a prior decompression.

Tasks that are common for all compressed representations of the XML document are isolated into a generic part. Therefore, the compression techniques being used for managing the client's cache do only have to implement a simple interface covering functions like basic navigation via first-child, next-sibling, and parent, as well as basic update functionalities in order to integrate the new results into the cache. Furthermore, the compression technique being used at the server-side additionally has to support computing the difference of two compressed node lists (with node unique node IDs).

Currently, we have implemented two different compression techniques within our caching framework: Succinct compression and DAG compression.

2.3.1   Succinct XML Compression

Succinct XML compression is an XML compressor that separates the XML constants from the XML element names and the attribute names and from the nesting of start tags and end tags, i.e. the compressed document structure of an XML document consists of the following parts:

1. A bit stream representing the tree structure of the element nesting in the XML tree, without storing any label information. In the bit stream, each start-tag is represented by a '1'-bit and each end-tag is represented by a '0'-bit.
2. Inverted element lists, containing a mapping of element and attribute names to '1'-bit positions within the bit stream.
3. Constant lists containing the text values and attribute values
4. Succinct compression can handle unbounded input streams and huge files and it allows query evaluation and updates directly on the compressed data.

A variant of succinct compression has been presented in [5][5].

Fig. 6 shows the succinct representation of the XML document given in Fig. 1.

Bit stream:	Inverted element lists:	
1 1 1 1 0 0 1 1 1 0 0 1 1 0 1 0 0 0 0 1 1 1 0 0 1 1 1 0 0 1 1 0 1 0 0 0 0 1 1 1 0 0 1 1 1 0 0 1 1 0 1 0 0 0 0 0		
	Label	**positions**
	orders	0
	order	1, 19, 37
	customer	2, 20, 38
Constant list:	Item	7, 25, 43
	@Name	8, 26, 44
Smith, pc500, EUR, 500, Jones, pc300, EUR, 299, Miller, pc300, EUR, 299	Price	12, 30, 48
	@Currency	13, 31, 49

Fig. 6. Succinct compression of the XML document given in Fig. 1

2.3.2 DAG-Based XML Compression

A variant of DAG-based XML compression has been presented in [6][6].

The constant data – i.e., text nodes and attribute values – are separated from the XML structure – i.e., element and attribute nodes – and compressed separately. Constant data is grouped according to their parent element name and each group of constant data is compressed via gzip.

DAG-based XML compression follows the concept of sharing repeated sub-trees in the XML structure. Whenever a sub-tree occurs more than once within the document tree structure, all but the first occurrence are removed from the document tree and are replaced by a pointer to the first occurrence.

The minimal DAG of an XML document tree structure can be calculated by a single pre-order pass through the document tree (e.g., by reading a linear SAX stream) with the help of a hash table, where all first occurrences of a sub-tree are stored.

As the DAG is stored in form of DAG nodes, where each node contains an address, the node label and pointers to its first-child and its next-sibling, the DAG compression allows for a very efficient basic navigation (similar to a DOM representation). In contrast, it does not reach as strong compression ratios as e.g. Succinct compression.

Besides query evaluation directly on the compressed data, DAG-based XML compression allows compressing unbounded and huge XML files as well as updating the compressed data directly.

Fig. 7 shows the DAG structure of the XML document given in Fig. 1. The constant list of the DAG is equal to that of the succinct representation as shown in Fig. 6.

Note that in the case of DAG compression, we sometimes have to transfer more text constants than it would be required to answer the query in order to keep the DAG structure consistent with the constant list.

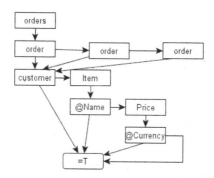

Fig. 7. DAG compression of the XML document given in Fig. 1

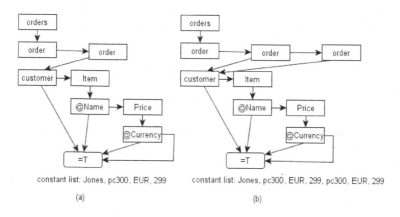

Fig. 8. Example for additional constants to be send

Fig. 8 shows such an example. Fig. 8(a) shows the content of the cache before the query evaluation of the query Q4=//Item[@Name='pc300']/Price. It contains 4 paths to the node with label '=T' and consistently, the constant list contains 4 entries, where the i-th entry belongs to the i-th path. Answering Q4 leads to an additional edge from the third order in the DAG structure to the customer node. The constants belonging to that order that are relevant for answering Q4 and that are not yet contained in the cache are 'pc300' (the value of @Name) and EUR and 299 (values of @Currency and Price). Fig. 8(b) shows the cache content after adding this information. But adding only this information would lead to an inconsistent cache content, as Fig. 8(b) contains 8 paths to the node with label '=T' but only 7 entries in the constant list. Therefore, in addition to the 7 constants, we have to transfer the text constant 'Miller', such that the constant list contains the values (Jones, pc300, EUR, 299, Miller, pc300, EUR, 299) and such that the DAG structure and the constant list are consistent.

2.4   Query Evaluation

The client and the server use an XPath evaluator based on a reduced instruction set that has to be provided by each compression technique. In order to simplify the presentation, we assume a simplified data model of an XML tree, where all nodes – no matter whether they are element, attribute or text nodes – are valid answers to the basic axes fc and ns:

- fc: Returns the first-child of the current context node ccn
- ns: Returns the next-sibling of the current context node ccn
- label: Returns the label of the current context node ccn if ccn is an element, the attribute name if ccn represents an attribute, the text value if ccn represents a text node, or an attribute value, if ccn represents an attribute value.
- parent: Returns the parent of the current context node ccn.
- node type: Returns the node type (i.e., either element, attribute or text node) of the current context node

We then use a technique like e.g. the one presented in [7][7] to evaluate XPath path queries on the compressed XML representation providing the reduced instruction set. Based on such a generic XPath evaluation technique, our approach allows to evaluate XPath queries containing the axes self, child, descendant, descendant-or-self, following-sibling, following, attribute and text as well as predicate filters with logical expressions containing comparisons of paths to constants. If additionally the backward axes ancestor, ancestor-or-self, preceding-sibling and preceding-sibling are required, this can be provided by a preprocessing step described in [8][8].

3   Evaluations

3.1   Performance Evaluation Environment

To evaluate the performance of the idea, a prototype has been developed and was tested using the XMark benchmark [9][9]. The prototype uses Java 6 Update 18 and was optimized for compression efficiency.

Each benchmark was performed ten times to account for external effects like operating system influences. The system used for the benchmarks was equipped with an AMD Phenom 9950 (Quad Core, each core runs with 2.6 GHz) and 4 GB main memory and running Windows 7 (64 Bit). Despite having a multi core processor, the prototype is single-threaded and does not use the complete system capacity.

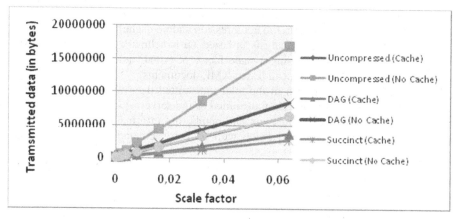

Fig. 9. Total aggregated sent data for growing documents

The benchmarks were performed on different XML documents, generated with increasing XMark scale factors, to determine the effect of different document sizes on the prototype. Table 1 shows the XMark scale factors being used and the resulting XML document size.

The generated documents were queried with a set of 22 different XPath queries that produce a mix of cache hits and cache misses. Queries 1-10 are closely related to the "XPath-A" benchmark of XPathMark [10][10] and are modified to overcome limitations in the used XPath evaluator. Queries 11-22 are selected to give an impression of (partial) cache-hits and cache-misses.

Table 1. Used XMark scale factors

XMark scale factor	XML document size
0.000	~ 35 kB
0.001	~ 154 kB
0.002	~ 275 kB
0.004	~ 597 kB
0.008	~ 1.178 kB
0.016	~ 2.476 kB
0.032	~ 4.899 kB
0.064	~ 9.514 kB

3.2   Performance Results

Fig. 9 shows the behavior of the prototype for each measured combination (Uncompressed, DAG or Succinct storage with or without cache) with growing document size. When the scale factor doubles, the transmitted data for each graph also doubles, meaning that the total amount of transmitted data scales linearly with the input data.

With an active cache, less data has to be transmitted in all cases. The additional use of compression techniques reduces the transferred data even further. Comparing the total data that is transferred (queries and query results including the compressed structure and the compressed constants of the XML representation), the best case scenario

(Succinct compression with active cache) uses only about 16% of the data volume being used by worst case scenario (no compression and no cache).

The following performance analysis is based on benchmark results of the XML document that was generated using a scale factor of 0.064, unless otherwise noted. The results are consistent through all tested XML documents.

Fig. 10 shows an aggregation of the total transmitted data of all 22 queries. The measured value consists of the data transmitted to the server (query information) and the result of the server (XML fragment and numbering information). For each compression technique, we measured twice with an activated and with a deactivated cache.

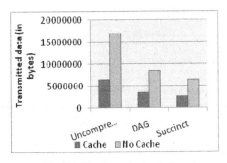

Fig. 10. Total transmitted data

Figure 10 shows the simulation of a real world scenario, considering different data rates on the channel between client and server, where the overall query evaluation time is calculated consisting of

— transferring data from client to server,
— evaluating query on server side,
— transferring data from server to client,
— integrating data into client's cache, and
— evaluating the query on the client's cache,

The left-most group of results in Figure 10, denoted as framework duration, is given as a lower bound for comparison purposes and includes only the time needed to evaluate the query on the server, to build the query difference on the server, to integrate the data into the client's cache and to evaluate the query on the client's cache, i.e. without the time needed to transfer data from server to client and from client to server.

Figure 11 shows that using the combination of caching and succinct compression consumes less time than using caching or compression alone up to a channel speed of about 128 kbit/s. Independent of the available data rate, the combination of caching and succinct compression transfers less data than using caching or compression alone. Using the combination of caching and DAG compression delivers speed improvements of up to 384 kbit/s, in comparison to using caching or using compression alone. Furthermore, in terms of total time, using caching only for uncompressed data outperforms the immediate query evaluation on the server up to a data rate of about 2 Mbit/s.

A breakdown of the total duration into each subtask (computing XPath result on client and server, identification of missing nodes on the client, integration of missing nodes in the client cache and data transfer from client to server and from server to client) shows that the XPath evaluation on server side as well as on the client side consumes the greatest part of the time. Depending on the compression algorithm, the client-side data integration can also lead to noticeable runtimes, because it may require renumbering or rearranging of existing data structures. The runtimes of all other operations are comparatively small and do not contribute much to the total runtime.

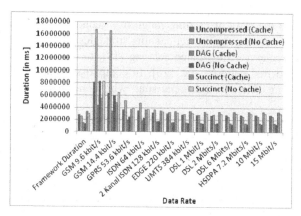

Fig. 11. Aggregated total duration (framework duration and simulated transmission duration)

3.3   Evaluation Summary

Our evaluation has compared transferred data volume and evaluation time being used in different combinations of caching and different compression techniques in comparison to caching and compression alone and in comparison to the immediate query evaluation on server site. Our evaluation has shown that using the combination of caching and compression not only reduces the data volume that is transferred from client to server and from server to client, but especially for data rates up to the data rate of UMTS reduces the total time that is needed to answer the query.

Clients with a limited bandwidth connection to the server will benefit from using the compressed XML cache as it is presented in this paper, whereas clients that are connected to the server via a high-speed connection might deactivate the cache and might request the query results from the server directly.

Our evaluation was using an unlimited cache size on the client side, thereby ignoring the following further advantage of the combination of compression and caching.

As the compressed data is significantly smaller than the non-compressed data, a cache of a fixed size can hold more XML data fragments in compressed format than in non-compressed format. Therefore, for limited cache size, we expect that the number of cache misses is significantly smaller for the combination of caching and XML compression than for caching only. In other words, if the cache size is limited, this leads to even stronger benefits of the combination of caching and XML compression over caching only.

4   Related Work

Although both, web data caching and XML compression, contribute to a reduction of the data transfer from server to client, the fields of web data caching and XML compression have mostly been investigated independently of each other.

There has been a lot of work in XML compression, some of which does not support query processing on compressed data, e.g.[11][11], and most of which support querying compressed data, but not querying cached compressed data, e.g. [12], [13], [14], [15], [16].

Contributions to the field of caching range from concepts of querying and maintaining incomplete data, e.g. [17], over caching strategies for mobile web clients, e.g. [18], caching strategies for distributed caching [19], to caching strategies based on frequently accessed tree patterns, e.g. [20]. In comparison, our approach allows for XPath queries using filters and comparisons with constants even on compressed cached XML.

Different approaches have been suggested for checking whether an XML cache can be used for answering an XPath query. On the one hand, there are contributions, e.g. [21], [1], [22] [21][22]that propose to compute a compensation query. These approaches can also be used on compressed XML data, but they are NP-hard already for very small sub-classes of XPath. On the other hand, containment tests and intersection tests for tree pattern queries have been proposed, and could in principle be used for deciding whether a given XPath query can be executed on the cached data locally. However, such intersection tests and containment tests are NP-hard for rather small subsets of XPath expressions [23], [24][23][24]. In comparison, our approach uses a fast difference computation that can be done within a single scan through the compressed XML file.

In contrast to[25][25], where the whole compressed structure was loaded into the cache and only the text values needed to answer the query was requested from the server, our approach stores only that part of the structure in its cache that was delivered from the server in order to answer previous queries.

In comparison to all other approaches, our technique is to the best of our knowledge the only strategy that combines the following advantages: it caches compressed documents – whereas the compression technique can be exchanged – and thereby reduces data transfer volume and data transfer time in comparison to caching non-compressed XML data and in comparison to transferring non-compressed or compressed XML data without caching the results.

5   Summary and Conclusions

Whenever the data exchange with XML-based information sources is a bottleneck, it is important to reduce the amount of exchanged XML data. Our approach combines two reduction techniques for exchanged data, i.e. caching and XML compression. Additionally, we have provided a performance evaluation that shows that a significant reduction in data transfer volume and transfer time can be achieved by our approach in comparison to caching only or to using only compression.

Altogether, our approach provides the following advantages:

— It provides a technique to combine caching and compression in such a way that any unnecessary decompression of data is avoided. The document is stored in a compressed format on the server, the results are transferred in a compressed format from server to client and all results are stored and integrated in a compressed format in the client's cache.

— The combination of compression and caching yields a reduced data transfer volume in contrast to each technique alone.

— Furthermore, the combination of compression and caching yields a reduced data transfer time for data rates up to that of UMTS in contrast to each technique alone.

We assume it to be an interesting task to combine our caching framework with other compression techniques to find a compressions technique that is most suitable in terms of strong compression capabilities and fast query evaluation such that the benefit in total evaluation time will be highest.

Finally, we assume that our approach will show even stronger benefits if it is combined with real world assumptions like a limited cache size.

References

1. Mandhani, B., Suciu, D.: Query Caching and View Selection for XML Databases. In: Böhm, K., Jensen, C., Haas, L., Kersten, M., Larson, P.-A., Ooi, B. (eds.) Proceedings of the 31st International Conference on Very Large Data Bases, Trondheim, Norway, pp. 469–480 (2005)

2. O'Neil, P., O'Neil, E., Pal, S., Cseri, I., Schaller, G., Westbury, N.: ORDPATHs: Insert-Friendly XML Node Labels. In: Weikum, G., König, A., Deßloch, S. (eds.) Proceedings of the ACM SIGMOD International Conference on Management of Data, Paris, France, pp. 903–908 (2004)

3. Böhme, T., Rahm, E.: Supporting Efficient Streaming and Insertion of XML Data in RDBMS. In: Bellahsene, Z., McBrien, P. (eds.) Third International Workshop on Data Integration over the Web, DIWeb 2004, Riga, Latvia, pp. 70–81 (2004)

4. Xu, L., Ling, T., Wu, H., Bao, Z.: DDE: from dewey to a fully dynamic XML labeling scheme. In: Cetintemel, U., Zdonik, S., Kossmann, D., Tatbul, N. (eds.) Proceedings of the ACM SIGMOD International Conference on Management of Data, SIGMOD 2009, Providence, Rhode Island, USA, pp. 719–730 (2009)

5. Böttcher, S., Hartel, R., Heinzemann, C.: Compressing XML Data Streams with DAG+BSBC. In: Cordeiro, J., Hammoudi, S., Filipe, J. (eds.) WEBIST 2008. LNBIP, vol. 18, pp. 65–79. Springer, Heidelberg (2009)

6. Buneman, P., Grohe, M., Koch, C.: Path Queries on Compressed XML. In: Proceedings of 29th International Conference on Very Large Data Bases, Berlin, Germany, pp. 141–152 (2003)

7. Böttcher, S., Steinmetz, R.: Evaluating XPath Queries on XML Data Streams. In: Cooper, R., Kennedy, J. (eds.) BNCOD 2007. LNCS, vol. 4587, pp. 101–113. Springer, Heidelberg (2007)

8. Olteanu, D., Meuss, H., Furche, T., Bry, F.: XPath: Looking Forward. In: Chaudhri, A.B., Unland, R., Djeraba, C., Lindner, W. (eds.) EDBT 2002. LNCS, vol. 2490, pp. 109–127. Springer, Heidelberg (2002)

9. Schmidt, A., Waas, F., Kersten, M., Carey, M., Manolescu, I., Busse, R.: XMark: A Benchmark for XML Data Management. In: Proceedings of 28th International Conference on Very Large Data Bases, VLDB 2002, Hong Kong, China, pp. 974–985 (2002)

10. Franceschet, M.: XPathMark: An XPath Benchmark for the XMark Generated Data. In: Bressan, S., Ceri, S., Hunt, E., Ives, Z.G., Bellahsène, Z., Rys, M., Unland, R. (eds.) XSym 2005. LNCS, vol. 3671, pp. 129–143. Springer, Heidelberg (2005)

11. Liefke, H., Suciu, D.: XMILL: An Efficient Compressor for XML Data. In: Proceedings of the 2000 ACM SIGMOD International Conference on Management of Data, Dallas, Texas, USA, pp.153–164 (2000)

12. Busatto, G., Lohrey, M., Maneth, S.: Efficient Memory Representation of XML Documents. In: Bierman, G., Koch, C. (eds.) DBPL 2005. LNCS, vol. 3774, pp. 199–216. Springer, Heidelberg (2005)

13. Cheng, J., Ng, W.: XQzip: Querying Compressed XML Using Structural Indexing. In: Hwang, J., Christodoulakis, S., Plexousakis, D., Christophides, V., Koubarakis, M., Böhm, K. (eds.) EDBT 2004. LNCS, vol. 2992, pp. 219–236. Springer, Heidelberg (2004)

14. Ng, W., Lam, W., Wood, P., Levene, M.: XCQ: A queriable XML compression system. Knowl. Inf. Syst., 421–452 (2006)

15. Skibiński, P., Swacha, J.: Combining Efficient XML Compression with Query Processing. In: Ioannidis, Y., Novikov, B., Rachev, B. (eds.) ADBIS 2007. LNCS, vol. 4690, pp. 330–342. Springer, Heidelberg (2007)

16. Zhang, N., Kacholia, V., Özsu, M.: A Succinct Physical Storage Scheme for Efficient Evaluation of Path Queries in XML. In: Proceedings of the 20th International Conference on Data Engineering, ICDE 2004, Boston, MA, USA, pp. 54–65 (2004)

17. Abiteboul, S., Segoufin, L., Vianu, V.: Representing and Querying XML with Incomplete Information. In: Proceedings of the Twentieth ACM SIGACT-SIGMOD-SIGART Symposium on Principles of Database Systems, Santa Barbara, California, USA, May 21-23 (2001)

18. Böttcher, S., Türling, A.: Caching XML Data on Mobile Web Clients. In: Proceedings of the International Conference on Internet Computing, IC 2004, Las Vegas, Nevada, USA, pp. 150–156 (2004)

19. Obermeier, S., Böttcher, S.: XML fragment caching for large-scale mobile commerce applications. In: Proceedings of the 10th International Conference on Electronic Commerce, ICEC 2008, Innsbruck, Austria, p. 26 (2008)

20. Yang, L., Lee, M.-L., Hsu, W.: Efficient Mining of XML Query Patterns for Caching. In: Proceedings of 29th International Conference on Very Large Data Bases, Berlin, Germany, pp. 69–80 (2003)

21. Balmin, A., Özcan, F., Beyer, K., Cochrane, R., Pirahesh, H.: A Framework for Using Materialized XPath Views in XML Query Processing. In: (e)Proceedings of the Thirtieth International Conference on Very Large Data Bases, Toronto, Canada, pp. 60–71 (2004)

22. Xu, W., Özsoyoglu, Z.: Rewriting XPath Queries Using Materialized Views. In: Proceedings of the 31st International Conference on Very Large Data Bases, Trondheim, Norway, pp. 121–132 (2005)

23. Benedikt, M., Wenfei, F., Geerts, F.: XPath satisfiability in the presence of DTDs. In: Proceedings of the Twenty-fourth ACM SIGACT-SIGMOD-SIGART, Baltimore, Maryland, USA, pp. 25–36 (2005)

24. Hidders, J.: Satisfiability of XPath Expressions. In: Lausen, G., Suciu, D. (eds.) DBPL 2003. LNCS, vol. 2921, pp. 21–36. Springer, Heidelberg (2004)

25. Böttcher, S., Hartel, R.: CSC: Supporting Queries on Compressed Cached XML. In: Bouguettaya, A., Lin, X. (eds.) Twentieth Australasian Database Conference on Database Technologies (ADC 2009), Wellington, New Zealand, pp. 153–160 (2009)

Part II

Web Interfaces and Applications

Systematically Evaluating Usability in Web-Based Electronic Government: An Empirical Study

Zhao Huang and Laurence Brooks

School of Information System, Computing and Mathematics, Brunel University
Middlesex, U.K.
{zhao.huang,laurence.brooks}@brunel.ac.uk

Abstract. Usability is an important factor influencing users' interaction and adoption of e-government, which needs to be considered in e-government development. However, current research has not paid much attention to assessing usability. This empirical study conducts a systematic approach to evaluate the usability of current e-government websites, identifying existing usability problems and providing proposed design solutions for further e-government usability development. Such research results can help designers and developers to understand the importance of usability and guide their particular attention to develop more usable e-government.

Keywords: e-Government website, Usability, Users' centered approach.

1 Introduction

Traditionally, government organizations deliver information and services using three channels: face to face, telephone and postal\mail services [1]. However, such methods are largely influenced by time and space limitations, which sometimes make access to information difficult and block users' engagement. With the widespread use of the Internet and web technology, it can be argued that a fourth method to deliver government services has been created – e-government. It provides all types of government information and services available online. In such a way, users can interact with government services 24/7 without physical distance requirements. Since these advantages have become apparent, governments worldwide have rapidly developed e-governments, which has now become a global phenomenon [2]. However, studies indicate that the actual use of information and services provided on e-government websites faces a challenge [3]. Website usability is one of the major reasons for the underuse of e-government. For example, Holden et al. [4] found that many users do not involve with government online services because of difficulty in finding their expected information on the site. Generally, website usability refers to how useful and user-friendly the site is. If websites fail to provide ease of use from a design standpoint and frustrate users interaction with government services, e-government will not be accepted and used by users [5]. Therefore, this suggests that e-government may not achieve greater users' participation unless the website usability is recognized and addressed.

J. Filipe and J. Cordeiro (Eds.): WEBIST 2011, LNBIP 101, pp. 133–148, 2012.
© Springer-Verlag Berlin Heidelberg 2012

However, current research has not paid enough attention to evaluating the usability of current e-government websites, especially identifying specific problems. Even studies that conduct usability investigations lack empirical evidence to provide concrete prescriptions for the identified problems in order to develop more usable e-government websites. Furthermore, an e-government website is used by a wide range of users, who have heterogeneous backgrounds in terms of skills and experience. These users may have different usability needs for e-government websites, which may increase the difficulty for designers in identifying users' requirements. In order to overcome this difficulty, a users' centered approach is considered as an appropriate method, which can involve users' participation and address users' point of view. This can be beneficial for designers to understand users and their usability requirements. Additionally, it can directly detect the e-government features that can cause users to have the most concerns about usability. Accordingly, there needs to be more attention directed toward users' evaluation of usability. In this way, it provides concrete prescriptions for developing more user-centered e-government websites that can generate greater users' participation.

Therefore, this study aims to evaluate the usability of current e-government websites in the UK, identifying existing usability problems. Moreover, in order to fulfill a systematic evaluation, based on the usability problems identified, this study proposes a set of design solutions and evaluates the effects of these proposed design solutions on the identified usability problems. This approach addresses design, evaluation and redesign processes in e-government website development, which is also reflected in user centered studies in HCI, where one of the major tasks is with problem detection and solutions provision to develop computer systems [6]. To implement the usability evaluation, an experimental study has been designed based on users' perception of Nielsen's set of usability heuristics to conduct a thorough and in-depth e-government website usability inspection. In addition, in order to reveal users' task performance within the e-government websites evaluated, users' performance is also measured by a number of performance criteria through observation. By doing so, a more comprehensive evaluation, which not only provides a deeper insight into e-government website usability, but also shows the levels of users' interaction with the specific e-government website, can be carried out.

This paper is structured as follows: section 2 reviews the literature to address the importance of usability to e-government. Section 3 describes the design of an empirical study with two linked experiments. Section 4 presents and discusses the results from experiment 1. Section 5 proposes the design solutions in relation to the usability problems identified. Section 6 shows the findings from experiment 2. Conclusions and limitations are drawn and future research suggested in section 7.

2   Literature Review

To consider a dynamic area of e-government and its application for the general public, e-government can be defined as the use of the Internet, especially web technology, as a tool to deliver government information and services to users [7]. The main purpose for e-government is to achieve better government, which enables easier access, higher quality services and more enjoyable experience [8]. Furthermore, other advantages of e-government include improving the level of public services, increasing cost-effectiveness in services provision [9], promoting engagement and strengthening trust between government and users [10]. Since such power has been recognized by traditional governments and e-government initiatives are evolving from the national to the local level, and being developed worldwide. Thousands of e-governments have now been established which make government information and services available online [11]. Users can conduct all government services provided by the national and local levels via information presentation, interaction, transaction and integration [12].

Although there is a rapid development of e-government, a challenge for e-government of how best to interact with users still remains [6]. Among the various reasons, usability has been found to be an important reason influencing users' interaction and adoption of e-government [5]. In essence, usability is a very broad concept [13]. It can be simply defined as effectiveness, efficiency and satisfaction [14]. However, in order to have more comprehensive understanding, usability can be explained by multiple criteria. Flavián et al. [15] described five elements in relation to usability, which are the perceived ease of understanding the structure of a system, simplicity of use of the website, the speed of locating the item, the perceived ease of navigating the site and the ability of the users to control their movement within the system. Moreover, usability can be used as a measurement related to how useful and user-friendly the system is. As such, it is no doubt that usability is a key factor in determining the computer system quality [16] and ensuring users' engagement [17]. Anthopoulos et al. [18] discovered user-oriented e-government services. The study addresses the importance of users' needs in order to guide service delivery improvement. Usability has been found to be the determinant in users' requirements, because if users failed to access and execute the proper service due to usability errors, their dissatisfaction increased. Such dissatisfaction may prevent users' return to an e-government website, and even cause these users to not recommend their use to others.

Furthermore, usability has a big impact on users' preference and attitude. Lee and Koubek [19] investigated the effects of usability and web design attributes on user preference. Their study found that a high level of usability results in a high level of user preference towards the website. In particular, user preference was largely dependent upon web attributes in terms of content arrangement, navigation function, visual organization, typography and color usage. Additionally, Casaló et al. [20] demonstrated that website usability not only has a positive influence on user attitude, but also builds user trust in the website loyalty formation process. Similarly, Barnes and Vidgen [21] observed users' interaction with an online government tax self-assessment facility. The findings show that users' activities, such as information seeking are largely concerned with usability, navigation and site communication. In order to generate greater users' interaction, there is a need to not only understand the usability requirements of users, but provide tailored solutions to improve the usability of e-government websites. These studies suggest that without addressing usability in sufficient level, e-government will not be fully used and accepted by the widest range of users. Accordingly, it is important to evaluate the usability of current e-government websites, identify existing problems and provide proposed design solutions in order to further develop e-government.

3   Methodology

Having established the importance of usability in e-government website development, an empirical study was conducted with two linked experiments. Experiment 1 aimed to evaluate usability of a target e-government website. Experiment 2 looked to examine the proposed design solutions regarding the usability problems found. To conduct both experiments, three research instruments were used: the task sheet, the usability questionnaire and the selected e-government website. The task sheet details a set of tasks for participants to perform. A usability questionnaire was developed to identify the participants' perception of usability. The e-government websites were selected as representative of e-government and used to evaluate its usability.

3.1   Task Design

To conduct the evaluation, the participants were required to complete a set of practical tasks on an e-government website. Such tasks are representative activities that users would be expected to perform with an e-government website. Based on relevant studies [22], there are two levels of e-government services. The first level relates to the publishing or static stage, which involves users' one-way communication, such as searching information, downloading forms. The second level refers to the interaction stage, which contains two-way communication, such as council tax payment and online service registration. According to these service categories, the set of tasks have been designed to represent different types of interaction that users 'normally' engage in with e-government.

3.2   Usability Questionnaire

A questionnaire was used to measure the participants' perception of usability of the target e-government website. The design of this questionnaire is based on Nielsen's set of usability heuristics [23]. The questionnaire design consists of three stages: extension of heuristics, development criteria and usability questionnaire design.

3.2.1   Extension of Heuristics

Nielsen's [23] set of heuristics (Table 1) is used as a starting point for evaluating e-government websites usability since a number of studies have proven its validity and usefulness [24];[25]. However, such heuristics were developed many years ago and used for general usability evaluation. In order to fit with the particular needs of e-government, there is a need to derive additional heuristics. Evidence from previous studies indicate that where e-government is used by the public, interoperability is important in terms of information and service exchange [26]; for example ensuring news is kept current between e-government and government. In addition, since e-government is used by diverse users, therefore, e-government should support users with different skills to access and complete services. Furthermore, during users' interaction, e-government should show respect for users at all times [27]. Therefore, the existing heuristics are extended by adding three new heuristics: 'Interoperability', 'Support users' skills' and 'Respectful interaction with users' (Table 1).

Table 1. Nielsen's [23] usability heuristics and extended heuristics

Heuristics	Interpretation
H1 Visibility of system status	To keep users informed about what is going on.
H2 Match system with real world	To follow real-world conventions.
H3 User control and freedom	To make undo and redo functions available.
H4 Consistency and standards	To keep the same design feature through the site.
H5 Error prevention	To support users to overcome errors.
H6 Recognition rather than recall	To make information easily remember.
H7 Flexibility, efficiency of use	To allow users to tailor frequent actions.
H8 Aesthetic design	To make minimalist design.
H9 Help user recover errors	To indicate the problem and suggest a solution.
H10 Help and documentation	To provide help to support user's task completion.
Extended heuristics	**Interpretation**
H11 Interoperability	To make all elements work as a whole.
H12 Support users' skills	To support users with different knowledge.
H13 Respectful interaction	To present pleased design, treat users with respect.

3.2.2 Development Criteria

Although Nielsen's set of usability heuristics is extended, it is still too general to develop a questionnaire, so that e-government website usability would be evaluated with enough depth. Furthermore, the lack of detailed analysis may lead to failure in specific usability problem identification. Therefore, associated criteria for each heuristic needed to be developed. Such criteria are developed from relevant usability [28] and e-government studies [5]. These studies reveal a number of elements that affect website usability and users' perception. Based on the analysis of these elements, relevant criteria are identified and grouped into corresponding heuristics. By doing so, it can provide a step-by-step approach to closely focus on specific usability aspects. In addition, relevant questions can be precisely developed.

3.2.3 Usability Questionnaire Design

A usability questionnaire was designed to capture the participants' perception of usability. The reasons behind choosing a questionnaire are that it can drive the participants directly to the research topics, which enables the participants to clearly see the focus. In addition, with an anonymous response style, it encourages respondents to offer more truthful responses. Furthermore, using a questionnaire can ensure that the same questions are delivered to each participant and their responses can be obtained quickly. In order to capture users' perception of usability before and after the redesign and to control the variables to support comparative analysis, the same questionnaire is used for the participants in both experiments 1 and 2.

3.3   E-government Website Selection

Among the variety of e-government websites, a local e-government website in the UK is selected in this study for a number of reasons. Firstly, the local level of e-government website is the closest level to users. Secondly, local e-government websites are frequently used by the general public, since local e-government provides more information and focuses on the needs of users in accessing information and services [29]. Thirdly, the local level of e-government can significantly indicate the effect of e-government on users [30]. Fourthly, previous studies show the big challenges at the local level of e-governments [31] and its website design [32]. Thus, the local e-government website, London Authority 1 (LA1) is used in this study.

3.4   Participants

To conduct heuristic evaluation, Nielsen and Molich [33] found that three participants can detect half of the major problems. Virzi [34] suggested that 80% problems can be identified with between 4 and 5 participants and 90% of problems can be found with 10 participants in usability evaluation. Moreover, Dumas and Redish [35] argued that additional participants are less and less likely to reveal new problems and pointed out that the most appropriate number of participants is between 6 and 12. As such, 12 participants were recruited to take part in the evaluation, participating in both experiments 1 and 2. These participants were recruited in public places, such as local libraries, leisure centers, universities, and found to be enthusiastic to do the evaluation. The participants found in public places can be assumed to be representative of the public and that they do normally use an e-government website.

3.5   Experimental Evaluation Procedure

In both experiments, each participant follows the same evaluation process: free-flow inspection, task-based interaction and usability questionnaire. Free-flow inspection allows users to freely look through the e-government website. They can focus on either the overall website or the specific website elements. As such, users can build their initial interaction and their general perception can be developed. Then, task-based interaction requires the participants to complete a set of tasks. During tasks completion, their performance was observed according to a number of performance criteria, including the amount of online help required; time spent completing tasks; number of steps to finish tasks and number of successful tasks completed. Having completed all tasks, the participants are asked to fill in the usability questionnaire to indicate their judgment of usability of the target e-government website.

4   Results of Experiment 1

The following section presents the results in terms of users' perception and performance. The former uses the results from the questionnaires to indicate usability assessment, while, the latter is measured by a set of performance criteria to indicate the level of users' interaction with the target e-government website. To conduct data analysis, the one-sample T-test is considered as an appropriate technique for experiment 1. More specifically, the one-sample T-test is applied to determine whether there is a significant difference between users' perception of overall usability and specific usability features. If a difference is indicated, then the mean score of the specific usability features is greater than the mean score of the overall usability features and these can be seen as 'usability strengths'. Similarly, where the mean score of the specific usability features is less than mean score for the overall usability features, then these usability elements have been selected as the 'usability problems'. In addition, a lower mean score indicates a more serious problem. Statistical analysis is conducted using SPSS for windows (version 13).

4.1 User' Perception

Generally, the target e-government website appears to be clear and fairly straightforward, and it is easy to operate the e-government website. Each page always follows the same display format, which is helpful to build website consistency. The site's functionality supports users to complete most tasks. A title on every page clearly indicates the subject of the content, so that users can quickly capture the subject information of the page and locate information to meet their needs. Moreover, key information is always placed in a central location on the page, which can support users quickly searching for information. Furthermore, it is quick to change the particular data in a previous section so users do not need to retype all the data when they go back. Additionally, forward and backward choices are always available within the different fields of the site, so that users can easily guide their movement.

Table 2. User' perception of usability problems

Usability problems		Mean (Std. deviation)
Confusion by links that have many different colors.		2.58 (0.669)
	Significance	T=-6.511, P=0.000
Subject categories are presented without a logical order.		2.83 (1.030)
	Significance	T=-3.386, P=0.006
Links already visited are not clearly marked.		2.92 (1.084)
	Significance	T=-2.952, P=0.013
Information is unbalanced between breadth and depth.		3.00 (0.853)
	Significance	T=-3.412, P=0.006

However, the results also indicate a number of usability problems (see Table 2). Among them, the most serious usability problem found is that users are confused by links that have many different colors. Link color is used to present different resources within the site. Links with limited colors can visually help users distinguish between the resources, so as to easily identify relevant subject information. As indicated by Kappel et al. [36], users with limited color vision can quickly recognize the differences among subjects. In contrast, failure to provide limited link colors can visually influence resource recognition, so that users may feel it difficult to locate target information among subject content.

The next usability problem is that subject categories are presented without a logical order. A logical order is used to indicate a sequence of information organization, which supports users having a sensible way to scan subject. It assists users' understanding of the overall subject arrangement and reduces memory load problems. Brinck et al. [37] suggested that when topics are arranged with a particular order, users are able to easily locate items; remember items of interest viewed previously. On the contrary, when subject categories are presented without a logical order, users may feel it is difficult to find target subjects among the categories.

Another usability problem found is that links already visited are not clearly marked. Marking visited links is used to support users' ability to distinguish which parts of the site they have already visited and which parts remain to be explored. As such, it can help users to locate information during information searching. As indicated by Nielsen [38], visited links that have been clearly marked can provide a sense of structure and location in the site and enable users to quickly find the subject information. However, failure to mark visited links can weaken navigational recognition, which results in users visiting the same place repeatedly, or even abandoning their search prematurely.

Finally, a usability problem found is that the information arrangement is out of balance between breadth and depth. Breadth and depth are used to distribute e-government content by designing a number of subject categories and a number of information levels. A medium condition of breadth and depth is considered as an optimal trade-off, which can help information retrieval [39]. It is because the appropriate number of categories displayed can keep content from getting cluttered and reduce the chance that users are confused by a vast number of options. Where a moderate level of information is designed it can avoid over-long subject information, so that users can follow a short path into the site in order to find the detailed information. However, unbalanced breadth and depth can cause problems in information acquisition. In such conditions, users are frustrated by increasing levels of depth or feeling lost in content space, when there are a large numbers of categories [39]. As such, the problem that information arrangement is out of the balance between breadth and depth in London Authority 1 may cause more difficulties and errors for users searching for available information resources on a page and locating detailed information through multiple information levels.

4.2   Users' Performance

Having provided the users' perception of usability, in order to indicate the level of the participants' interaction, users' performance is measured based on a set of performance data, including the amount of online help required; average time spent completing all tasks; average number of steps to finish tasks and ratio of successful tasks completed. More importantly, this performance measurement in experiment 1 will be used as the baseline to compare users' performance in experiment 2. Table 3 presents the participants' performance with the target e-government website. Overall, all participants are able to complete most of the tasks assigned. In addition, during their performance, the participants' required some assistance through online help information. The time spent and the steps used for completing all tasks are 16.209 and 50.167 with standard deviation of 8.102 and 16.297 respectively.

Table 3. Experiment 1: users' performance results

	Mean	Std. Deviation
Online help required	0.000	0.000
Steps used	50.167	16.297
Successful tasks completion	1.065	0.088
Time spent for all tasks (minutes)	16.209	8.102

5   Design of the Proposed Solutions

The findings in experiment 1 indicate a number of usability problems that have been identified in the target e-government website. These problems suggest that usability has not been considered in sufficient detail in e-government website design. For an e-government to be accepted and used by the widest range of users, the e-government website should improve its usability to support users' interaction with e-government. As previously indicated [26], improving usability of e-government can enhance service effectiveness and users' satisfaction, which may involve more users' participation. As such, it is important to develop more usable e-government websites that can meet different users' requirements. Thus, this study takes further action by providing the proposed design solutions in relation to the usability problems found in experiment 1.

Usability Problem 1 (UP1): Users are Confused with Links that have Many Different Colors. A limited number of link colors can visually help users to distinguish resource differences so as to easily identify relevant subject information. Conversely, links with many different colors hamper resource recognition, which may result in users' difficulty with information identification. As such, designers of e-government websites should consider applying the minimum number of link colors, thereby supporting users' subject recognition during information seeking. One proposed design solution is to reduce link colors used in London Authority 1. In this way, it may reduce users color visual confusion and visually support users when locating information objects. Figure 1a presents an example of links that have many different colors in London Authority 1. Whereas, Figure 1b shows that some link colors are reduced in the redesigned London Authority 1 website.

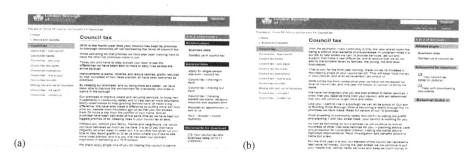

(a)   (b)

Fig. 1. UP 1 and the Proposed Design Solution

Usability Problem 2 (UP2): Subject Categories are Presented without a Logical Order. A logical order is used to show a sequence of information arrangement, which helps users quickly scan subject information to identify objects and reduce memory load problems. Similarly, failure to present subject categories with a logical order hinders information arrangement, which may lead to more complex information seeking. Accordingly, designers of e-government websites should consider organizing subject categories in a particular order in order to support users identifying a sensible way to scan subject information. One proposed design solution is to arrange subject categories in an alphabetical order on each page of London Authority 1. In this way, users may quickly understand the overall subject arrangement and easily identify relevant information to meet their needs. Figure 2a shows that initially, the subject categories are randomly presented on London Authority 1. However, Figure 2b presents an example in which the subject categories are organized alphabetically.

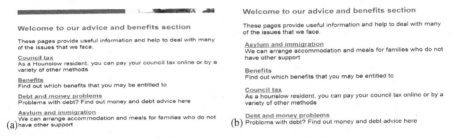

Fig. 2. UP 2 and the Proposed Design Solution

Usability Problem 3 (UP3): Links Already Visited are not Clearly Marked. Marking visited links is used to indicate which parts of the site users have already visited and which parts remain to be explored. It can help users build a sense of structure and location in the site, and navigate quickly to their target information. However, when visited links are not clearly marked, it weakens the site's navigational recognition, so that users may very likely revisit the same page and have difficulty locating information. Thus, designers should consider providing an approach that will help users recognize the unvisited and visited links within the site during the information seeking process. One proposed design solution is to mark visited links in italics within London Authority 1. As shown in Figure 3a, initially, the visited links in London Authority 1 have not been clearly marked. Whereas, Figure 3b shows that the visited links are clearly marked using italics on the site.

Apply for it »	Report it »	Pay it »	Say it »
Dispute parking fine	Abandoned vehicle	Council tax	Enquiry
Halls for hire	Benefit fraud	Parking ticket	Consultations
Housing benefit	Missed bin	Rent	Request a form/leaflet
Leisure centres	Street cleaning	Other payments	Find councillor

(a)

Apply for it	Report it	Pay it	Say it
Dispute parking fine	*Abandoned vehicle*	*Council tax*	*Consultations*
Halls for hire	*Benefit fraud*	*Parking ticket*	*Enquiry*
Housing benefit	*Missed bin*	*Rent*	*Find councillor*
Leisure centres	*Street cleaning*	*Other payments*	*Request a form/leaflet*

(b)

Fig. 3. UP 3 and the Proposed Design Solution

Usability 4 (UP4): Users become Lost due to being given too Many Choices during Information Seeking. An appropriate number of options can be used to keep content from getting cluttered and reduce the chance that users are confused by a large number of choices. Hence, it helps information retrieval. On the contrary, an excessive number of choices may cause difficulty in information acquisition [38], so that users may feel frustration when searching for information in a particular content space. Therefore, designers of e-government websites should consider providing an approach that will allow users to feel comfortable with the number of subject options. One proposed design solution is to design a drop-down menu for each subject category that visually hides its sub options. When users move the mouse to the subject category, a type of stretch sub list is used to present the various sub options associated with this subject category. In this way, the number of choices is visually reduced on the page, which is not only helpful in preventing content from getting cluttered, but also beneficial for users to read and locate information (see Figure 4a and 4b).

Fig. 4. UP 4 and the Proposed Design Solution

6   Results of Experiment 2

Have provided the design solutions, to investigate the effects of the proposed design solutions on the usability problems found, experiment 2 is conducted. This section provides the results of experiment 2 in terms of users' perception and performance. To control the variables under the same conditions between experiments 1 and 2, the same research instruments used in experiment 1 are used in experiment 2; including the questionnaire, the task sheet, the participants and the procedure. However, in order to avoid the participants learning from their experience with experiment 1, the tasks designed for experiment 2 focus on different service activities, but remain the same type of tasks as used in experiment 1. The results obtained from the participants' perception and performance is analyzed by using a paired-sample T-test.

6.1   Users' Perception

Table 4 reveals users' perception in experiment 2. Regarding the specific usability feature of links having many different colors, and subcategories not being present with a logical order, a significant difference is found between experiments 1 and 2. However, although no significant difference is indicated between experiments 1 and 2 with respect to the usability problems of visited links not being clearly marked and many choices being given during information seeking, the results still show that the participants' assessments are influenced after the design solutions have been applied to the redesigned London Authority 1.

Table 4. Experiment 2: User' Perception Results

	Experiment 1	Experiment 2
Confusion with links that have many different colors.		
Mean	2.58	4.33
Std. Deviation	0.669	0.492
Significance		T= -8.042, P=0.000
Difficult to choose the option in subcategories because no logical order of sub options is used in subcategories.		
Mean	2.83	4.17
Std. Deviation	1.030	0.577
Significance		T= -4.000, P=0.002
It clearly indicates which choices/links are already visited because they have been marked.		
Mean	2.92	3.58
Std. Deviation	1.084	1.165
Significance		T= -1.685, P=0.120
I sometimes get lost due to being given too many choices over sequences.		
Mean	3.00	3.75
Std. Deviation	0.853	1.215
Significance		T= -1.567, P=0.145

In other words, for each specific usability feature, the participants' assessment is changed for the better in experiment 2. As indicated earlier, the proposed design solutions have been applied to the target e-government website in experiment 2. The results show that the usability problems perceived in experiment 1 have been improved in the redesigned e-government website. Therefore, the findings suggest that the proposed design solutions have improved the usability problems identified in experiment 1. In addition, it increases overall users' perception of usability of London Authority 1.

6.2   Users' Performance

Given that the usability problems have been improved by the proposed design solutions in the redesigned London Authority 1, and in order to reveal the level of users' interaction with the redesigned London Authority 1, users' performance in experiment 2 is also measured based on the same performance criteria used in experiment 1. By focusing on such criteria, a comparative analysis of performance before and after the proposed design solutions have been applied can be derived. The detailed results are presented in the following subsections.

Table 5 shows the participants' performance in experiments 1 and 2. As indicated in Table 5, the results of the Paired-Samples T-test reveals a significant difference in terms of the time spent completing all tasks between experiments 1 and 2 (T=2.523, P=0.028). More specifically, the participants in experiment 2 use less time to complete all tasks, compared with experiment 1.

Table 5. Experiment 2: Users' Performance Results

		Experiment 1	Experiment 2
Total time spent completing tasks			
Mean		16.209	10.009
Std. Deviation		8.102	2.334
	Significance		T=2.523, P=0.028
Number of steps to finish tasks			
Mean		50.167	40.333
Std. Deviation		16.297	4.1141
	Significance		T=2.046, P=0.045
The amount of online help required			
Mean		0.000	0.000
Std. Deviation		0.000	0.000
	Significance		T= N/A, P= N/A
Successful tasks completion			
Mean		1.065	1.000
Std. Deviation		0.088	0.000
	Significance		T= N/A, P= N/A

In addition, a significant difference in terms of steps used for all tasks completion is found between experiments 1 and 2 (T=2.046, P=0.045). In detail, the participants in experiment 2 take fewer steps to finish all the tasks than those who are in experiment 1.

The results of the Paired-Samples T-test show that the difference in terms of number of online help actions required for all tasks completion is not significantly different between experiments 1 and 2. However, according to the mean score, it emerges that the participants in experiment 2 required less online help to complete all the tasks compared with experiment 1. Similarly, although the difference in terms of number of successful tasks completion is not significant between experiments 1 and 2, the mean score also indicate that the participants finish more tasks in experiment 2 than experiment 1.

Based on the performance results, it seems that the participants' performance with the redesigned London Authority 1 is enhanced in experiment 2. This result is also reflected in the results of users' perception, which reveal that the proposed designed solutions on the redesigned London Authority 1 have improved the usability problems identified in experiment 1. A possible explanation is that since the proposed design solutions have improved the usability problems, it increases the overall users' perception of usability, which in turn, makes for better users' performance. This is also supported by previous studies [5], which suggested that the overall users' perception of usefulness and ease of use has positively influenced users' performance and intention to use the technology.

7   Conclusions

This study has evaluated the usability of one current UK e-government website, which uncovered a number of usability problems. This suggests that this e-government website has some reason to improve its usability. As such, this study offers and assesses a set of proposed design solutions regarding the usability problems found for the target e-government website. The results show that the proposed design solutions have improved the usability problems identified. More significantly, after the proposed design solutions have been implemented in the redesigned e-government website, users' task performance has been also significantly improved. Accordingly, it suggests that the proposed design solutions may improve the overall users' perception of usability of the target e-government website, which makes for better users' performance. Therefore, it is important to show that usability of e-government websites meet users' needs, so that users' interaction with e-governments may be promoted. To achieve this goal, this study conducts a user centered approach, which can help understand the usability requirements of users. In addition, this study combines usability evaluation and redesign of an e-government website, which provides guidance for designers to identify existing usability problems and offer specific prescriptions for further usability improvement of e-government websites. The final target is to develop more usable e-government that can generate greater users' participation in e-government.

However, there are also some limitations to this study. For example, this study only evaluates one e-government website, as an example. Further research may be conducted with more distributed e-government websites in the UK. Another limitation relates to the redesigned e-government website in experiment 2. The redesigned e-government website is based on the target e-government website used in experiment 1, keeping the same structure, layout and content. However, the redesigned e-government website does not include all the website pages from the target e-government website. This may influence users' general perception when they conduct a free-flow inspection. In addition, this study applies a set of extended heuristics to evaluate usability of current e-government websites. In order to support designers' usability knowledge and skills for e-government development, there is also a need to conduct future study to develop usability guidelines that contain detailed usability design features, specifically for the development of better e-government websites.

References

1. Brown, M.M.: Digital government innovation, School of Government, University of North Carolina at Chapel Hill (retrieved from 2003), http://ncinfo.iog.unc.edu/pubs/electronicversions/pdfs/dgib0301.pdf
2. Jaeger, P.T.: The endless wire: e-government as global phenomenon. Government Information Quarterly 20(4), 323–331 (2003)
3. Donker-Kuijer, M.W., Jong, M., Lentz, L.: Usable guidelines for usable websites? an analysis of five e-government heuristics. Government Information Quarterly 27, 254–263 (2010)
4. Holden, S.H., Norris, D.F., Fletcher, P.D.: Electronic government at the local level: progress to date and future issue. Public Performance and Management Review 26(4), 325–344 (2003)
5. Barker, D.L.: Advancing e-government performance in the United States through enhanced usability benchmarks. Government Information Quarterly 26, 82–88 (2009)
6. Kossak, F., Essmayr, W., Winiwarter, W.: Applicability of HCI research to e-government. In: 9th European Conference on Information Systems, pp. 957–968 (2001)

7. Muir, A., Oppenheim, C.: National Information policy developments worldwide in electronic government. Journal of Information Science 28(3), 173–186 (2002)
8. OECD: OECD E-Government Studies: the e-government imperative, OECD, Paris (2003)
9. Følstad, A., Jørgensen, H.D., Krogstie, J.: User involvement in e-government development projects. In: Nordic Conference on Human-Computer Interaction, vol. 82, pp. 217–224 (2004)
10. Wang, L., Bretschneider, S., Gant, J.: Evaluating web-based e-government services with a citizen-centric approach. In: Proceedings of the 38th Annual Hawaii International Conference on System Sciences, vol. 5, pp. 129–139 (2005)
11. Steyaert, J.C.: Measuring the performance of electronic government services. Information and Management 41(3), 369–375 (2004)
12. Layne, K., Lee, J.: Developing fully functional e-government: a four stage model. Government Information Quarterly 18, 126–136 (2001)
13. Gillan, D.J., Bias, R.G.: Usability science I: foundations. International Journal of Human Computer Interaction 13(4), 351–372 (2001)
14. ISO 9241-11: Ergonomic requirements for office work with visual display terminals part II: guidance on usability. International Organization for Standardization (1998)
15. Flavián, C., Guinalíu, M., Gurrea, R.: The role played by perceived usability, satisfaction and consumer trust on website loyalty. Information and Management 43, 1–14 (2006)
16. Karahoca, A., Bayraktar, E., Tatoglu, E., Karahoca, D.: Information system design for a hospital emergency department: a usability analysis of software prototypes. Journal of Biomedical Informatics 43, 224–232 (2010)
17. Sauer, J., Sonderegger, A.: The influence of prototype fidelity and aesthetics of design in usability tests: effects on users behaviour, subjective evaluation and emotion. Applied Ergonomics 40, 670–677 (2009)
18. Anthopoulos, L.G., Siozos, P., Tsoukalas, I.A.: Applying participatory design and collaboration in digital public services for discovering and re-designing e-government services. Government Information Quarterly 24(2), 353–376 (2006)
19. Lee, S., Koubek, R.J.: The effects of usability and web design attributes on user preference for e-commerce web sites. Computers in Industry (2010) (in press, Corrected Proof)
20. Casaló, L., Flavián, C., Guinalíu, M.: The role of perceived usability, reputation, satisfaction and consumer familiarity on the website loyalty formation process. Computers in Human Behavior 24(2), 325–345 (2008)
21. Barnes, S.J., Vidgen, R.: Interactive e-government services: modelling user perceptions with eQual. Electronic Government 1(2), 213–228 (2004)
22. Shareef, M.A., Kumar, V., Kumar, U., Dwivedi, Y.K.: E-government adoption model (GAM): differing service maturity levels. Government Information Quarterly 28, 17–35 (2011)
23. Nielsen, J.: Heuristic evaluation: usability inspection methods, New York (1994)
24. Hvannberg, E.T., Law, E.L., Larusdottir, M.K.: Heuristic evaluation: comparing ways of finding and reporting usability problems. Interacting with Computers 19(2), 225–240 (2007)
25. Delice, E., Güngör, Z.: The usability analysis with heuristic evaluation and analytic hierarchy process. International Journal of Industrial Ergonomics 39(6), 934–939 (2009)
26. Garcia, A.C.B., Maciel, C., Pinto, F.B.: A Quality Inspection Method to Evaluate E-Government Sites. In: Wimmer, M.A., Traunmüller, R., Grönlund, Å., Andersen, K.V. (eds.) EGOV 2005. LNCS, vol. 3591, pp. 198–209. Springer, Heidelberg (2005)
27. Reddick, C.G.: Citizen interaction with e-government: From the streets to servers? Government Information Quarterly 22(1), 38–57 (2005)

28. Sonderegger, A., Sauer, J.: The influence of design aesthetics in usability testing: effects on user performance and perceived usability. Applied Ergonomics 41, 403–410 (2010)
29. Reddick, C.G.: The adoption of centralized customer service systems: a survey of local governments. Government Information Quarterly 26(1), 219–226 (2009)
30. Tolbert, C., Mossberger, K.: The effects of e-government on trust and confidence in government. In: Proceedings of the 2003 Annual National Conference on Digital Government Research, Digital Government Research Center, pp. 1–7 (2003)
31. Yang, J.Q., Paul, S.: E-government application at local level: issues and challenges: an empirical study. International Journal of Electronic Government 2(1), 56–76 (2005)
32. Henriksson, A., Yi, Y., Frost, B., Middleton, M.: Evaluation instrument for e-government websites. International Journal of Electronic Government 4(2), 204–226 (2007)
33. Nielsen, J., Molich, R.: Heuristic evaluation of user interface. In: Proceedings of the ACM CHI 1992, pp. 249–256 (1990)
34. Virzi, R.: Refining the test phase of usability evaluation: how many subjects is enough? Human factors 24, 457–468 (1992)
35. Dumas, J.S., Redish, J.C.: A practical Guide to usability testing. Intellect Ltd., USA (1999)
36. Kappel, G., Pröll, B., Reich, S., Retschitzegger, W.: Web engineering, the discipline of systematic development of web applications. John Wiley & Sons (2006)
37. Brinck, T., Gergle, D., Wood, S.D.: Usability for the web: designing web site that work. Morgan Kaufmann Publishers, San Francisco (2002)
38. Nielsen, J.: Deigning web usability: the practice of simplicity. New Riders Publishing, Indiana (2000)
39. Larson, K., Czerwinski, M.: Web page design: implications of memory, structure and scent for information retrieval. In: Proceedings of CHI 1998 Conference on Human Factors in Computing Systems, pp. 25–32 (1998)

OP2A: How to Improve the Quality of the Web Portal of Open Source Software Products

Luigi Lavazza, Sandro Morasca, Davide Taibi, and Davide Tosi

Università degli Studi dell'Insubria, Varese, Italy
{luigi.lavazza,sandro.morasca,
davide.taibi,davide.tosi}@uninsubria.it

Abstract. Open Source Software (OSS) communities do not often invest in marketing strategies to promote their products in a competitive way. Even the home pages of the web portals of well-known OSS products show technicalities and details that are not relevant for a fast and effective evaluation of the product's qualities. So, final users and even developers who are interested in evaluating and potentially adopting an OSS product are often negatively impressed by the quality perception they have from the web portal of the product and turn to proprietary software solutions or fail to adopt OSS that may be useful in their activities. In this paper, we define OP2A, an evaluation model and we derive a checklist that OSS developers and web masters can use to design (or improve) their web portals with all the contents that are expected to be of interest for OSS final users. We exemplify the use of the model by applying it to the Apache Tomcat web portal and we apply the model to 47 web sites of well-known OSS products to highlight the current deficiencies that characterize these web portals.

Keywords: Open source software, Quality perception, Web portals quality assessment, Web portal quality model.

1   Introduction

The usage of Open Source Software (OSS) has been continuously increasing in the last few years, mostly because of the success of a number of well-known projects.

However, the diffusion of OSS products is still limited if compared to the diffusion of Closed Source Software products. There is still reluctance to massive adoption of OSS, mainly due to two reasons: (1) lack of trust, as final users are often skeptical in trusting and adopting software products that are typically developed at no charge by communities of volunteer developers that are not supported by large business companies; (2) lack of marketing strategies, as OSS developers often do not pay attention to marketing, commercial and advertising aspects because these activities require a huge amount of effort and are not very gratifying. OSS developers are more focused on and interested in developing competitive software products than creating a commercial network that can support the diffusion of their products. Thus, OSS products may not have the success and the recognition that they should deserve.

Instead, as a mark of quality, commercial software and software producers may claim adherence to well-known standards, such as ISO9001 [8]. Such product and

J. Filipe and J. Cordeiro (Eds.): WEBIST 2011, LNBIP 101, pp. 149–162, 2012.

process certifications require detailed documentation and clearly defined organizational responsibilities, which are likely to exist only for an established organization with a solid and clear infrastructure. Such an accreditation is not easy to obtain for OSS produced by globally spread individuals or virtual teams who often operate without much infrastructure and / or specialized tools.

The websites and web portals of an OSS product may suffer from similar problems, as they are created by non professional web masters who, on the one hand, tend to focus on technicalities that are not relevant for the evaluation of the OSS product from the point of view of the end-user, and, on the other hand, often do not provide in a systematic and exhaustive way the technical information needed by other developers that intend to modify the code or to incorporate it into their products.

Websites and web portals are very important for creating the initial quality perception that end-users or other developers have about an OSS product. A website may be viewed as a shop window: if the window is ordered, clean and well-organized, customers will probably go inside the shop to either have a look or buy a product. Conversely, if the window is dusty and messy, buyers will not enter the store and they will turn to another store. This may seem an obvious consideration, but OSS portals often do not provide the contents that are most relevant to the end-users [11], or, if they do, they provide this information in hidden sections of the website, thus not favoring usability [13]. This may have a strong impact on the diffusion of OSS products.

In this paper, we introduce OP2A (Open source Product Portal Assessment), a model for evaluating the quality of web portals that store OSS products. OP2A can be used as the starting point for certifying the quality of OSS portals. The model is built upon the results of a survey [4, 5] – conducted in the context of the European project QualiPSo [19] – carried out to (1) identify the factors most commonly used to assess the trustworthiness and the quality of an OSS product, and (2) understand the reasons and motivations that lead software users and developers to adopt or reject OSS products. The model can be used by OSS developers to assess and improve the quality of their own web portals in order to present their products clearly, and minimize the effort required for presenting and promoting the OSS product in a competitive manner. OP2A takes into account a number of factors that are considered very important for the trustworthiness of an OSS product and describes the way this information should be presented to users that access the web portal of the product. OP2A is based on a checklist that summarizes the factors and simplifies the computation of the site maturity score. The checklist can be used by OSS developers to evaluate the maturity of their web portals and identify the maintenance actions required to meet attractiveness, clarity, and completeness requirements. We applied the assessment model to a real-life web portal (the Apache Tomcat portal) to show (1) the limitations of this portal, (2) how to use the checklist, and (3) how our model can actually drive the improvement of the portal. We also apply OP2A to 47 well-known OSS portals to assess the general quality level of these famous projects.

The paper is structured as follows. Section 2 introduces the OP2A assessment model and the related checklist. Section 3 presents the application of the model to the Apache Tomcat web portal and to the 47 OSS portals. Section 4 describes related works in the field of web quality and usability. We conclude and provide an outline for future work in Section 5.

2   The Assessment of OSS Web Portals

In this section, we detail the OP2A assessment model we derived from the results of our survey.

2.1   Which Factors Influence the Quality Perception of OSS Products

We conducted a survey [4, 5] in the context of QualiPSo [19] to find out which factors are most commonly used by developers and end-users to assess the trustworthiness of an OSS product. Our goal was to understand the reasons and motivations that lead software users and developers to adopt or reject existing OSS products, and, symmetrically, software developers to develop OSS. We called these factors "trustworthiness factors." Specifically, we focus on the trustworthiness of OSS, since OSS users and developers will not adopt a specific OSS product unless they can trust it. On the other hand, OSS developers need to promote the trustworthiness of their products, so that they may be more appealing to end-users and other developers that want to integrate existing OSS products in their software solutions or build on top of them.

We used the results of this survey [4, 5], specifically the trustworthiness factors and the relevance score they obtained in the survey, to derive our OP2A.

2.2   The OP2A Assessment Model

Assessing and certifying the quality of a web portal can help achieve the goals of different stakeholders. From the developer's point of view, the assessment provides guidelines for the definition of the website structure. Certified websites speed up the assessment of new OSS products and guarantee the availability of all the needed information for both OSS users and developers that may need to reuse OSS source code. OSS web masters may benefit from the website quality model used in the assessment, because it helps assess if all the product's contents are correctly organized and published in their portals: they can simply compute the maturity level of their web portal, and then, improve the "goodness" and "attractiveness" of the portal, if needed.

OP2A is built upon two sources of data: the trustworthiness factors highlighted in [4, 5] and the literature that describes well-known usability and accessibility rules for developing websites and web portals [14]. OP2A has been defined with emphasis on simplicity and ease of use. To this end, we defined a checklist that OSS developers and web masters can use to determine the maturity level of their own OSS web portals. OP2A is thus a tool for self-assessment, rather than an instrument for formal certifications. The core of the checklist is reported in the Appendix and in [17].

The checklist is structured in five areas: company information; web portal information; reasons of assessment; availability of information concerning trustworthiness factors; web portal usability information. So, when using the checklist, the evaluator first inserts general information about the company, about the portal under analysis and the reasons of assessment. Then, the evaluator goes through a sequence of entries that drive developers and web masters to identify whether contents and data related to the relevant trustworthiness factors are published in their OSS web portal.

Specifically, the core of the checklist is the evaluation of the project information availability in which trustworthiness factors are considered and further detailed into subfactors. In turn, trustworthiness factors are grouped into the following categories:

1. *Requirements*: disk usage, memory usage, supported operating system, etc.;
2. *License*: reference to the license, use conditions, and law conformance;
3. *Documentation*: user documentation, technical documentation, etc. The detailed description of the OSS features is expected to be found here;
4. *Downloads*: the number of downloads and related information;
5. *Quality reports*: information about important properties like Reliability, Maintainability, Performance, Product Usability, Portability, etc.;
6. *Community & Support*: the availability of various forms of support and the possible existence of a community around the project are investigated.

Every item of the information availability area is associated with a weight. Items corresponding to trustworthiness factors are weighted according to the average grade obtained in the survey [4, 5]. If a trustworthiness factor is evaluated through subfactors, its value is equally divided among the subfactors.

As an example, Fig. 1 shows an excerpt of the checklist that refers to the *"License"* category. The interviewees of our survey [4, 5] assigned to factor *"Type of license"* an average grade of 6.45 and to factor *"Law conformance aspects"* an average grade of 6.89. In the checklist, we have three items: *"Law conformance aspects"*, which is a factor, so it has the weight obtained through the survey, and *"Main license"* and *"Sub-licenses"*, which are sub-factors of *"Type of license"* and thus get half of the weight that was obtained for factor *"Type of license"* in the survey.

The total value for the *"License"* category of the checklist is: 6.45+6.89 = 13.34.

Project Information Availability	Overall Assessment		
3. License		_____ / 13.34	
	Presence		
	Y	N	Weight
- Main license			3.22
- Sub licenses (if applicable)			3.22
- Law conformance (if applicable)			6.89

Fig. 1. Excerpt of the checklist for the area "project information availability", category "License"

The assessor evaluates the availability of each type of information by ticking the box "Y" if the information is available, "N" otherwise. Some trustworthiness factors and sub-factors may be not applicable to the target portal: if a factor is not applicable, its weight is not meaningful to compute the final score of the portal. For example, if the sub-factor *"Law conformance"* is not applicable to a specific OSS product, the total value for the *"License"* category for that OSS product is 6.45 instead of 13.34.

When this process is completed and all the entries have been checked, the evaluator simply sums the values of the information classified as available: the result is the actual total score of the portal.

The weighted percentage of covered factors is equal to:

$$OP2A\_Score\ (\%) = (Tot\_Portal\_Score/Tot\_Applicable\_Score)*100$$

where *Tot_Portal_Score* is the sum of the scores for all the sub-factors that received the Y evaluation (or equally the sum of the scores for the seven categories), while *Tot_Applicable_Score* is the sum of all the scores for the sub-factors that are applicable for the portal under assessment. *OP2A_Score* is a valid indicator about the quality of the target portal and can be used by final users and web developers to understand the quality level of the portal. A high value of *OP2A_Score* suggests that the quality of the portal is good, while a low value of *OP2A_Score* indicates that the portal needs refactoring. The checklist suggests how to improve the quality of the portal.

Referring to our previous example, if the web portal under analysis provides only information about the main license used in the project and sublicenses and law conformance aspects are applicable but not published on the web portal, the final score for category "*License*" will be 3.22.

3   Validation of OP2A

In this section, we illustrate the application of the OP2A model to the Apache Tomcat website [1], and to 47 well-known OSS portals. The goal of this activity is threefold: (1) showing the simplicity of OP2A and the real support provided by the checklist; (2) showing how it is possible to actually improve the quality of the web portal by refactoring it according to the indications provided by the analysis; (3) providing an evaluation of the quality of well-known OSS products. The Appendix reports on the evaluation results of the Apache Tomcat website. Here, we also propose a refactoring of the portal to improve its quality.

3.1   Applying OP2A to the Apache Tomcat Website

Apache Tomcat is an open source servlet container developed by the Apache Software Foundation. It provides a platform for running Web applications developed in Java. We decided to take Apache Tomcat as an example because of its notoriety and diffusion.

Figure 4 shows the Apache Tomcat website at the time of writing. A quick look at the home page shows a very long menu on the left, with several links grouped by topic. We notice a lack of the general product description. On the home page the overview says: "*Apache Tomcat is an open source software implementation of the Java Servlet and JavaServer Pages (jsp) technologies...*" but an inexperienced user or developer may not understand if Apache Tomcat is just a utility or a set of libraries for Java Servlet and jsp or something else able to manage jsp.

The download area is well structured, but it contains too much information, while users usually want to be presented with a link for downloading the latest stable version of the product. Nevertheless, we scored this area as good in our checklist, because it provides all the information required by OSS final users and developers.

Other areas like "problems?", "get involved" and "misc" fulfill several entries of the checklist. More than 90% of the information is correctly shown on the website for the categories: *Overview, License, Documentation and Downloads*. Conversely, we noticed that information about *Requirements and Quality Reports* –such as reliability, maintainability, performance and product usability– is only marginally discussed on the Apache Tomcat website. The current version of the website covers 60% of the category *Community&Support*. In conclusion, as shown in the Appendix, the Apache Tomcat website earned a *Tot_Apache_Score* = 98.19 over a theoretical *Tot_Applicable_Score* = 147.50 (*OP2A_Score* = 66.6%).

3.2   A Proposal for Refactoring the Apache Tomcat Website

As described in Section 3.1, the Apache Tomcat website gained an *OP2A_Score* of 66.6% thus indicating that more than 30% of trustworthiness factors have not been taken into account when designing the Apache Tomcat website. In this section, we make a proposal for refactoring the Apache Tomcat portal to improve the quality of the website and to increase the *OP2A_Score*, so that OSS users and also developers will be able to quickly find all required information, and the probability of adoption/reuse of the Apache Tomcat product will increase.

Table 1. Evaluation data for the assessment of the Apache Tomcat website

Original Website			*Refactored Version*	
overall time	*quality perception*	*OP2A score*	*overall time*	*quality perception*
1h30m	2	98.19 (66.6%)	26m	3
1h18m	2	95.65 (64.8%)	30m	4
1h00m	2	96.99 (65.7%)	30m	4
1h15m	2	94.59 (64.1%)	25m	4
1h10m	2	97.59 (66.2%)	22m	3
1h14m (avg)	2 (avg)	1.46 (st.dev)	27m (avg)	3.6 (avg)

To this end, we need to consider all the factors included in the OP2A checklist. In Fig. 5, we propose a new menu structure for the home page. This menu is shorter than the original one and enables users to reach the most important information directly from the home page. The idea of grouping all the information comes out by looking at the views of Nielsen [13].

To validate the quality of the refactored version of the website against the original one, we asked ten Computer Science Master's students, who had never accessed the Apache Tomcat portal before, to surf the original web portal and the refactored one and rank their perception of the quality of the website, in a scale from 1 (poor quality) to 4 (very good quality). Then, we asked our sample to fill out the OP2A checklist. Five students evaluated the original Apache tomcat website, and the five other evaluated the refactored version. We were interested in observing the ease of the information retrieval process, the time taken to fill out the checklist, the perceived quality of the two versions of the website, and the subjectivity degree of the checklist. In Table 1, we show the time taken by our testers for applying the OP2A checklist to the original Apache Tomcat website in column <<*overall time*>>, the users' perceived quality of the Apache Tomcat website in column <<*quality perception*>>, and the total score achieved by applying the checklist to the website in column <<*OP2A score*>>. The other two columns show the overall time, and the quality perception for the refactored version of the website. Based on these results, we can state that the refactoring actually seems to have improved the quality of the portal (that now obtained an *OP2A_Score* near to 100%). It is interesting to observe that the quality perception is actually increased from an average value of 2 to an average value of 3.6 after the refactoring activity. These values are in line with the maturity level computed by OP2A. Moreover, the relatively low value of the standard deviation (equal to 1.46), computed over the five OP2A scores, suggests the low degree of subjectivity of the proposed checklist.

For our empirical study, we selected ten students, following [15]. We are conducting additional experiments with a larger number of students in order to strongly validate these preliminary results.

3.3   Analysis of OSS Portals

We analyzed the portals of 47 OSS projects to get a preliminary assessment of their quality. The purpose was not actually to show the feasibility of OP2A, but to provide the evidence that techniques like OP2A are actually needed, as the quality of OSS projects portals is far from adequate, with respect to the quality of OSS products and their ambitions to substantially increase their user basis.

The set of portals has been selected by taking into account different types of software products, generally considered well-known, stable, and mature. In [17] it is possible to find the details of this experimentation.

Figure 2 summarizes the results of the assessment, by reporting the *OP2A_Scores*, computed as the ratio between the obtained score and the total achievable score. The empirical study shows that the quality of the analyzed portals is generally inadequate (the mean value of the *OP2A_Score* achieved by the portals is 57.3%), thus calling for heavy portal refactoring to achieve an acceptable level of quality.

Figure 2 shows that the situation is quite homogeneous: over 26 portals out of 47 achieved an *OP2A_Score* between 40 and 60%. Nineteen portals achieved a 60% or higher score, but only 7 are above 70%.

The overall quality per portal section is described in Figure 3. It is easy to see that the areas of portals with the lowest quality are those concerning requirements, quality reports, licenses, and the community and support. On the one hand, it is natural that most OSS projects rely on spontaneous spreading of information concerning the functionality and quality of their products; on the other hand, it is clearly a problem if a potential user, having heard of product XYZ, looks for the site of XYZ and does not find clear information about the product functionalities, under what license it is released, what quality claims and evidence are available, etc.

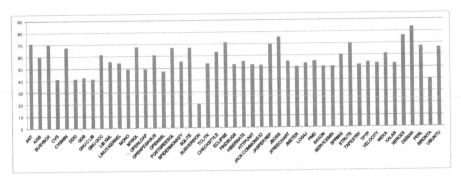

Fig. 2. OSS portal scores

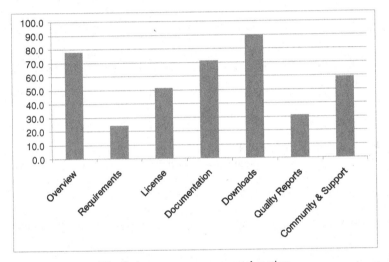

Fig. 3. Average scores per portal section

4   Related Work

Before committing to using a software product, people want to collect information about the product, in order to be able to evaluate its trustworthiness. Usually, during the selection of software, users and developers collect information about the products from the official websites. This is especially true for OSS products, which are typically distributed exclusively via the web.

The type of the information commonly used by the users when they evaluate OSS projects has been investigated in the last few years, and several OSS evaluation methods have been proposed. Their aim is to help potential adopters understand the characteristics of the available products, and evaluate the pros and cons of its adoption. Some of the most known OSS evaluation models are: OpenBRR [23], QSOS [3], OSMM [7] and OpenBQR [21]. OSMM is an open standard aimed at facilitating the adoption of OSS based on the evaluation of some maturity aspect of OSS like documentation, provided support, training availability and third parties integration possibilities. QSOS extends the information to be evaluated by adding new quality areas like the documentation quality and the developer community. Finally, OpenBRR and OpenBQR address additional quality aspects and try to ease the evaluation process. The evaluation process of all these methods is mainly organized into an evaluation step and a scoring step. The evaluation step aims at collecting the relevant information concerning the products from the OSS website. In this phase, the goal is to create an "identity card" for every product with general information, functional and technical specifications, etc. The quality aspects of the selected products are evaluated and a score is assigned according to the evaluation guidelines provided by each method. In the scoring phase, the final score is computed by summing all the scores calculated in the previous step.

In [7] a method for OSS quality certification is proposed. Like the other evaluation methods, it is based on the evaluation of a common set of information but differs whilst the process is based on ISO/IEC 9126. The biggest problem of the evaluation model is the definition of the information to be evaluated. This information has been defined according to experience and the literature, but they are often unavailable and not useful for most users. To reduce the amount of information to be evaluated, we carried out a survey [10] to study the users' perception of trustworthiness and a number of other qualities of OSS products. We selected 22 Java and 22 C++ products, and we studied their popularity, the influence of the implementation language on trustworthiness, and whether OSS products are rated better than Closed Source Software products.

Another important research field for this paper is the website certification. In 2001, a certification schema proposal for Italian Public Administration website quality has been defined [12]. This certification model is based on a set of information that Public Administration websites must publish on their own website. The set of information has been defined by investigating the quality aspect –e.g., usability and accessibility– of 30 Italian Public Administration websites.

Since 1994, the World Wide Web Consortium (W3C) has defined several standards, guidelines and protocols that ensure the long-term Web growth and accessibility to everybody, whatever their hardware, software, language, culture, location, or physical or mental ability.

In 2008, W3C released the second version of the "Web Content Accessibility Guideline," aimed at making Web contents more accessible [22]. Usability is defined by the International Organisation for Standardisation (ISO) as: "the extent to which a product can be used by specified users to achieve specified goals with effectiveness, efficiency and satisfaction in a specified context of use." Some usability studies show problems in Sourceforge [20]: Arnesen et al. [2] showed several problems, mainly concerning the link structure and the information organization. Another study [18] identified usability problems both with Sourceforge and with the Free Software Foundation [6] website by means of eye tracker techniques [9].

Currently, the vast majority of OSS websites does not provide the information needed by end-users. OP2A aims at ensuring both the availability of information and its accessibility.

5   Conclusions

A survey that we conducted in the context of the QualiPSo European project led to the identification of the trustworthiness factors that impact on the choices of users in adopting OSS products. On such basis, we defined the OP2A assessment model, which contains a checklist that OSS developers and web masters can use to design their web portals so that all the contents that are expected by OSS users are actually provided. We exemplified the use of OP2A through its application to the Apache Tomcat website, to show the simplicity and the actual potentialities of the model and of the checklist, and we evaluated the quality of 47 OSS portals. Preliminary results suggest that the model can be effectively used to improve the quality of OSS web portals.

The proposed evaluation model can be applied also to the websites of closed source products. Of course, a few trustworthiness factors (namely those addressing source code qualities) are not applicable in the case of closed source software.

We are conducting additional experiments to understand whether: (1) the weight of subfactors should be refined, for example asking OSS developers and users to weight also subfactors; (2) define targeted weights for the different OSS stakeholders such as managers, developers, and end-users; (3) collecting additional statistical data about the analyzed portals; (4) using degrees of presence of factors, instead of yes/no values.

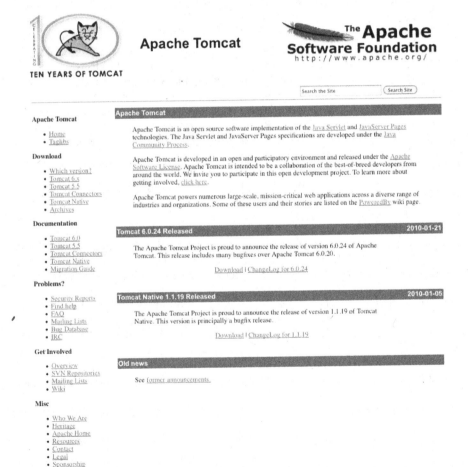

Fig. 4. Original Apache Tomcat website

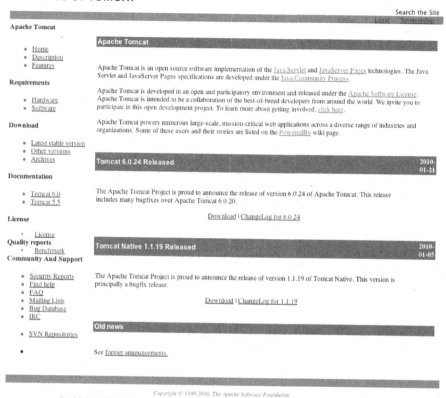

Fig. 5. Apache Tomcat website Refactored

Acknowledgements. The research presented in this paper has been partially funded by the IST project QualiPSo (http://www.qualipso.eu/), sponsored by the EU in the 6th FP (IST-034763); the FIRB project ARTDECO, sponsored by the Italian Ministry of Education and University; and the projects "Elementi metodologici per la specifica, la misura e lo sviluppo di sistemi software basati su modelli" and "La qualità nello sviluppo software," funded by the Università degli Studi dell'Insubria.

References

1. Apache Tomcat Web Site, http://tomcat.apache.org/ (last visited: January 2011)
2. Arnesen, L.P., Dimiti, J.M., Ingvoldstad, J., Nergaard, A., Sitaula, N.K.: SourceForge Analysis, Evaluation and Improvements. Technical Report, University of Oslo (May 2000)

3. Atos Origin, Method for Qualification and Selection of Open Source Software (QSOS). Web published, http://www.qsos.org (last visited: January 2011)

4. Del Bianco, V., Chinosi, M., Lavazza, L., Morasca, S., Taibi, D.: How European software industry perceives OSS trustworthiness and what are the specific criteria to establish trust in OSS. Deliverable A5.D.1.5.1 – QualiPSo project – (October 2008), Web published, http://www.qualipso.eu/node/45 (last visited: January 2011)

5. Del Bianco, V., Lavazza, L., Morasca, S., Taibi, D.: A Survey on Open Source Software Trustworthiness. IEEE Software (to appear)

6. FSF Free Software Foundation Web Page, http://www.fsf.org (last visited: January 2011)

7. Golden, B.: Making Open Source Ready for the Enterprise: The Open Source Maturity Model, from "Succeeding with Open Source". Addison-Wesley (2005)

8. International Standardization Organization. "ISO 9001:2008". Web published, http://www.iso.org (last visited: January 2011)

9. Jacob, R.J.: The use of eye movements in human-computer interaction techniques: what you look at is what you get. ACM Transaction on Inf. Syst. 9(2), 152–169 (1991)

10. Del Bianco, V., Lavazza, I., Morasca, I., Taibi, D., Tosi, D.: An Investigation of the users' perception of OSS quality. In: Proceedings of the 6th International Conference on Open Source Systems (OSS), Notre Dame, IN, USA (May/June 2010)

11. Lavazza, L., Morasca, S., Taibi, D., Tosi, D.: Analysis of relevant open source projects. Deliverable A5.D.1.5.2 – QualiPSo project – (October 2008), Web published, http://www.qualipso.eu/node/84 (last visited: January 2011)

12. Minelle, F., Stolfi, F., Raiss, G.: A proposal for a certification scheme for the Italian Public Administration web sites quality. In: W3C – Euroweb Conference, Italy (2001)

13. Nielsen, J.: User Interface Directions for the Web. Communications of the ACM 42(1), 65–72 (1999)

14. Nielsen, J., Norman, D.: Usability On The Web Isn't A Luxury. Information Week (February 2000)

15. Nielsen, J., Landauer, T.K.: A mathematical model of the finding of usability problems. In: Proceedings of ACM INTERCHI 1993 Conference, pp. 206–213 (1993)

16. O'Reilly CodeZoo SpikeSource community initiative, being sponsored by Carnegie Mellon West Center for Open Source Investigation and Intel. Business Readiness Rating for Open Source – A Proposed Open Standard to Facilitate Assessment and Adoption of Open Source Software (August 2005)

17. OP2A, http://www.op2a.org (last visited: January 2011)

18. Pike, C., Gao, D., Udell, R.: Web Page Usability Analysis. Technical Report, Pennsylvania State University (December 2003)

19. QualiPSo Web page, http://www.qualipso.org (last visited: January 2011)

20. Sourceforge Web page, http://www.sourceforge.net (last visited: January 2011)

21. Taibi, D., Lavazza, L., Morasca, S.: OpenBQR: a framework for the assessment of OSS. In: Proceedings of the Third International Conference on Open Source Systems (OSS), Limerick, Ireland, pp. 173–186. Springer, Heidelberg (2007)

22. W3C recommendation, Web Content Accessibility Guidelines (WCAG) 2.0, 2008. Web published, http://www.w3.org/TR/WCAG20/ (last visited: September 2010)

23. Wasserman, A., Pal, M., Chan, C.: Business Readiness Rating Project. Whitepaper 2005, RFC 1, http://www.openbrr.org/wiki/images/d/da/BRR_whitepaper_2005RFC1.pdf (last visited: January 2011)

Appendix

Here, we present the core of the OP2A checklist and the results of its application to the Apache Tomcat website before the refactoring process.

Project information availability		Overall Assessment		
1	**Overview**	**22.86 / 29.09**		
		Presence		
		Y	N	Weight
	• Product general description	x		3.92
	• Product age	x		3.92
	• Best Practices		x	6.23
	• Features high level description	x		4.29
	• Detailed Features description	x		4.29
	• License	x		6.44
2	**Requirements**	**2.86 / 8.59**		
		Presence		
		Y	N	Weight
	• Hardware requirements			
	• Disk usage		x	1.43
	• Memory usage	x		1.43
	• Min CPU required		x	1.43
	• Other HW requirements		x	1.43
	• Software requirements			
	• Supported operative systems	x		1.43
	• Required 3rd parties components (if applicable)		x	1.43
3	**License**	**13.34 / 13.34**		
		Presence		
		Y	N	Weight
	• Main license	x		3.22
	• Sub licenses (if applicable)	x		3.22
	• Law conformance (if applicable)	x		6.89
4	**Documentation**	**20.25 / 20.85**		
		Presence		
		Y	N	Weight
	• Technical documentation			
	• Code documentation (javadoc, etc.)	x		0.60
	• Code examples	x		0.60
	• Architectural documentation	x		0.60
	• Documentation on customization	x		0.60
	• Installation guide	x		0.60
	• Technical related F.A.Q.	x		0.60
	• Technical forum	x		0.60
	• Technical related mailing list	x		0.60
	• Testing documentation		x	0.60
	• Documentation about additional tools for developing, modifying or customizing the product (if applicable)	x		6.84
	• Security aspects analysis (if applicable)	x		6.21
	• User documentation			
	• User manual	x		0.60
	• Getting started guide	x		0.60
	• User related F.A.Q.	x		0.60
	• Mailing list	x		0.60

		Y	N	Weight
5	**Downloads**			**9.00 / 12.00**
			Presence	
		Y	N	Weight
	• Download page	x		3.00
	• The download page is easily reachable	x		3.00
	• More than one archives	x		3.00
	• Specified the dimension of each downloads		x	3.00
6	**Quality reports**			**17.31 / 37.11**
			Presence	
		Y	N	Weight
6.1	**Reliability**			1.64 / 8.20
	• Correctness		x	1.64
	• Dependability		x	1.64
	• Failure frequency		x	1.64
	• Product maturity	x		1.64
	• Robustness		x	1.64
6.2	**Maintainability**			1.96 / 7.86
	• Code size		x	1.96
	• Standard architectures (if applicable)		x	1.96
	• Language uniformity	x		1.96
	• Coding standard (if applicable)		x	1.96
6.3	**Performance**			0.00 / 7.34
	• Performance tests and benchmarks (if applicable)		x	3.67
	• Specific performance-related documentation		x	3.67
6.4	**Product Usability**			7.20 / 7.20
	• Ease of installation/configuration	x		3.60
	• ISO usability standard (ex. ISO 14598)	x		3.60
6.5	**Portability**			6.51 / 6.51
	• Supported environments	x		2.17
	• Usage of a portable language	x		2.17
	• Environment-dependent implementation (e.g., usage of hw/sw libraries)	x		2.17
7	**Community & Support**			**12.58 / 26.52**
			Presence	
		Y	N	Weight
7.1	**Community**			4.88 / 14.52
	• Size of the community		x	7.20
	• Existence of mid / long term user community			
	• Trend of the number of users		x	2.44
	• Number of developers involved	x		2.44
	• Number of posts on forums / blogs / newsgroups	x		2.44
7.2	**Training and Support**			7.70 / 12.00
	• Availability of training			
	• Training materials	x		2.54
	• Official training courses (if applicable)		x	2.54
	• Bugs number	x		1.72
	• Number of patches / release in the last 6 months	x		1.72
	• Average bug solving time		x	1.72
	• Availability of professional services (if applicable)	x		1.72
	Total Score:			**98.19 / 147.50 (66.6%)**

User-Friendly Interaction in an On-line System Based on Semantic Technologies

Anna Goy and Diego Magro

Dipartimento di Informatica, Università di Torino, C. Svizzera 185, Torino, Italy
{annamaria.goy,diego.magro}@unito.it

Abstract. Nowadays, SME have to take into account new business and management approaches, like CRM, as well as the support provided by ICT. In this scenario, SME would take advantage from a Web-based service like ARNEIS, supporting an intelligent matching between supply and demand of CRM-related tools. Such a service needs a detailed knowledge base, and a friendly user interface (UI) enabling users to interact with the formal knowledge base. In this chapter we claim that both the knowledge representation and the user interaction mechanisms have to be based on a domain analysis (how users talk about CRM). The chapter presents three UI, based on on-line forms, business processes, and natural language. All three exploit semantic templates, i.e., formal representations of dialog topics (key concepts in the descriptions of CRM activities). The proposed approach suggests a general solution to enable users to enter formal representations in systems based on semantic technologies.

Keywords: User interaction, User interfaces, Ontology, e-Business, Semantic Web.

1 Introduction

In order to be competitive in the globalized market Small-to-Medium sized Enterprises (SME) have to take care of two major aspects: (a) The support provided by Information and Communication Technologies (ICT) to their business and, in particular, the trend of relying more and more on Internet and Web technologies: Web-based solutions are available for almost any kind of application, supported by innovative technologies at different levels, ranging from Cloud Computing infrastructures [12] [15], to Web Services [1], to Semantic Web [2]. (b) New business and management approaches and, in particular, the way to handle relationships with customers. The new market, in fact, requires personalized approaches to the single customer and flexible offers that need to be updated frequently. Moreover, in order to be aware of the market and customer behavior trends, data about offers, sales, communications with customers, and so on have to be elaborated very rapidly, to support management and marketing decisions.

For these reasons, Customer Relationship Management (CRM) [16], and ICT products and services supporting it, have received an increasing attention in the last couple of decades, not only from large enterprises, but also from SME. The key

J. Filipe and J. Cordeiro (Eds.): WEBIST 2011, LNBIP 101, pp. 163–176, 2012.

principle of the CRM approach is a one-to-one marketing strategy that implies establishing personalized relationships with the single customer, by producing personalized offers, pricing, after-sale services, etc. Moreover, technological innovative solutions could effectively support the CRM approach, given that CRM requires the processing, integration, and analysis of a huge amount of heterogeneous knowledge (about customers, sales, communications, etc.), as well as effective, fast and integrated communication tools.

Within this scenario, SME would get great benefits from a Web-based service supporting an intelligent matching between supply and demand for CRM-related tools, and such a service can only be based on a clean, complete, and sharable formal knowledge representation of the concepts related to CRM.

In order to face this challenge, we designed an architecture for a Web-based intelligent system supporting SME in finding suitable software solutions for their business, and we chose CRM as a testbed for this architecture. On the basis of this architecture, we developed ARNEIS (Advanced Repository for Needs of Enterprises and Innovative Software), a prototype implementation of a Web-based repository of descriptions of software solutions for CRM, that exploits Web Services and Semantic Web technologies. ARNEIS users are: (a) ICT companies (i.e., software houses) that offer software solutions for CRM, but can find it difficult to get in contact with their potential customers; (b) SME that aim at finding software products or services supporting their CRM activities, but lack the know-how to find the ICT solution fitting their needs.

Such an intelligent repository has to be equipped with a large and detailed knowledge base, e.g. an ontology [20], which represents the shared conceptual vocabulary and is the basis for the matching mechanism used to suggest SME the most suitable software solutions, given their needs. Moreover, ARNEIS requires a Web-based user interface (UI) enabling ICT companies to describe their software solutions and SME to express their requirements and needs. We claim that both these goals, i.e. building the CRM ontology and designing the system UI, have to be based on a domain analysis that takes into account how users, both from ICT companies and from SME, talk (and think) about CRM activities (see Section 2.2).

The CRM ontology developed for the ARNEIS project is described in [23] and [24], while this paper focuses on the definition of the UI enabling the users to interact with it. In particular, Section 2.1 briefly describes the system architecture and Section 2.2 reports the main results of the domain analysis; Section 3 focus on the user interaction management: it provides a brief survey of the relevant related work in the field (Section 3.1), it discusses the UI design choices and describes the mechanisms supporting UI management (Section 3.2). Section 4 briefly discusses some open issues and concludes the chapter.

2   The ARNEIS System

In this section we will describe the ARNEIS architecture and then we will briefly present the domain analysis that enabled us to define the system knowledge base and the user interface design.

2.1   System Architecture

Fig. 1 shows a simplified version of the basic architecture of the ARNEIS system, which is described in details in [19].

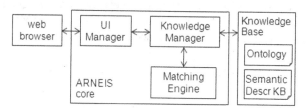

Fig. 1. ARNEIS system architecture (a simplified version taken from [19]).

It is a standard three-tiers architecture, where the presentation layer is represented by a standard Web browser.

The application logic layer is represented by the *ARNEIS core*, which includes three main components: the *UI Manager*, the *Knowledge Manager*, and the *Matching Engine*. The *UI Manager* generates the UI taking as input the concepts, properties and relations provided by the Knowledge Manager and represented in the Ontology; moreover, it collects information provided by the user and forwards it to the Knowledge Manager, that builds the semantic representation of software descriptions and SME requirements. The *Knowledge Manager* mediates the interaction between the UI Manager and the data layer (its role will be discussed in more detail in Section 3.2). Moreover, it dialogs with the *Matching Engine* (whose description is out of the scope of this chapter), by providing it the semantic representations on the basis of which the Matching Engine calculates the correspondence between SME requirements and software house offers.

The data layer contains the *Knowledge Base*, whose main components are the *Ontology*, representing the system semantic competence about the domain (CRM), and the semantic representation of software descriptions and SME requirements (*Semantic Descr KB*). Both the Ontology and the Semantic Descr KB are written in OWL (http://www.w3.org/2004/OWL/). The OWL domain Ontology is based on a CRM *Reference Ontology* [20], described in [23] and [24]), which in turn is based on DOLCE (http://www.loa-cnr.it/DOLCE.html). The CRM Reference Ontology basically models: (1) business activities (e.g., sales, offers, communications, appointments, etc.); (2) business relationships which the company is involved in (e.g., relationships with actual or potential customers); (3) the knowledge that the company has on (or derives from) business activities and relationships; (4) software supporting business activities and knowledge management.

2.2   CRM Domain Analysis

In this section we will describe the type of knowledge used by the UI Manager to generate the UI, as well as the kind of information that should be elicited from the users in order to build a structured and formal representation of the offered software solutions and of the SME requirements.

The definition of the knowledge and information just mentioned has been based on a detailed domain analysis, aimed at understanding how users (both software houses and SME) talk about CRM. We analyzed two types of information sources: (a) Documents (e.g., brochures, white papers), produced by ICT companies, describing their CRM software tools. (b) Interviews with salesmen from ICT companies, aimed at eliciting the way they describe software solutions for CRM for SME, and managers of SME, aimed at understanding which concepts and terms they use to think about their activities related to customer management.

The analysis of documents and interviews provided us with the following outcomes:

(1) We identified the main concepts, properties and relations involved in the description of CRM activities in SME, which represent the basic requirements for building the CRM Ontology.

(2) We identified a set of *dialog topics*, i.e. concepts that emerged to be the keys of the description of CRM activities. As we will describe in detail in Section 3.2, within the system these concepts are represented as *templates*, i.e. general conceptual patterns that are instantiated with more specific concepts in the different documents/interviews, by means of various linguistic forms. Each template is formally represented as a concept in an Application Ontology: basically, each description of a software solution or a set of SME requirements is an instantiation of a number of such templates (see Section 3.2).

(3) We extracted the linguistic expressions used to refer to dialog topics. The list of such expressions (after a normalization process aimed at eliminating morphological variants) represents a *controlled vocabulary* that is used to provide users with a list of *semantic tags*. Such tags are "semantic" because they are associated with dialog topics, which are represented within the system as concepts in an Application Ontology (see Section 3.2).

Moreover, we proposed to people from SME a short additional interview aimed at eliciting their preferred ways to describe CRM activities. From this additional interview, it emerged that the most natural ways to describe their CRM activities are business processes and natural language. This outcome led us to design a prototype user interface based on Business Process Modeling (BPM) and to start a study to evaluate the feasibility of a Natural Language (NL) UI (see Section 3.2).

3   User Interaction in Knowledge-Based Systems

As mentioned in Section 2, the system needs a formal representation of the descriptions of software solutions and of SME technological in order to find the software solutions best matching the SME requirements. Since it is unrealistic to ask users to write descriptions in a formal Semantic Web language, such as OWL, the generation of a user-friendly UI turned out to be an issue of major importance.

3.1   Related Work

The importance of the UI to access complex knowledge bases is a topic studied in different research fields. Many authors recognize that there has been an increase of interest in the design of UI for systems based on semantic technologies (see, for instance, the SWUI workshops series: http://swui.semanticweb.org/). The main issue to be faced is the fact that the user interacting with a formally encoded knowledge base (e.g., an ontology) should not be exposed to the formal details of the representation: in other words, "semantic technologies should be invisible to users" [5], p. 76.

The most traditional approaches facing this issue aim at supporting user queries that have the goal of searching for information encoded in formal knowledge bases (databases or ontologies). These approaches are mainly based on the translation of keywords (provided by the users) into formal queries (being SQL, or DL, or other formal languages); see, for instance, [29].

Within this thread, some approaches propose graphical (Web-based) UI to enable users to easily access knowledge bases; e.g.,[27]. Other approaches propose to use NL-based UI; e.g. [6], [10], [14]. In [22], for example, a mechanism is presented for providing a natural language access to databases: a NL query is firstly translated into a query expressed in terms of concepts and relations specified in a domain ontology; in a second step, such a query is translated into a computer language for accessing databases (such as SQL).

In all the mentioned approaches the user input is a query aimed at retrieving information from a (formal) knowledge base. In ARNEIS, the two categories of users interacting with the system have different goals: the goal of a user from a software house is to provide the system with a description of a software solution, while the goal of a representative from a SME is to "explain" the system the SME technological requirements and needs in order to find a suitable software solution. Thus, in ARNEIS, in both cases, the user input is a complex description, based on an existing ontology. In order to elicit this kind of information the system requires a more complex UI with respect to the UI typically provided by the previously mentioned approaches, where the user simply provides the system with a query.

With the broader goal of supporting friendly user interfaces to knowledge-based systems, [7] presents K-Forms, a tool enabling users to define knowledge structure and content through a user-friendly form-based UI; the tool then translate such a knowledge into a formal (RDF/OWL) representation. In [8] K-Search, another tool supporting knowledge search and sharing, is described. Moreover, some authors propose to use Controlled Natural Languages (CNL), i.e., subsets of natural languages that are simpler and less ambiguous [26]. Several CNL have been defined that enable domain experts to specify formal knowledge bases and ontologies, without the need for them to know the formal languages in which the knowledge is ultimately encoded or the knowledge engineering tools. Among these CNL it is worth mentioning CLOnE [18], SOS [13], ACE [17] and Rabbit [21]. As regards ARNEIS, even though SME users should not be forced to learn any "constrained" language, the role of CNL (perhaps for complementing on-line forms in the UI for users from software houses) should be investigated. In [4] the authors describe a user interface for semantic wiki systems which enables users to enter semantic knowledge by filling in a set of "semantic forms". The interface renders that knowledge as embedded Rabbit sentences on wiki pages. Their approach exploits a set of "semantic templates", expressing information about elements of the OWL language (classes, properties, individuals, restrictions, etc.). As explained in the following sections, our approach relies on semantic templates, linked to the domain ontology. However, differently from the above-mentioned work, in ARNEIS templates represent (skeleton of) domain knowledge fragments instead of meta-model elements.

Other works concerned with user interaction with formal representations are authoring tools: in these cases the UI is aimed at enabling the user to design and populate a complex knowledge structure such as an ontology (e.g. [25], Protégé: http://protege.stanford.edu/). However, ARNEIS users are not expert in knowledge representation and they could find it difficult to interact with an authoring system, even if provided with a smart (maybe graphical) UI.

Some approaches to Semantic Search study ontology-based Information Retrieval (IR) systems, i.e. systems in which both resources and user queries are represented in a formal semantic language. For example [28] proposes a resource model based on various integrated ontologies, expressed in OWL, enabling resources (documents) representation in terms of ontology elements (i.e., entities and axioms). As discussed by the authors, the issue of how to acquire formal semantic representations of resources is still open. Some steps have been made towards the automatic extraction of such representations from (textual) documents (e.g., [3], [11]), but the results in this field are still not completely satisfactory, especially in those contexts in which complex and detailed concepts should be extracted, as in ARNEIS. As an alternative, "a manual approach can be undertaken" [28], p. 65. In particular, a manual approach makes sense in those cases in which resources are not already available as documents. For instance, in the ARNEIS scenario, a software house may have only simple brochures describing its software products, and thus it seems to be reasonable to provide it with a tool supporting the construction of a formal semantic representation describing their software products, which can be handled as resources by an ontology-based IR system. Our proposal is as a step in this direction.

3.2   User Interaction in the ARNEIS System

In order to face the issue regarding the choice of the most suited user interface for the ARNEIS system, we initially opted for on-line forms, since they are very familiar to Web users; see [7]. In particular, a form-based UI seems to be suited for ICT company users, which are usually skilled enough about the functional and technological aspects of their software products or services. Moreover, such users are probably used to Web-based interaction, often consisting in a sequence of on-line forms. Finally, such users may be motivated to complete a possibly boring task like filling in long on-line forms, since they are describing the software solutions they offer, and this can be viewed as an effective promotion of their products and services.

However, typical users from SME interacting with ARNEIS in order to look for software solutions supporting their CRM activities are not technical experts and they can be in trouble in filling in large on-line forms, possibly requiring technical skills in order to be completed. Thus, on the basis of the results of the additional interview with SME representatives mentioned in Section 2.2, we designed two different types of UI for these users: (a) a UI based on a graphical representation of business processes (BP), based on the idea that business processes are the form in which some companies think about their business and management activities; (b) a Natural Language (NL) UI, in which the SME users can freely express their requirements using natural language texts. These two UI will be available to users from SME as a possible alternative to the form-based UI.

The user interaction supported by all the three types of UI should be based on an analysis of the way in which users (representatives from ICT companies and SME) talk about CRM. For this reason, as we mentioned in Section 2.2., in the domain analysis phase, besides Ontology requirements, we also identified dialog topics, (i.e., key concepts of the descriptions of software solution supporting CRM, and of the descriptions of CRM activities provided by SME), and the linguistic expressions used to refer to such dialog topics (see Section 2.2).

We will present an example to clarify how dialog topics are exploited in the system. One of the templates representing dialog topics we extracted from our analysis corresponds to the concept of "(dynamic) acquisition of data from (another) enterprise application" [1], which means that the described CRM software application can acquire data by directly communicating with another application. Such a general concept is instantiated in different documents/interviews with more specific concepts by various linguistic expressions: specific instances of this template include more specific concepts in place of "data" and in place of "enterprise application"; for example "real time acquisition of customers info from Ms Outlook", or "(management of) product records acquired from ERP software".

Within ARNEIS templates are represented as ontological concepts belonging to an *Application Ontology* [20] linked to the CRM Ontology.

A template represents a structured concept in which there are some *slots* (i.e., *variables*). By default, such slots are filled in by generic concepts (e.g. "data"), that can be replaced by more specific concepts (e.g. "product data").

Fig. 2 shows the OWL logical representation (generated by Protégé) of the Application Ontology class representing the template corresponding to the concept of "(dynamic) acquisition of data from (another) enterprise application".

Slots within a template are identified by adding to each concept that represents a default slot filler the expression *and S_i*, where S_i is a unique identifier (automatically generated) for that slot. Thus, for example, in Fig. 2 the expression *(CRM_element and S_1)* identifies a slot (labeled S_1) filled in, by default, by the *CRM_element* class (intuitively speaking, *CRM_element* represents all the items that are typically involved in CRM: customers, products, orders, sales, and so on). In order to express

---

[1] Within the ARNEIS system, templates do not have a linguistic form, but only a formal one (in OWL). For the sake of readability, here we provide also a rough linguistic "translation".

the acquisition of data about customers (e.g., "customers info"), in a template instantiation, the class *CRM_element* is replaced by a more specific one, i.e. *Customer* (subclass of *CRM_element*) and the expression *and S_1* is deleted; in order to express the acquisition of data about products (e.g., "product records"), *CRM_element* is replaced by *Product_or_service* (subclass of *CRM_element*).

It is worth stressing that the expression *and S_i* is used merely as a label, to identify slots within a template. This solution preserves the syntactic correctness of the OWL representation, without producing any odd semantic result, since not instantiated templates are never used in any form of semantic reasoning.

Templates based on dialog topics are the basis of the mechanism underlying all three UI we are going to describe in the following, i.e.: (a) the form-based UI devoted to the acquisition of descriptions of software solutions by ICT companies and available also to SME representatives; (b) the BPM-based UI available to SME users in order to provide ARNEIS with a description of their CRM activities in the form of business processes; (c) the study we carried on in order to evaluate the feasibility of a NL-based UI, enabling SME users to express their requirements about CRM support using natural language texts.

```
T₃
Software_process
and has_input some (Digital_encoding
      and encodes some (Information_object
           and refers_to some (CRM_Element and S₁) )
      and has_message_role some (Communication_to_software_processes
           and sees_as_encoder some (Software_process and execution_of some (Application_software and S₂) )
           and sees_as_sender some (Software_process and execution_of some (Application_software and S₃) ))
      and completely_realized_by some Information_realization_by_physical_bits
      and output_of some (Software_process
           and execution_of some (Application_software and S₄) ))
and has_output some (part_of some (Digital_encoding
           and encodes some (Information_in_CRM_system and S₅) ))
and has_decoder_role some (Communication_to_software_processes
      and sees_as_encoder some (Software_process and execution_of some (Application_software and S₆) )
      and sees_as_message some (Digital_encoding
           and encodes some (Information_object and refers_to some (CRM_Element and S₇) )
           and completely_realized_by some Information_realization_by_physical_bits
           and output_of some (Software_process and execution_of some (Application_software and S₈) ))
      and sees_as_sender some (Software_process
           and execution_of some (Application_software and S₉) ))
and has_receiver_role some (Communication_to_software_processes
      and sees_as_encoder some (Software_process and execution_of some (Application_software and S₁₀) )
      and sees_as_message some (Digital_encoding
           and encodes some (Information_object and refers_to some (CRM_Element and S₁₁) )
           and completely_realized_by some Information_realization_by_physical_bits
           and output_of some (Software_process and execution_of some (Application_software and S₁₂) ))
      and sees_as_sender some (Software_process and execution_of some (Application_software and S₁₃) ))
```

Fig. 2. "(Dynamic) acquisition of data from (another) enterprise application" template

Form-based UI. For each template, the UI Manager generates a set of Web-forms, aimed at eliciting the information needed for filling in the slots.[2]

In order to enable the UI Manager to generate the Web forms, the Knowledge Manager performs two (nested) steps:

---

[2] Since, typically, the knowledge on the basis of which such forms are generated does not change in time, Web forms are pre-compiled off-line; they are re-generated only in case the knowledge bases are modified.

(1) For each template in the Application Ontology, it extracts all the slots by looking for the expressions of the form *(C and S_i)*, where *C* is a named class of the reference Ontology.

(2) For each slot (identified by S_i), it extracts from the Ontology all the subclasses of *C* and provides the UI Manager with this information.

The UI Manager, in turn, generates a Web form in order to ask the user which subclass of *C* (if any) she wants to consider. For example, Fig. 3 shows the form asking the user to select the subclasses of *CRM_element*.

Would you like to acquire data concerning...

- O Sales_agents
- ⊙ Customers [view more]
- O Communications [view more]
- O Appointments

- O Estimates
- O Sales
- O Orders
- O Product_or_service offer

Fig. 3. Web form for filling in the first slot of the template corresponding to "(dynamic) acquisition of data from (another) enterprise application"

The user selects the desired subclass *(C_x)* and the UI Manager sends this information back to the Knowledge Manager, that substitutes C_x in place of *(C and S_i)* within the corresponding template slot. The result (that refers to the example presented above) is shown in Fig. 4.

Software_process
and has_input some (Digital_encoding
and encodes some (Information_object
and refers_to some Customer)

Fig. 4. Part of the instantiated template after the user answer

There are some issues to be faced in order to make this mechanism work: we will briefly comment them in the following.

The knowledge engineer who configures ARNEIS on a new domain is in charge of defining the Application Ontology containing the templates. When doing this, she identifies the slots and, for each slot, she provides a natural language question that will be used by the UI Manager to generate the form referring to that slot (e.g., "Would you like to acquire data concerning..." in Fig. 3). The link between the slot S_i within the template T_j *($T_j.S_i$)* and the corresponding question is stored in a *Configuration KB* which is accessed by the UI Manager during the form generation process.

When filling in the forms, the user may want to specify a more specific class (e.g., she wants to acquire data about golden customers, which are represented, within the Ontology, by the class *Golden_customer*, subclass of *Customer*).When extracting from the Ontology all the subclasses of *C* (step (2) mentioned above), the Knowledge Manager actually extracts not only the direct subclasses of *C*, but the whole subtree. The UI Manager, on the basis of this information, includes a link to enable the user to optionally expand the subtree ("view more" links in Fig. 3): in this way she is enabled to select any (direct or indirect) subclass she is interested in.

However, given the complexity of the Ontology, listing all the (named) subclasses of a given class C could result in a too long list, containing concepts that are relevant from the formal point of view, but not from the user perspective. For this reason, the knowledge engineer can add to the Configuration KB, for each slot $T_j.S_i$, a list of the (direct and indirect) subclasses of C that should be asked to the user, as shown for example in (1)[3]:

$$T_3.S_1 \rightarrow \{ \text{Sales\_agent, Customer, ...} \} . \tag{1}$$

The final issue to discuss concerns the dependencies between slots. It is quite common that the suited value for filling in a slot depends on the value assigned to another slot (of the same template). In the example above (see Fig. 2), if we fill in slot S_1 with *Customer* (meaning that we want to acquire information about customers) slot S_5 (representing the knowledge structure that is modified by the data acquisition) has to be filled in with *Customer_database*. In order to take into account possible dependencies between slot fillers, the Configuration KB contains if-then rules representing such dependencies, as shown for instance in (2):

$$\text{IF } T_3.S_1 = \text{Customer THEN } T_3.S_5 = \text{Customer\_database}. \tag{2}$$

These dependency rules enable the UI Manager to avoid asking the user useless questions: after having asked the filler for slot S_1, slots S_5 will be filled in automatically.

When the user has completed all the forms proposed by the ARNEIS system, the instantiated templates are saved in the Semantic Descr KB (see Section 2.1): the set of such instantiated templates is the OWL representation of the software solution supporting CRM, proposed by an ICT company, or the set of user requirements, provided by a SME.

BPM-based UI. SME users, besides the UI based on on-line forms, can choose the BPM-based UI. In this last case, the user can draw a diagram representing the CRM business processes of her SME, using the tool she prefers. The only requirements are that the output diagram must be compliant with BPM Notation (http://www.bpmn.org/) and must be exportable in XPDL (http://www.wfmc.org/xpdl.html). When the diagram representing the CRM process is ready and saved as an XPDL file, the user can upload it on the ARNEIS server. The UI Manager acquires the XPDL file and, on the basis of the information it contains, it "re-draws" the diagram in a Web page, as shown in Fig. 5. When the user clicks on an activity, she accesses the tagging page, shown in Fig. 6, that presents her the list of available *semantic tags* (see section 2.2), among which she can select those to be associated to the activity in focus. For instance, in the page shown in Fig. 5 the user selected the "customer contact" ("contatto cliente") activity and, in the following page (Fig. 6), she associated the semantic tag "multichannel communication" to this activity.

---

[3] The Configuration KB is an XML document; here we show its content in a more readable way.

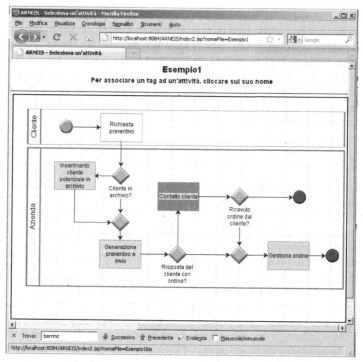

Fig. 5. The BPM-based UI: selecting an activity

Each semantic tag is associated to one or more (possibly instantiated) templates. As a consequence, the user tagging activity corresponds to template selection and thus results in a set of template instances that represent the semantic (OWL) representation of the SME requirements concerning CRM. The OWL representation of the SME requirements is then compared with the software descriptions stored in the Software Repository by the Matching Engine (see Section 2.1).

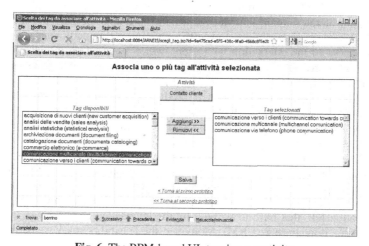

Fig. 6. The BPM-based UI: tagging an activity

NL-based UI. The study to evaluate the feasibility of a Natural Language (NL) UI started from an analysis of the type of texts that users could provide to the system. We thus asked SME representatives who indicated NL as the preferred interaction modality (see Section 2.2) to provide us with textual descriptions of their CRM activities and needs. On the basis of these texts, and taking into account the various NLP approaches that emerged from a preliminary survey, we advanced the hypothesis of exploiting Information Extraction (IE) techniques [9], to extract from NL texts the information needed by ARNEIS.

The UI we designed contains a number of questions referring to CRM activities (e.g., "Which are the main activities for Customer Relationship Management, within your company?"). The user can answer these questions by inserting (or uploading) free texts, which are then sent to the ARNEIS interpretation module (which is an additional module within the Knowledge Manager). Such a module takes as input the user answers, extracts relevant information and builds the OWL representation of the description of CRM activities, representing SME requirements, to be matched with the OWL representation of CRM software descriptions.

The goal of the IE phase is to instantiate the templates representing dialog topics. This phase is based on semantic rules that extract from the text the information needed to fill in the template slots. For instance, the IE module contains a semantic rule that matches various linguistic patterns that refer to "(dynamic) acquisition of data from (another) enterprise application" (e.g., "real time acquisition of customers info from Ms Outlook", or "management of product records acquired from ERP software"); the results of the application of such a rule is an instantiated template (see the fragment shown in Fig. 4).

4   Discussion and Conclusions

In this paper, we described the management of the user interaction within the ARNEIS system, an "intelligent" Web-based repository of descriptions of software solutions. ARNEIS enables ICT companies to upload a description of their software solutions supporting CRM, and SME to find software products or services supporting their CRM activities. The functionality of ARNEIS is based on a semantic representation of the domain knowledge, which represents the shared vocabulary to express both software descriptions and SME requirements. In particular, we described the management of the interaction with users, which is based on the instantiation of templates that represents *dialog topics*. Different types of user interfaces (i.e., form-based, BPM-based, and NL-based) enable software houses to upload the semantic representation of the description of their products or services and SME to express their requirements concerning CRM support.

The approach we proposed within the ARNEIS scenario suggests a general solution to face the issue of how to build formal representations of resources in a those systems based on semantic technologies. However, our approach is strongly based on a domain analysis that takes into account how users talk about their business activities and the software applications that could support such activities. In fact, the mechanism described in this chapter relies on templates stored in an Application Ontology and on a Configuration KB, that have to be built by the knowledge engineer who configures the system on a domain (e.g., CRM). Moreover, the feasibility study we carried on the NL-based UI, showed that in such a type of UI there is an additional effort, i.e., the definition of the semantic rules devoted to the extraction of the information needed to instantiate the templates These tasks could represent a considerable knowledge acquisition effort. However, the definition of templates and Configuration KB, as well as the definition of extraction rules for the NL-based UI, are typically done once and usually do not require frequent updates. Moreover, the Configuration KB definition can be easily supported by a user-friendly tool that provides the knowledge engineer with simple mechanisms supported by system defaults. The development of such a tool, supporting the knowledge engineer in the system configuration on new domains, is an issue of major importance, given that the knowledge acquisition effort is a key challenge of knowledge-based systems like ARNEIS.

References

1. Alonso, G., Casati, F., Kuno, H., Machiraju, V.: Web Services. Springer, Heidelberg (2004)
2. Antoniou, G., Van Harmelen, F.: A Semantic Web Primer. The MIT Press, Cambridge (2004)
3. Banko, M., Cafarella, M.J., Soderland, S., Broadhead, M., Etzioni, O.: Open Information Extraction from the Web. In: 20th International Joint Conference on Artificial Intelligence, pp. 2670–2676. Morgan Kaufmann, San Francisco (2007)
4. Bao, J., Smart, P.R., Braines, D., Shadbolt, N.R.: A Controlled Natural Language Interface for Semantic Media Wiki Using the Rabbit Language. In: Workshop on Controlled Natural Language. CEUR, Aachen (2009)
5. Benjamins, V.R.: Near-Term Prospects for Semantic Technologies. IEEE Intelligent Systems 23(1), 76–88 (2008)
6. Bernstein, A., Kaufmann, E.: GINO - A Guided Input Natural Language Ontology Editor. In: Cruz, I., Decker, S., Allemang, D., Preist, C., Schwabe, D., Mika, P., Uschold, M., Aroyo, L.M. (eds.) ISWC 2006. LNCS, vol. 4273, pp. 144–157. Springer, Heidelberg (2006)
7. Bhagdev, R., Chakravarthy, A., Chapman, S., Ciravegna, F., Lanfranchi, V.: Creating and Using Organisational Semantic Webs in Large Networked Organisations. In: Sheth, A.P., Staab, S., Dean, M., Paolucci, M., Maynard, D., Finin, T., Thirunarayan, K. (eds.) ISWC 2008. LNCS, vol. 5318, pp. 723–736. Springer, Heidelberg (2008)
8. Bhagdev, R., Chapman, S., Ciravegna, F., Lanfranchi, V., Petrelli, D.: Hybrid Search: Effectively Combining Keywords and Semantic Searches. In: Bechhofer, S., Hauswirth, M., Hoffmann, J., Koubarakis, M. (eds.) ESWC 2008. LNCS, vol. 5021, pp. 554–568. Springer, Heidelberg (2008)
9. Cunningham, H.: Automatic Information Extraction. In: Brown, K. (ed.) Encyclopedia of Language and Linguistics, 2nd edn., pp. 665–677. Elsevier, Amsterdam (2005)
10. Cimiano, P., Haase, P., Heizmann, J., Mantel, M.: ORAKEL: A Portable Natural Language Interface to Knowledge Bases. Data & Knowledge Engineering 65(2), 325–354 (2008)
11. Cimiano, P., Mädche, A., Staab, S., Völker, J.: Ontology Learning. In: Staab, S., Studer, R. (eds.) Handbook on Ontologies, 2nd edn., pp. 245–267. Springer, Heidelberg (2009)
12. Creeger, M.: CTO Roundtable: Cloud Computing. Communications of the ACM 52(8), 50–65 (2009)
13. Cregan, A., Schwitter, R., Meyer, T.: Sydney OWL Syntax – towards a Controlled Natural Language Syntax for OWL 1.1. In: Third International Workshop on OWL: Experiences and Directions. CEUR, Aachen (2007)

14. Damljanovic, D., Agatonovic, M., Cunningham, H.: Natural Language Interfaces to Ontologies: Combining Syntactic Analysis and Ontology-Based Lookup through the User Interaction. In: Aroyo, L., Antoniou, G., Hyvönen, E., ten Teije, A., Stuckenschmidt, H., Cabral, L., Tudorache, T. (eds.) ESWC 2010, Part I. LNCS, vol. 6088, pp. 106–120. Springer, Heidelberg (2010)
15. Dikaiakos, M.D., Pallis, G., Katsaros, D., Mehra, P., Vakali, A.: Cloud Computing. Distributed Internet Computing for IT and Scientific Research. IEEE Internet Computing 13(5), 10–13 (2009)
16. Freeland, J.: The Ultimate CRM Handbook. McGraw-Hill, New York (2005)
17. Fuchs, N.E., Kaljurand, K., Kuhn, T.: Attempto Controlled. English for Knowledge Representation. In: Baroglio, C., Bonatti, P.A., Małuszyński, J., Marchiori, M., Polleres, A., Schaffert, S. (eds.) Reasoning Web 2008. LNCS, vol. 5224, pp. 104–124. Springer, Heidelberg (2008)
18. Funk, A., Tablan, V., Bontcheva, K., Cunningham, H., Davis, B., Handschuh, S.: CLOnE: Controlled Language for Ontology Editing. In: Aberer, K., Choi, K.-S., Noy, N., Allemang, D., Lee, K.-I., Nixon, L.J.B., Golbeck, J., Mika, P., Maynard, D., Mizoguchi, R., Schreiber, G., Cudré-Mauroux, P. (eds.) ASWC 2007 and ISWC 2007. LNCS, vol. 4825, pp. 142–155. Springer, Heidelberg (2007)
19. Goy, A., Magro, D., Prato, F.: ARNEIS: A Web-based Intelligent Repository of ICT Solutions for E-business. In: 10th Int. ACM Conference on Information Integration and Web-Based Application & Services, pp. 403–406. ACM Press, New York (2008)
20. Guarino, N.: Understanding, Building and Using Ontologies. Int. Journal of Human-Computer Studies 46, 293–310 (1997)
21. Hart, G., Johnson, M., Dolbear, C.: Rabbit: Developing a Control Natural Language for Authoring Ontologies. In: Bechhofer, S., Hauswirth, M., Hoffmann, J., Koubarakis, M. (eds.) ESWC 2008. LNCS, vol. 5021, pp. 348–360. Springer, Heidelberg (2008)
22. Lesmo, L., Robaldo, L.: From Natural Language to Databases via Ontologies. In: 5th International Conference on Language Resources and Evaluation, pp. 1460–1465 (2006)
23. Magro, D., Goy, A.: The Business Knowledge for Customer Relationship Management: an Ontological Perspective. In: 1st Int. ACM Workshop on Ontology-Supported Business Intelligence. ACM Press, New York (2008)
24. Magro, D., Goy, A.: Towards a first Ontology for Customer Relationship Management. In: 1st IEEE/ACM Workshop on Applied Ontologies in Distributed Systems, pp. 637–643. ACM Press, New York (2008)
25. Rector, A.L., Drummond, N., Horridge, M., Rogers, J., Knublauch, H., Stevens, R., Wang, H., Wroe, C.: Designing User Interfaces to Minimise Common Errors in Ontology Development: The CO-ODE and HyOntUse Projects. In: 3rd UK E-Science All Hands Meeting, pp. 493–499. EPSRC, Swindon (2004)
26. Schwitter, R.: Controlled Natural Languages for Knowledge Representation. In: 23rd International Conference on Computational Linguistics, pp. 1113–1121 (2010)
27. Thoméré, J., Barker, K., Chaudhri, V., Clark, P., Eriksen, M., Mishra, S., Portr, B., Rodriguez, A.: A Web-based Ontology Browsing and Editing System. In: 18th AAAI National Conference on Artificial Intelligence, pp. 927–934. AAAI Press, Menlo Park (2002)
28. Tran, T., Bloehdorn, S., Cimiano, P., Haase, P.: Expressive Resource Descriptions for Ontology-Based Information Retrieval. In: 1st International Conference on the Theory of Information Retrieval, pp. 55–68. Alma Mater Foundation for Information Society, Budapest (2007)
29. Tran, T., Cimiano, P., Rudolph, S., Studer, R.: Ontology-Based Interpretation of Keywords for Semantic Search. In: Aberer, K., Choi, K.-S., Noy, N., Allemang, D., Lee, K.-I., Nixon, L.J.B., Golbeck, J., Mika, P., Maynard, D., Mizoguchi, R., Schreiber, G., Cudré-Mauroux, P. (eds.) ASWC 2007 and ISWC 2007. LNCS, vol. 4825, pp. 523–536. Springer, Heidelberg (2007)

Vizgr: Linking Data in Visualizations

Daniel Hienert, Benjamin Zapilko, Philipp Schaer, and Brigitte Mathiak

GESIS – Leibniz Institute for the Social Sciences, Lennéstr. 30, 53113, Bonn, Germany
{Daniel.Hienert,Benjamin.Zapilko,Philipp.Schaer,
Brigitte.Mathiak}@gesis.org

Abstract. Working with data can be very abstract without a proper visualization. Yet, once the data is visualized, it presents a dead end, so the user has to return to the data level to make enrichments. With Vizgr (vizgr.org), we offer an elegant simplification to this workflow by giving the opportunity to enrich the data in the visualization itself. Data, e.g. statistical data, data entered by the user, from DBpedia or other data sources, can be visualized by graphs, tag clouds, on maps and in timelines. The data points can be connected with each other, with data in other visualizations and any web address, regardless of the source. It allows users to make data presentations without changing to the data level, once the data is in the system. In an evaluation, we found that over 85% of the participants were able to use and understand this technology without any training or explicit instructions.

Keywords: Visualization, Web, Linked visualizations, Social software, Social data analysis, Collaboration, Visual analytics.

1 Introduction

Presenting data in an appealing or at least understandable way is a common task in the modern working environment. While the classical business application is presenting company data to support decision making, it has also become important in any teaching job or marketing. The reason for this is that raw data that can be found in databases is easy to collect, but the pure tables are hard to understand.

Since it is such a widespread task, it is clear that most of the people that are making such visualizations are not experts in data visualization or statistics. They are domain experts on the data they want to present and this data is typically complex and interconnected.

The classical spreadsheet approach often does not adequately represent either the complexity or the interconnectedness. Also, the people who are typically using such applications are not willing to learn complex data-centered techniques to represent this interconnectedness, as they are typically just modifying the data so it can be visualized more appropriately.

The solution to this dilemma is the option to interconnect the visualizations directly. Since the visualized data is what users are thinking of anyway when handling the large arrays of data, it is only logical to allow them to work on the visualizations directly.

J. Filipe and J. Cordeiro (Eds.): WEBIST 2011, LNBIP 101, pp. 177–191, 2012.

In Vizgr, we allow users to interconnect their data visualizations like they could do with any other object on the Internet. The web-based framework allows sharing of visualizations (connecting to people), connecting visualizations with each other on a data level and connecting visualizations with web resources to fully embed it into the World Wide Web.

As our survey shows, the user acceptance and usability of Vizgr is very high. Most of the participants can imagine scenarios in which they would like to use this tool in their daily work.

In the next few sections, we will, first, discuss related products and ideas. In section three, we will give an overview on the capabilities and technical details of Vizgr. We will proceed in section four with some use cases we have been studying. In section five we present the survey and the results of the survey we have conducted, to investigate both the usability of the tool and the usability of the idea. We conclude with some final remarks.

2   Related Work

Vizgr integrates the key ideas of collaborative sharing of visualizations on the web, the coordinated views of multiple visualizations on one web page and extends the concept to manual, semiautomatic and automatic linking of visualizations for browsing and coordination purposes. In this section, we first present related systems and their key ideas and conclude how Vizgr distinguishes to them.

2.1   Visualization on the Web

IBM Many Eyes [1], Data360 [2] and Socrata [3] are online tools for sharing data and visualizations on the web. The user can upload data, choose a visualization type and create a visualization that can be viewed and commented by the community. By integrating an HTML snippet the visualization can be embedded on other sites or blogs. The underlying data set can be reused by other users to build their own visualizations. Heer et al. [4] gives an overview of online visualization tools, their functionality and impacts. There are a number of Visualization Toolkits, which provide functionality to create visualizations in different programming languages and with different priorities, i.e. the InfoVis Toolkit [5], Prefuse [6], Flare [7], Processing [8], Protovis [9] and the Google Chart Tools [10].

VisGets [11] uses different visualizations to show and filter retrieved web resources in several dimensions like time, location and topic. Based on the concept of dynamic queries, results can interactively be filtered by manipulating the visualizations. VisGets also implements coordinated interactivity. Hovering with the mouse over a visual element highlights all related elements in the visualizations and in the result list. The new introduced approach of Weighted Brushing is used to highlight strongly related items more than weakly related ones.

Tableau [12] or Spotfire [13] are commercial solutions which also allow creating dashboards with different visualizations. Dashiki [14] is a wiki-based collaborative platform for creating visualization dashboards. Users can integrate visualizations that contain live connections to data sources. Data sets are embedded into data pages by a special markup, via Copy & Paste from spreadsheets or by an URL. Live data is dynamically fetched and stripped from formatting tags, so the user can wrap the content with needed markup. Dashiki uses a simple technical approach for coordinated selecting among multiple views. Simple attribute-value pairs are propagated to all visualizations via JSON format.

Exhibit [15] is a lightweight framework for easy publishing of structured data on the web. Users can import data via JSON, which is presented on the web page in different views including maps, table, thumbnails and timelines.

2.2 Coordinated Views

Wang Baldonado [16] set up a model for coordinated multiple views and provide guidelines for not disrupting the positive effect through increased complexity. The main idea is that data in different views can be linked. If data is selected in one view, it is also highlighted in other views (brushing-and-linking).

North & Shneiderman [17] provide an alternative visualization model which is based on the relational data model. The system Snap [18] is an implementation of this model. It allows the user to select databases and assign visualizations. In a second step, the user can then connect different visualizations and generate coordinated visualizations. Highlighting or other actions are coordinated between the different views. For example, if data is selected in one view it is also selected in the other views. In Improvise [19] users can create multi-view visualizations with a visual abstraction language that allows a finer control of the appearance of data in different coordinated views by selection or navigation interaction.

VisLink [20] is a system for revealing relationships amongst different visualizations. Multiple visualizations are drawn on 2D planes and can be placed in a 3D space. Relationships are displayed between them by propagating edges from one visualization to another. Relationships, connections and patterns between these visualizations can be explored by several interaction techniques.

2.3 Unique Features of Vizgr

Vizgr is similar in certain aspects to the presented systems, but differs in some others. On a basic level Vizgr can create visualizations like the aforementioned systems. However, most tools concentrate on one or some information types like tabular data, text, maps and so on; in contrast Vizgr supports heterogeneous information types like tabular data, text, locations, events and network data and heterogeneous visualizations like business graphics, tag clouds, maps, timelines and network graphs in one tool. Vizgr supports the user with easy creation of visualizations with different forms, possibilities for copy & paste from spreadsheets and automatic data import from Wikipedia.

Similar to Dashiki and Exhibit Vizgr supports the integration of several visualizations on one webpage. But in contrast to those systems, the selection of visualizations in Vizgr is based on the relationships between visualizations.

Vizgr has a similar approach to highlight related visual items in different visualizations to VisGets or Dashiki. But in Vizgr the coordinated view is not only based on the same data items in different visualizations, but also on relationship data.

A completely new aspect in Vizgr is the support for the manual, semiautomatic and automatic mapping of heterogeneous visualization types and from visualizations to web resources. This allows the creation of networks of visualizations for browsing and coordination purposes.

3   Vizgr

In the following section we describe the architecture of Vizgr and the workflows to create and map visualizations to each other and to websites. We introduce the browsing approach and the possibility of coordinated views.

Vizgr includes components to create, view, modify, save and connect visualizations. Figure 1 gives an overview of the system's architecture. All modules are integrated in a web framework, which is implemented in PHP. The creation and editing of visualizations can be done in one single HTML form, the workflow and exact details are described in section 3.1. The entered data is stored in the user session and in the Vizgr database. In a second step the user can either connect two visualizations to each other or a visualization to web resources. The workflows for connecting visualizations are further described in section 3.2. Connection data is also stored in the user session and in the database. Visualization data and properties are committed to the visualization component via XML. The framework creates an XML file that contains all information that is necessary for the visualization component to create the visualization, set the linking icons and mark individual items.

The core component for building and viewing the visualization is a Flash application that is implemented in ActionScript 3. We have chosen Flash, because it is widely distributed, does not need any preloading time to start a virtual machine and offers all available possibilities to implement advanced graphics and user interaction. The module parses the XML and builds the appropriate visualization.

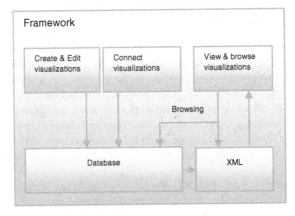

Fig. 1. Vizgr system overview

3.1   Creating Visualization

The user can create different visualizations with the help of an HTML form. For creating a visualization the user has to go through four steps: (i) enter a title, (ii) enter a description, (iii) enter data and (iv) choose a visualization type. As a result, a preview of the created visualization is shown. All steps are accomplished in one single HTML form. This makes it possible to edit and correct certain entries and to see the result immediately in the preview. Title and description are metadata fields the user can fill out to identify and describe the visualization. Data can be entered with (i) different data input templates belonging to the information type, (ii) by copy and paste from spreadsheets or (iii) by automatically loading the data from Wikipedia or the DBpedia database.

For small amounts of data the user can enter the information manually. The framework offers data input templates for (i) tabular data, (ii) text, (iii) locations, (iv) events and (v) network data. The tabular data template is structured like an excel sheet. The user can enter different attributes and the respective data. Textual data can be entered simply by copying it into a text field. The location template offers fields for title, description and address details like street, house number, post code, city and country. The framework has a built in geocoder to add latitude and longitude information to the record. Events can be entered with the attributes title, description, start and end date. The network data template is a simplified table data template with three columns. Related nodes can be entered in columns one and two. Column three is an optional field for entering the relationship between nodes.

Copy and Paste from spreadsheets is appropriate for large data collections already available in CSV (Comma Separated Values) format, like for example finance data from Yahoo. For locations, events and network data the user has to format the columns in a certain order. Then data can just be marked in the spreadsheet, copied to the clipboard and pasted in the form.

For the information types text, location and event exist the possibility to load the data directly from Wikipedia and the DBpedia database that offers structured information from Wikipedia articles. To get the text of a Wikipedia article the user can enter a topic in the search field. Via an autocomplete list the user can identify existing topics and choose one. With a click on a button the text is loaded and can be used for tag clouds. The benefit is that links to other Wikipedia articles are automatically extracted and provided by linking icons (further described in section 3.3). For locations on a map the user can enter different location names in the fields. Coordinates, description and links are loaded from DBpedia. The user is again supported by an autocomplete list of relevant topics. For events in a specific time period the user can enter a start and an end date. Vizgr checks for appropriate events in the DBpedia database that can be visualized in a timeline.

Depending on the chosen information type, the framework offers appropriate visualization types. Figure 2 shows the different types of visualization which can be created. For tabular data as follows: line chart, area chart, bar chart, pie chart, scatter plot; for text: tag cloud and 3D tag cloud; for locations: a Google map; for events: a timeline; and for network data: a network graph. Users can choose visualization types and see the created visualization in the preview section.

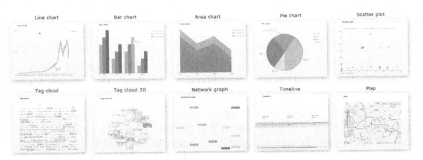

Fig. 2. An overview of visualizations that can be created with Vizgr: for tabular data: line chart, bar chart, area chart, pie chart, scatter plot; for text: tag cloud and 3D tag cloud; for network data: a network graph; for events: a timeline; and for locations: a Google map.

3.2   Connecting Visualizations

In order to connect two visualizations, some kind of relationship data is needed. This can be automatically derived, e.g. from relational data in a database, an RDF store or by a matching attribute/value pair in a table. Also an editor for entering and editing the relations by hand is provided. The editor is directly based on the created visualization and is thus seamlessly integrated into the workflow of creating and viewing visualizations. Vizgr supports the connection of all its visualization types.

Connecting Two Visualizations. Graphical objects of two different visualizations can be manually connected using the Mapping Editor. The system supports the user by making suggestions for possible connections.

Graphical objects of the different types of visualization are, for example, a location marker on a map or a bar in a bar chart. A graphical object or glyph represents several data fields or properties in one simple graphical representation. The Mapping Editor utilizes this to simplify the mapping process. The user does not have to deal with the complex information structure on a data level, but can select graphical objects directly in the visualization. For the simple identification of a graphical object, the user receives additional information in a popup window by hovering with the mouse.

The user interface is organized as follows: at the top, the two chosen visualizations are shown side by side. The visualizations appear with the same functionality as in the view modus, this means that information for the graphical object is available by hovering with the mouse. A list of the connected graphical objects can be found below the visualizations. On the left side, each record displays the graphical object value of the origin visualization, and on the right side, the visual object value of the target visualization. A button is available to delete each record. There are buttons for Save, Cancel and Suggest Mapping actions at the bottom of the list. Figure 3 gives an overview of the Mapping Editor.

The first step in the mapping workflow is to choose the visualizations to be connected. To create a connection, a graphical object from the left or right visualization is selected. Objects that are available for selection are marked with a thin red border when moused over. Clicking the mouse selects the object and it is then marked with a thicker, red border. Moving the mouse towards the target visualization makes a red connection line appear that will visually connect the origin and target object. Clicking the mouse a second time will select the target object. Once a connection has been created, it appears in the list and is visible in the visualizations as two marked objects.

All connections are similarly color-coded in the visualization and in the list. This allows connections to be easily identified, for example, to find them in the visualization in order to delete them from the list. Clicking *Save* completes the workflow. The two visualizations are now connected, and the mapping process can be continued for other visualizations. All created connections can again be loaded into the Mapping Editor and edited.

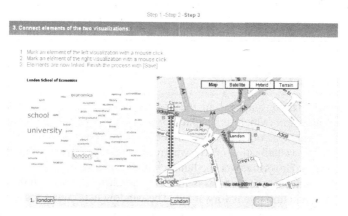

Fig. 3. The Mapping Editor: mapping the word London in a tag cloud to the place on a map

Semiautomatic Mapping. The system can support the manual mapping process by making suggestions for connections between information items. By clicking on the button *Suggest Mapping* the system analyses the underlying data set and shows possible links in the visualization and in the mapping table. The user can check these mappings and delete unwanted links.

The algorithm for automatic search of mappings works by pre-processing the underlying data for both visualizations. For graphics with tabular data we build an array of attribute/value pairs in a simple format. The mappings are created on a graphical level, but visual elements need a different number of attribute/value pairs to be visually created and identified for different visualizations. For tag clouds, we take the whole text, for Google maps the title and description and so on. Text elements are again split into single words. The algorithm then checks for every array element if there is an equal element in the array of the other visualization.

For example, if we connect a network graph of persons with a visualization of a timeline with publications, for every network node value the system searches for any occurrence of the name in the title or description. Meaning that all names are compared to all publications and immediately connected if a match is found.

Connecting a Visualization to Web Resources. Connecting items of visualizations to web resources offers the possibility to create links from visual items to any resource on the web. This can be websites, DOIs for literature references, queries to web APIs or visualizations in other portals. IBM ManyEyes e.g. supports addressing different states of visualizations via URL. The benefit is that visualizations and their visual items are included in the process of web hyperlinking and thus elevated from being fixed non-interactive illustrations.

Connecting visualizations to URLs works similar to the workflow described for connecting two visualizations. The user chooses a visualization in the gallery. Now he can mark any graphical object in the visualization with a mouse click. The object is then highlighted with a colored border. For every marked object a list element appears where on the left side appears the object's name and on the right side one can enter a title and an URL for a website. The elements in the list are also visually connected with a frame in the same color as in the visualization. The user can continue the process until he finishes it with a click on the save button. He then can have a look at the created connections in the visualization or start a new mapping process. The connections are listed in the personal area and can be edited later.

3.3   Browsing in Visualizations

All created visualizations appear in the gallery with title and thumbnails. Users choose a visualization which is displayed with functionality to edit, share and comment. If a graphical object in the source visualization is connected to another object in any target visualization or to a web resource, it is marked with a linking icon (compare figure 4). Hovering over the button with the mouse pointer shows a window with the explanation that the element is linked to another visualization or website and with a click on the button one is forwarded. The window lists connected visualizations with title, visualization type and thumbnail and websites with title and URL. If the element has just one connection, clicking the button directly forwards the user to the connected visualization or website. Otherwise if a graphical object has connections to other, multiple visualizations or websites, a click on the button opens again a window listing the target visualizations by title and visualization type and websites by title and URL. The related visual element in the target visualization is highlighted with a red border. The target object is also marked with the linking icon, which leads directly back to the origin visualization or other related visualizations and websites.

Fig. 4. Hovering over the linking icon of New York City shows a window with a link to the tag cloud of the Wikipedia article

3.4   Coordinated Multiple Views

Beside the possibility to explore relations between visualizations by browsing from one to another in full view, the original and all related visualizations are also shown on the individual visualization page in half the scale. This way it is possible to see at once multiple related visualizations. Based on the approach of highlighting the same data item in different views, we choose an approach to highlight connected data in the different heterogeneous visualizations. Hovering the mouse pointer over a linked visual item in the original visualization highlights all connected items in the connected visualizations with a green frame (compare figure 5). If these items are linked to other items again, they send secondary events to all related visualizations that appear with a yellow frame. So, the user can interactively explore which visualizations are directly or indirectly connected to the chosen item. For example, when hovering with the mouse pointer over a person in a network graph, the connected location on the map is highlighted with a green frame. The location itself is connected with several events on a timeline that are highlighted with a yellow frame. The user can see that the person is indirectly connected with these events.

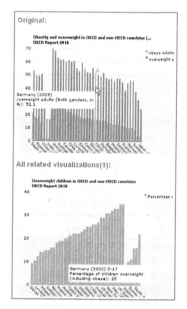

Fig. 5. Coordinated Multiple Views: Hovering with the mouse pointer over a graphical object highlights all related object in other views

4   Use Cases

In this section we demonstrate the capabilities of Vizgr by giving two examples of visualization that can be produced within minutes. Simple mappings produce graphics showing relationships which may be retrievable in the web. But with Vizgr they are much easier to explore and produce. In our first example, we show relationships between 60 years stock prices and historical events on financial crisis. Relationships between minima and maxima of stock prices and related historical events can be explored with a mouse click. Our second example is also the basis scenario for our user study. We show the workflows to create a tag cloud and a map of chosen Wikipedia data and connect the visualizations to each other and to the web.

In the first example, we connect a line chart of historical data for S&P 500 stocks with historical events on financial crisis on a timeline. The stock data is taken from Yahoo, consists of about 15,000 rows of daily adjusted closing stock prices from 1950 to 2009. The data is entered via Copy & Paste from the provided CSV file. Selected historical events on financial crisis with title, details, start and end date is entered manually. In a second step, we connect the visualizations in the Mapping Editor. Both data sets have a date field, so the system propose a mapping automatically. The result is a line chart with historical stock prices connected with a timeline of historical events on financial crisis. The user can click on certain points of the line charts maxima and minima marked with the linking icon. A click forwards to the appropriate historical event on the timeline which is highlighted with a red rectangle. A click on an event leads back to the appropriate stock price of that date. Figure 6 shows the line chart with historical stock prices and the timeline with historical events across financial crisis. The visualizations could be connected simple and fast and result in interactive linked visualizations that can be explored with a mouse click.

In our second example we show the workflow to create two visualizations from Wikipedia data, connect them to each other and to a website. First visualization is a tag cloud of the Wikipedia article on *London School of Economics*. We choose *Create Visualization* and enter a title and a description for the visualization. In the data input menu we choose *Wikipedia*. We now enter the first letters of *London School of Economics* and Vizgr proposes matching articles from Wikipedia in a drop down list. We select the entry with the mouse and click on *Load text from Wikipedia*. In the next step we choose *tag cloud* as a visualization type and click on *Create* to see the preview. The visualization has been created and can now be saved. Second visualization is a map with Wikipedia data from *London*. The workflow is similar: enter a title and a description, choose *Wikipedia*, then *Places*. We enter the first letters of *London*, choose the matching article from the drop down list and click on *Load places from Wikipedia*. *Map* is already chosen as a visualization type; we can click on create and save the visualization. Now both visualizations can be connected in the Mapping Editor. Therefore we choose *Connect Visualizations* from the main menu. We choose both visualizations from the drop down lists. In the Mapping Editor we click in the tag cloud on the word London and a second click on the location marker of London in the map. The visualizations now are already connected and the mapping can be saved. Then we connect the word London in the tag cloud to a website. Therefore we choose the menu entry *Connect visualization with websites* to enter the Mapping Editor. We choose the visualization and mark the word London with a mouse click. We now can enter a title and an URL of a website and save the connection. The visualizations now have multiple connections to other resources of which some were created automatically. The tag cloud contains links to Wikipedia for every word that represent a Wikipedia article, the location London in the map links to related websites. The visualizations are linked to each other and additionally we have created a link from London to a related website manually. Within minutes we have what could serve as a info graphic for tourism etc.

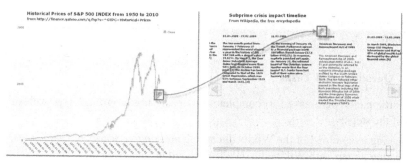

Fig. 6. The left visualization presents historical stock prices of S&P 500 index in a line chart. The right visualization shows events on the financial crisis on a timeline. The user can browse from a minima of the line chart directly to the event on a timeline by clicking on the linking icon.

5   Evaluation

We carried out a user study to approve that users can create visualizations simple and fast and can connect them to other visualizations or websites with the help of the Mapping Editor. We asked for a detailed assessment of each task, asked questions to approve the user understood the concept and asked for scenarios.

5.1   Method

We gathered the participants of our user study by using Mechanical Turk, an online workers marketplace offered by amazon.com. For 4US$ each, 100 participants were asked to complete 6 tasks with Vizgr and then fill out an online survey about it. We deleted all surveys that did not contain the basic information on demographics. Three of the surveys were only half-filled. As the corresponding accounts did not suggest technical difficulties (all tasks were fulfilled), we removed the unanswered question from the evaluation.

5.2   Demographics

The demographics seem quite typical for the internet population and surprisingly unbiased towards the archetypical heavy internet users (although we do have them). For the evaluation, we asked four demographical questions: Gender, Age, Education level and average internet usage.

Out of the valid surveys we received 53.6% were male and 46.4% female. The most common age group was 18 to 29 with 59.1%, followed by 32.7% 30 to 39. All participants have a high school degree; most (52.7%) even have a college degree. The average time spent on the internet was given at 29.4 hours per week, but varying from as little as 4 hours to an unrealistic 105 hours.

Although we did not explicitly ask for country of birth, the IP addresses used suggest that the vast majority (over 90%) of the users were logging in from the United

States, with small minorities from a variety of rich first-world countries (Germany, Singapore, ...).

5.3   Questions and Tasks

The participants were asked to complete four basic tasks on the Vizgr website. For each of the steps:

1. creating a tag cloud of the Wikipedia article on *London School of Economics*,
2. creating a map with Wikipedia data from *London*,
3. connecting both visualizations,
4. connecting the word *London* in the tag cloud to a website,

we asked whether the participants had succeeded in the task, how long it took them, how difficult it was and how they would judge the usability of this in their life and in general.

The success rate was (in order): 97.3%, 94.5%, 87.7% and 87.6%. Failure was consecutive, all three that failed at the first step, also failed at the other steps, e.g. one person did not find the save button and was thus not able to finish any of the visualizations. When asked about obstacles, many participants found the first step "easy" or "simple", even though some of them never knew what a tag cloud was, before they entered the survey. There were some complaints about the save functionality or other minor user interface issues. 74.6% managed to finish the task in less than five minutes and 82.8% found it normal to very easy, compared to only 17.2%, who found it difficult or very difficult.

In the second step, creating a map, the three new failures were based on a misunderstanding. They had simply found and then used the prepared map for them, without even trying to create a new one. Only one of them also failed at the next steps. The commentary on this step was very mixed; some found it easier than the last step, others exactly the other way around. 75.5% finished in less than five minutes, 23.7% found it difficult or very difficult. This is somewhat comparable to the last step.

Connecting the visualizations seemed to be more difficult, with only 87.7% success rate. Besides the inherited failures from the tasks before, many participants were unsure on their actions, because they had no clear picture on what a successful link would look like, both visually and conceptually. This made some of the participants to give up on the task, but it also is the predominant theme in the commentary of the more successful participants. 81.1% of the participants managed to finish in less than five minutes, 21.7% found it difficult or very difficult. When we asked the participants, what the effect of the connection was, 69.8% of all participants explained it visually and/or conceptually. 11.9% either answered very generally ("it combines") or off-topic ("user friendly"); the rest (18.8%) either did not finish the task or did not understand the idea.

Although the success rate for linking the visualizations and linking a visualization to a website are very similar, the participants failing were not identical to each other. No one seemed to be confused about the purpose of linking to a web page. The failures and negative comments were mostly due to technical or GUI problems. A common comment at that point was that fulfilling the steps before was helpful in understanding and executing this step as well. 83.8% finished in less than five minutes, 20.0% found it difficult or very difficult.

5.4   Evaluation of Symbols for Links in Visualizations

A problem in our evaluation seems to be the symbol for the linking. We originally used a simple green dot as a linking icon. About 10% of the users had not understood what the green dot symbolizes in the visualization, although they had created the link themselves. This is a rather high rate, when compared to better known symbols, such as underlined text in a website. We did a follow-up evaluation to test different symbols and their acceptance as a linking icon. Therefore we identified different categories of linking symbols in the web and designed a set of icons (compare figure 7) that we could evaluate in different visualizations.

Fig. 7. Different linking icons: arrow, chain, pin, flag, road sign, link logo, green dot

For links in normal websites exist some standardized characteristics that mark text as a link. This includes for example a different color, underlining and a different mouse cursor while hovering over. As a baseline icon for the test we included an icon with the underlined word *LINK* and the original green dot.

Participants for our user study were gathered again by using Mechanical Turk. For 0.30US$ each, 100 participants were asked to view prepared visualizations with different icons and then fill out an online survey. We prepared five different screenshots of existing visualizations in Vizgr and equipped them with the created icons. For table data we took a line chart, for location data a Google Map, for text data a tag cloud, for historical events a timeline and for network data a network graph. Six questions were asked to identify the icons that are most suitable for links in visualizations and are accepted by a majority of users. The questions are the following:

1. Which icons in the graphic represent a link (for example to a website)?
2. Which icons most likely symbolize a link? Enter a sequence.
3. Which icon would you click most likely?
4. Which icon do you like best?
5. Do you know a better symbol for links in visualizations?
6. Which symbol you would take for visualizations?

Question 1, 3 and 4 could be answered by selecting the check boxes for *Flag, Pin, Arrow, Globe, Link Logo, Road Sign, Green Dot, Chain* and *None*. In question 2 the user had to enter a sequence of the icons that most likely symbolize a link. Questions 5 and 6 are answered with free text. Table 1 shows the summarized results. Clearly most accepted is the baseline icon, followed by the arrow symbol. In question 5 the majority of users had no suggestions, some mentioned the provided icons, a few users mentioned new symbols like a star, down arrow, computer mouse or the Internet Explorer logo.

Table 1. Summarized results of the evaluation of linking icons

Question	Link Logo	Arrow	Green dot	Globe	Chain	Flag	Pin	Road Sign
1 (in %)	**30.33**	**15.57**	11.48	9.43	8.20	7.79	6.97	6.97
2 (position)	**2.22**	**3.22**	4.86	4.61	5.49	5.08	4.90	5.27
3 (in %)	**45.24**	**15.87**	5.56	11.9	7.94	5.56	4.76	3.17
4 (in %)	17.92	**28.30**	9.43	**22.64**	6.60	7.55	4.72	2.83
6 (in %)	**26.74**	**24.42**	9.30	15.12	12.79	3.49	4.65	3.49

6 Conclusions

We have presented a user-friendly approach to map heterogeneous information on a visual level. Benefits of information visualization are not only used by encoding large and complex data into user-understandable visualizations, but also to map this information to other heterogeneous information types. Results are connections on the data level and interactive graphics that are included in the hyperlinking process of the web. Graphical elements can be used as links to other visualizations, web resources and can define search queries for web APIs.

The great majority of the users had no or only small difficulties when working on the tasks. The difficulty of the different tasks seems to be stable when looking at time consumption and perceived difficulty. The failure rate seems to be much higher when being confronted with a new concept, be it tag clouds or connecting visualizations. The last step of connecting the visualization to a website was technically the most difficult, counting e.g. the number of distinct mouse clicks. Yet, its conceptual simplicity ranked it near the technically much simpler task of connecting the visualizations.

References

1. Viegas, F.B., Wattenberg, M., van Ham, F., Kriss, J., McKeon, M.: ManyEyes: a Site for Visualization at Internet Scale. IEEE Trans. Visual. Comput. Graphics 13, 1121–1128 (2007)
2. Data360, http://www.data360.org/index.aspx
3. Socrata, http://www.socrata.com/
4. Heer, J., Viégas, F.B., Wattenberg, M., Agrawala, M.: Point, Talk, and Publish: Visualisation and the Web. In: Jain, L., Wu, X., Liere, R., Adriaansen, T., Zudilova-Seinstra, E. (eds.) Trends in Interactive Visualization, pp. 1–15. Springer, London (2009)
5. Fekete, J.: The InfoVis Toolkit. In: Proceedings of the IEEE Symposium on Information Visualization, pp. 167–174. IEEE Computer Society, Washington, DC (2004)

6. Heer, J.: Prefuse: a Toolkit for Interactive Information Visualization. In: CHI 2005: Proceedings of the SIGCHI Conference on Human Factors in Computing Systems, pp. 421–430. ACM Press (2005)
7. Flare, http://flare.prefuse.org/
8. Processing, http://processing.org/
9. Bostock, M., Heer, J.: Protovis: A Graphical Toolkit for Visualization. IEEE Trans. Visualization & Comp. Graphics (Proc. InfoVis) (2009)
10. Google Chart Tools, http://code.google.com/apis/chart/
11. Dork, M., Carpendale, S., Collins, C., Williamson, C.: VisGets: Coordinated Visualizations for Web-based Information Exploration and Discovery. IEEE Trans. Visual. Comput. Graphics 14, 1205–1212 (2008)
12. Mackinlay, J., Hanrahan, P., Stolte, C.: Show Me: Automatic Presentation for Visual Analysis. IEEE Transactions on Visualization and Computer Graphics 13, 1137–1144 (2007)
13. Ahlberg, C.: Spotfire: an information exploration environment. SIGMOD Rec. 25, 25–29 (1996)
14. McKeon, M.: Harnessing the Information Ecosystem with Wiki-based Visualization Dashboards. IEEE Trans. Visual. Comput. Graphics 15, 1081–1088 (2009)
15. Huynh, D.F., Karger, D.R., Miller, R.C.: Exhibit. In: Proceedings of the 16th International Conference on World Wide Web - WWW 2007, Banff, Alberta, Canada, p. 737 (2007)
16. Wang Baldonado, M.Q., Woodruff, A., Kuchinsky, A.: Guidelines for using multiple views in information visualization. In: Proceedings of the Working Conference on Advanced Visual Interfaces - AVI 2000, Palermo, Italy, pp. 110–119 (2000)
17. North, C., Shneiderman, B.: Snap-together visualization: a user interface for coordinating visualizations via relational schemata. In: Proceedings of the Working Conference on Advanced Visual Interfaces, pp. 128–135. ACM, New York (2000)
18. North, C., Conklin, N., Indukuri, K., Saini, V.: Visualization schemas and a web-based architecture for custom multiple-view visualization of multiple-table databases. Inf. Vis. 1, 211–228 (2002)
19. Weaver, C.: Building Highly-Coordinated Visualizations in Improvise. In: Proceedings of the IEEE Symposium on Information Visualization, pp. 159–166. IEEE Computer Society, Washington, DC (2004)
20. Collins, C., Carpendale, S.: VisLink: Revealing Relationships Amongst Visualizations. IEEE Trans. Visual. Comput. Graphics 13, 1192–1199 (2007)

A Multi-factor Tag-Based Personalized Search

Frederico Durao[1], Ricardo Lage[1], Peter Dolog[1], and Nilay Coskun[2]

[1] Intelligent Web and Information Systems, Aalborg University, Computer Science Department
Selma Lagerlöfs Vej 300, DK-9220 Aalborg-East, Denmark
[2] Istanbul Technical University, Science and Technology Institution Building
34469 Maslak, Istanbul

Abstract. With the growing amount of information available on the Web, the task of retrieving documents of interest has become increasingly difficult. Personalized search has got significant attention because it considers the user's preference into the search process to improve the results. However, studies have shown that users are reluctant to provide any explicit input on their personal preference. In this study, we investigate how a search engine can elicit users' preferences by exploring the user's tagging activity from various sources. We propose a simple yet flexible model to succinctly represent user preferences based on multiple factors. Our experiments show that users' preferences can be elicited from a multi-factor tagging data and personalized search based on user preference yields significant precision improvements over the existing ranking mechanisms in the literature.

1 Introduction

Users often have different intentions when using search engines [26]. According to [18], queries provided by users to search engines are under-specified and, thus, poorly translate fully the meaning users have in mind. In fact, the same query provided by different users can have semantically different intentions. For example, one user searching for "stars" may be interested in famous actors or actresses while another may be looking for astronomical objects. As a consequence, according to [12], only 20% to 45% of the results match a user's intentions. One approach to increase user satisfaction is to personalize search results.

Recently, strategies intended to disambiguate the true intention of a query began to collect and analyze user preferences in order to personalize the search retrievals. The user preferences have been modeled in many ways in the literature [4,26,18], including analysis of explicit data such as user profile and preference models, or the implicit collection of data such as user click history, visited pages log, or tagging activity. All of these are indicators of user preferences utilized by search engines to decide which items in the collection of search results are more or less relevant for a particular individual.

In this work, we analyze user's tagging activity to learn the user preferences and personalize the search results. For this purpose, we consider tags because they represent some sort of affinity between user and resource. By tagging, users label resources freely and subjectively, based on their sense of value. Tags, therefore, become a potential source for learning user's interests [8].

J. Filipe and J. Cordeiro (Eds.): WEBIST 2011, LNBIP 101, pp. 192–206, 2012.

In our approach, we build our user model incorporating various tag indicators of user's preference, i.e., each indicator relates to a factor for personalizing searches. We therefore formalize the term *factor* as an indicator of user's preference denoted by a particular set o tags. For instance, a factor Z may represent the set of tags assigned to the most visited pages of a user and a factor Y may represent the set of tags assigned to the pages marked as favorites by the same user. Our belief is that a multi-factor approach can produce a more accurate user model, and thereby facilitate the search for what is more suitable for a given user. The contributions of this paper are:

1. We provide a personalized component to investigate the problem of learning a user's preference based on his tagging activity. We propose a simple yet flexible model to succinctly represent user preferences based on multiple factors.
2. Based on the formal user model, we develop a method to automatically estimate the user's implicit preferences based on his and the community's tagging activity. We provide theoretical and experimental justification for our method.
3. We describe a ranking mechanism that considers a user's implicit interest in ranking pages for a query, based on the users' tagging activity.
4. Finally, we conduct an experimental and comparative analysis to evaluate how much the search quality improves through this personalization. Our experiments indicate reasonable improvement in search quality — we observed about **61.6%** of precision improvement over traditional text-based information retrieval and **6,13%** of precision gain over the best method compared — demonstrating the potential of our approach in personalizing search.

The rest of this paper is organized as follows. We first provide an overview of personalized search and social tagging activity in section 2, on which our work is mainly based. In section 3 we describe our models and methods. Experimental evaluation, results and discussion are presented in section 4. Section 5 addresses the efficiency of the approach and presents the results of retrieval latency. In section 7, we review the related work and finally conclude the paper in section 8.

2   Background

In this section we briefly revise traditional text-based information retrieval concepts followed by an overview of collaborative tagging systems.

2.1   Information Retrieval and Personalized Search

Traditionally, search engines have been the primary tool for information retrieval. According to [2], they appeared to supply the need of human capabilities in storage and retrieval. In brief, they operate by maintaining a comprehensive index of available information. Typically an index represents an information item (such as a Web page or a document) in terms of a set of relevant index terms. When a user submits a query to a search engine, the query terms are compared against index terms for relevant items in the search engine index. An overall relevancy score for each information item (i.e.

document) is computed according to how many of the user's query terms occur in the index, and how important these terms are for that item. The relevant items are then ranked according to their relevancy score before being presented to the user. To produce a composite weight for each term in each document, usually the search score is computed in terms of *term frequency* and *inverse document frequency* (i.e. tf-idf) [2]. The tf-idf weighting scheme assigns to term t a weight in document d given by:

$$\text{tf-idf}_{t,d} = \text{tf}_{t,d} \times \text{idf}_t \tag{1}$$

In other words, tf-idf$_{t,d}$ assigns to term t a weight in document d that is: i)highest when t occurs many times within a small number of documents (thus lending high discriminating power to those documents); ii) lower when the term occurs fewer times in a document, or occurs in many documents (thus offering a less pronounced relevance signal); iii)lowest when the term occurs in virtually all documents.

Eventually the search score of a document d is the sum, over all query terms q, of the tf-idf weights given for each term in d.

$$\text{Score}(q, d) = \sum_{t \in q} \text{tf-idf}_{t,d} \tag{2}$$

In order to achieve personalization, a further step consists of selecting which documents d are relevant or not for a given user. Technically, the traditional scoring function must be adapted/integrated with a personalization model capable of modeling the users' preferences. This is usually done by tracking and aggregating users' interaction with the system. In general, such aggregation includes users' previous queries [22], click-through analysis [13], tagging activity analysis [26,16], etc. A user profile information is also usually employed through personalized query expansion, i.e., adding new terms to the query and re-weighting the original query terms based on the user profile. Similar to [26,16], we explore user's tagging activity as means of learning user's preferences for personalizing search results.

2.2 Collaborative Social Tagging

Collaborative tagging systems have become increasingly popular for sharing and organizing Web resources, leading to a huge amount of user generated metadata. Tags in social bookmarking systems such as *Del.ici.ous*[1] are usually assigned to organize and share resources on the Web so that users can be reminded later on. Invariably, tags represent some sort of affinity between user and a resource on the Web. By tagging, users label resources on the Internet freely and subjectively, based on their sense of values. Tags then become a potential source for learning user's interests.

Tagging Notation. Formally, tagging systems can be represented as hypergraphs where the set of vertices is partitioned into sets: $U = \{u_1, ..., u_k\}, R = \{r_1, ..., r_m\}$, and $T = \{t_1, ..., t_n\}$, where U, R, and T correspond to users, resources, and tags. A tag annotation, i.e. a resource tagged by a user, is an element of set A, where: $A \subseteq U \times R \times T$. The final

---

[1] http://delicious.com

hypergraph formed by a tagging system is defined as G with: $G = \langle V, E \rangle$ with vertices $V = U \cup R \cup T$, and edges $E = \{\{u, r, t\} \mid (u, r, t) \in A\}$.

Particularly to understand the interests of a single user, our models concentrate on the tags and resources that are associated with this particular user, i.e. in a *personalized* part of the hypergraph G. We then define the set of interests of a user as $I_u = (T_u, R_u, A_u)$, where A_u is the set of tag annotations of the user: $A_u = \{(t, r) \mid (u, t, r) \in A\}$, T_u is the user's set of tags: $T_u = \{t \mid (t, r) \in A_u\}$, R_u is the set of resources: $R_u = \{r \mid (t, r) \in A_u\}$.

The introduction on information retrieval as well as on tagging notations will serve as basis for describing our personalized search model in the following sections.

3   Multi-factor Tag-Based Personalized Search

We now discuss how we personalize search results. In Section 3.1 we first describe our multi-factor representation of user preferences. Then in Section 3.2, we describe how to use this preference information in ranking search results.

3.1   User Preference Representation

Among the numerous amount of resources available on the Web and their diverse subject areas, it is reasonable to assume that an average Web user is interested in a limited subset of articles. Because of this, his activities on the Web such as visiting a page, tagging an item, or bookmarking an interesting Web site are often affected by his preferences. Given these observations, it is convenient to represent the user's preference as a multi-factor user model rather than rely on a single indicator of preference. In this work, tags from different factors such as tags assigned to the user's bookmarks and his own tags serve as our learn units of user preferences. Further, we understand that some tags are preferred over another, meaning that the frequency of usage of a given tag can denote its affinity with the tagger. In this sense, we define the tag preference set, for each factor, as a tuple $(tag, tagFreq(tag))$, where $tagFreq(tag)$ is a function that measures the user's degree of interest in that tag. Formally, we define this set for a particular user u and factor $f \in F$ (let F be the set of all possible factors) as:

$$T_f = \{(t, tagFreq(t)) \mid t \in T_f\}, \tag{3}$$

where $tagFreq(t) = \frac{n_t}{|T_f|}$, n_t is the number of occurrences of the tag $t \in T_f$ and $|T_f|$ is the amount of tags in a given factor f. The set T_f is normalized such that $\sum_{i=1}^{|T_f|} tagFreq(i) = 1$. To illustrate the user tagging preference representation, suppose a user has only two tags in one particular factor: "semantic web" and "data mining", and the first has been utilized three times while the second has been utilized only once. This means the user has been interested in "semantic web" three times as much as he has been interested in "data mining". Then, the tag preference set of the user for that factor will be represented as {("semantic web",0.75),("data mining",0.25)}.

The composition of our multi-factor tag-based user model T'_u extends the traditional set of user tags T_u (see subsection 2.2), with a disjoint union of tag sets:

$$T'_u = \bigsqcup_{f \in F} T_f, \tag{4}$$

where T_f is the set of tags assigned to each factor $f \in F$. Next section explains how the tag-based multi-factor approach is applied to personalize search results.

3.2 Tag-Based Personalization Approach

The tag-based personalization approach decides which resource $r \in R$ is relevant to each user $u \in U$ based on his preferences established in the multi-factor tag-based user model. In the context of this work, we re-rank the search results by measuring the similarity of tags that denote user preference and the tags assigned to the retrieved items. With this, we promote the items closer to user's preferences at the first positions in the collection of search results.

Technically, we calculate the cosine similarity between *each* vector of tag frequencies $\overrightarrow{T}_f \subset \overrightarrow{T}'_u$ from $T_f \subset T'_u$ and the vector of tag frequencies $\overrightarrow{T}_r$ from the retrieved resources T_r of a given user query q. Further, we weigh each vector $\overrightarrow{T}_f$ with a coefficient, α_f that determines its degree of importance over the other factors in the model. We incorporate the coefficients because different users may rely on tag factors differently. As a consequence, the importance of each factor may vary accordingly.

The coefficient values for each factor are automatically estimated using the Ordinary Least Square (OLS) linear regression. The goal of using OLS is to minimize the sum of squared distances between the observed tag frequencies of each factor in the dataset and the best coefficient values predicted by linear approximation [25].

Once the coefficient values are estimated, the Tag-based Similarity Score (TSS) can be calculated as:

$$TSS(\overrightarrow{T}_r, \overrightarrow{T}'_u) = \sum_{f=1}^{|F|} \alpha_f * \frac{\overrightarrow{T}_r.\overrightarrow{T}_f}{|\overrightarrow{T}_r||\overrightarrow{T}_f|}, \tag{5}$$

The TSS value is then utilized to weigh the ordinary search score and thereby promote the items matching the user interests to higher positions in the search ranking. The Personalized Search Score (PSS) over a resource r triggered by a query q in the set of resources R is then defined as follows:

$$PSS(q, r, u) = \sum_{t \in q} \text{tf-idf}_{t,r} * TSS(\overrightarrow{T}_r, \overrightarrow{T}'_u). \tag{6}$$

In the following section, with the intuit of demonstrate the how the personalized search takes place, we simulate a user search since the user's initial query until the re-ranking of search results.

3.3 Personalized Search in Action

In this section we describe how the personalized ranking is realized when a user $u \in U$ submits a query q for a search engine:

1. Assume that a user u, whose preferences are denoted by the multi-factor tag-based model T'_u, submits a query q for a given search engine;

2. The search engine returns a set of resources $S \subseteq R$ that matches the entry query q. Each retrieved resource $s \in S$ is assigned with a set of tags defined by $T_s = \{t1, .., t_z\}$. The retrieved items in S are initially ranked respecting the tf-idf ordering $\tau = [s_1, s_2, ..., s_k]$, where the ordering relation is defined by $s_i \geq s_j \Leftrightarrow$ tf-idf$(q, s_i) \geq$ tf-idf(q, s_j).

3. For each $s \in S$, we weigh the τ with $TSS(\vec{T}_s, \vec{T}'_u)$. The outcome is a personalized ranking list of pages represented by S'. The rank list will follow a new ordering $\tau' = [s_1, s_2, ..., s_k]$, where $s_i \in S'$ and the ordering relation is defined by $s_i \geq s_j \Leftrightarrow PSS(q, s_i, u) \geq persScore(q, s_j, u)$.

4. The personalized result set $S' \subseteq R$ is then returned to the user.

4   Experimental Evaluation

To evaluate our approach, we analyze and compare how the different similarity measures re-rank the returned result list. For the matter of comparison, the best personalization approaches will rank the relevant/preferable retrieved items to the higher positions in the result list.

We utilize the precision metric to measure and compare the performance of our personalization approach over other similarity measures. By doing so, the research goal of this evaluation is *to assess whether the multi-factor tags improve the precision of traditional text-based information retrieval mechanism in leading users to find the information they are actually looking for.* We intend to address (and attenuate) the problem witnessed by searchers when the search results do not meet their real needs and, instead, present them with undesired information.

4.1   MovieLens Dataset

We have utilized the MovieLens dataset for evaluating our approach. The data set contains 1,147,048 ratings and 95,580 tags applied to 10,681 movies by 13,190 users. The dataset was chosen because it allowed us to build multi-factor user model base on two distinct factors corresponding to two different user activities: tagging and rating. The first factor refers to T_u as the set of user' tags and the second refers to V_u, the set of tags assigned by other users to the pages rated four or five stars by user u. In a scale from one to five, we consider movies rated four or five as strong indicators of user's preferences. The evaluated multi-factor user model is defined as follows:

$$T'_u = \gamma.T_u + \beta.V_u \qquad (7)$$

where γ and β are the coefficients used to weigh the importance of each tag factor.

Because the MovieLens dataset only provides little information about the movies such as title and category, we crawled the synopses of the movies in order to create our search space. The synopses were extracted from *The Internet Movie Data Base* (IMDb) [2], a movie repository that catalogs information about movies, including information about casting, locations, dates, synopses, reviews, and fan sites on the Web.

---

[2] http://www.imdb.com/

4.2 Methodology and Evaluation Metrics

In order to evaluate whether the proposed approach matches our research goal, we performed a quantitative evaluation in terms of precision of the search results. Precision refers to the proportion of retrieved items that are actually relevant to the user's query. We calculated the precision as $prec(q, u) = \frac{|R_{q,u} \cap R'_{q,u}|}{|R_{q,u}|}$, where $|R_{q,u}|$ is the amount of retrieved items for a query q triggered by an user u and $|R'_{q,u}|$ is the amount of *relevant* pages expected to be retrieved. This set was composed by movies rated four or five stars besides the query q as a term in the text content. In this way, we could distinguish what was relevant or not for each user. Further, we statistically computed the most representative number of users to be assessed. The sample size was calculated with confidence level set to 95% and confidence interval set to 2%.

Queries and Search Space. For each user, we ran the top n queries using the most popular terms that appeared in all indexed pages. We prioritized the most frequent terms along all documents and the most frequent ones in each document. It is important to mention that we filtered out the stop words prior to processing the list of indexed terms. This list was calculated as a mean of tf-df [2]. This decision was taken to avoid that any particular group of individuals was favored over another.

Once we have selected the queries, we focused on defining the most appropriate search space. Since our goal was centered on the precision, we decided to focus the search only at the top 30 ranked items. This focused observation was motivated by the fact that users usually don't go further to encounter what they are looking for, instead they reformulate queries to better convey the information they are actually seeking [2].

Pruning. Although substantial data was available, we pruned the dataset for our analyses of the personalized search. We focused on a set of movies with a minimum threshold of tags and ratings. We began pruning the present dataset by selecting items that had been tagged with at least 5 distinct tags. We wanted to focus on tag sets with high lexical variability and less redundancy. This care was taken to prevent that tags from distinct factors could overlap with tags from expected documents in the case of low tag variability. We iteratively repeated this pruning until reach a stable set of items and tags. Further, since we wanted to explore the precision of the personalized search, we only included users that had distributed ratings higher than or equal to four stars. Otherwise we would not have any source of information on user's preference about the retrieved items. The complete overview of the dataset size is shown in Table 1.

Similarity Measure Comparison. The core of the tag-based personalization approach is the computation of the Tag-based Similarity Score (TSS) (see in section 3.2). In order to compare our approach with other similarity measures, we changed the TSS algorithm using other similarity algorithms without considering the coefficients assigned to the factors involved. Besides the cosine similarity, the other similarity measures utilized are the *Matching Coefficient, Dice, Jaccard* and *Euclidean Distance* (all refer to [5]).

Table 1. Size of different datasets we utilized in this paper. *Count* is the number of movies the dataset contains. *N. users* is the number of users that generated those entities. For example, the second and third columns of the second row indicate that 4,009 users assigned 95,580 tags to movies. Total is the number of times the users rated or tagged the movies. The last three columns indicate the same numbers after the pruning is being applied.

	Before Pruning			After Pruning		
Dataset	Count	N. Users	Total	Count	N. Users	Total
Movies rated	8,358	9,753	1,147,048	7,075	6,476	211,746
Movies tagged	7,601	4,009	95,580	4,029	3,871	88,181

- The *Matching Coefficient* approach is a simple vector based approach which simply counts the number of terms (tags in our case), (dimensions), on which both vectors are non zero. So, for vector set $\vec{v}$ and set $\vec{w}$ the matching coefficient is calculated as $matching(\vec{v}, \vec{w}) = |\vec{v} \cap \vec{w}|$. This can be seen as the vector based count of similar tags.
- The *Dice Coefficient* is a term based similarity measure (0-1) whereby the similarity measure is defined as twice the number of terms common to compared entities divided by the total number of tags assigned in both tested resources. The Coefficient result of 1 indicates identical vectors (e.g. $\vec{v}$ and $\vec{w}$) as where a 0 equals orthogonal vectors. The coefficient can be calculated as $dice(\vec{v}, \vec{w}) = \frac{2|\vec{v} \cap \vec{w}|}{|\vec{v}| + |\vec{w}|}$.
- The *Jaccard Coefficient* measures similarity between sample sets, and is defined as the size of the intersection divided by the size of the union of the sample sets. The coefficient can be calculated as: $jaccard(\vec{v}, \vec{w}) = \frac{|\vec{v} \cap \vec{w}|}{|\vec{v} \cup \vec{w}|}$.
- The *Euclidean Distance* approach works in vector space similar to the matching coefficient and the dice coefficient, however the similarity measure is not judged from the angle as in cosine rule but rather the direct euclidean distance between the vector inputs. The standard Euclidean distance formula between vectors $\vec{v}$ and $\vec{w}$ is defined as follows: $euclidean(\vec{v}, \vec{w}) = \sqrt{\sum_{i=1}^{n}(\vec{v}_i - \vec{w}_i)^2}$.
- The *Cosine Similarity* is utilized to measure the similarity between two vectors of n dimensions by finding the cosine of the angle between them. The cosine similarity for two vector between vectors is calculated as: $cosSim(\vec{v}, \vec{w}) = \frac{\vec{v} \cdot \vec{w}}{|\vec{v}||\vec{w}|}$.

Unlike our proposed TSS algorithm, here we do not consider the coefficients assigned to the tag factors. For the sake of differentiation, we call the cosine similarity with coefficient applied to our TSS algorithm as $Cosine^{Coef}$.

4.3   Evaluation Results

Figure 1 shows the mean of precision (Subfigure 1(a)) and the box plot displays the distribution differences between the five similarity measures (Subfigure 1(b)). The higher precision values correspond to better performance. The precision of our approach is displayed in the first bar ($Cosine^{Coef}$) followed by the compared similarity measures with

Table 2. Mean of Precision

	Cosine^{Coef}	Cosine	Jaccard	Dice	Euclidean	Matching
Min.	0.723	0.616	0.576	0.575	0.600	0.510
1st Qu.	0.765	0.710	0.576	0.577	0.600	0.583
Median	0.776	0.761	0.634	0.633	0.634	0.583
Mean	**0.796**	**0.755**	**0.694**	**0.694**	**0.667**	**0.641**
3rd Qu.	0.841	0.845	0.841	0.842	0.756	0.766
Max.	0.912	0.909	0.912	0.913	0.886	0.865
Std.Dev	0.052	0.087	0.131	0.130	0.083	0.105

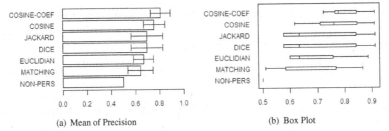

(a) Mean of Precision   (b) Box Plot

Fig. 1. Overall result and statistics from the experiment. Note that each of the similarity measure are utilized in the TSS algorithm to personalize the search.

their respective standard errors. We also include the non-personalized precision result for the sake of comparison. This ranking was based on the traditional tf-idf weighting scheme where the text-based search has no support from personal tags. It is important to emphasize that all compared similarity measures produce a personalized score except the non-personalized search.

Table 2 summarizes the statistics from our sample of precision values regarding the evaluated metrics. It shows the five-number summary (sample minimum, lower quartile, median, upper quartile and sample maximum), the mean value, and the standard deviation of the samples. It is worth noting that the sample minimum value of our approach has higher precision than any other similarity measure compared. This behavior is also noticed when compared with the sample maximum value. Similarly, the standard deviation of the sample of our approach is lower than the standard deviation of the other samples. This indicates less dispersion within the precision values of our approach. Furthermore, differences between all pairs of similarity measures are significant ($p \leq 0.01$) except for those between Jaccard and Dice similarity.

As results show, our approach (Cosine^{Coef}) achieved the highest precision rates. In particular, it achieved 61.6% of precision improvement over traditional text-based information retrieval (non-pers) and 6,13% of precision gain over cosine similarity. The overall result also indicates that the cosine-based similarity measures (regarding or not the coefficients) perform better than the other approaches. As expected, all similarity measures applied to the personalized search outperformed the non-personalized method.

5 Assessment of Efficiency

The efficiency of information retrieval systems is of utmost importance, because it ensures that systems scale up to the vast amounts of information needing retrieval. Efficiency research over the past years has focused on efficient indexing, storage (compression) and retrieval of data (query processing strategies). In the previous section we explored the comparative evaluation of the quality of the search results. Although, our approach shows significant improvement over the compared methods, there is still always a cost of performance involved. In this Section, we aim at demonstrating the impact of the personalization on the retrieval latency as well as the cost for building the personalized ranking.

To quantify the efficiency of our approach, we run a large number of keyword queries on an Intel Core 2 Duo E8400 with 8GB Ram running Sun Java 6 on a 32-bit installation of Windows XP. The structure of the data as well as the indexed terms are stored in a PostgreSQL object-relational database. The algorithm is not parallelized and runs entirely on a single core. We do not use any partitioning or segmentation techniques, but hold all individual searches in memory, using about 2 GB of main memory.

5.1 Indexing Time and Personalization Cost

The total indexing time of the all 211,746 test documents (rated and tagged) was 135 seconds. Within this time, the invalid characters are steamed out the term frequency are calculated. To conduct this task, we utilized the Apache Lucene search engine [3]. We consider this time relatively feasible in case there is a need to re-index the whole corpus in a real time application.

Invariably, the calculation of the user preferences adds additional cost to the overall search. The cost is related to the computation of tag frequencies along the tag factors. Regardless this work, personalization does not take place. We therefore measured the cost of personalization for 500 users randomly chosen from our dataset. We ran ten queries for each user and the response time is given as the mean of them. As a result, we evidenced that, on average, the calculus of user preferences takes approximately 910 ms. This value is latter added to the overall retrieval.

5.2 Data Retrieval Latency

In order to evaluate the retrieval latency, we analyzed how the latency scales according to different scenarios setups. The scenarios are assembled in terms of number of documents, number of tags and number of users. We then collected the latency for the non-personalized method and our approach (called Cosine^{Coef}). In this evaluation, the users' preferences are calculated on demand. The other similarity approaches were not considered in this evaluation since the difference of retrieval latency are not significant and the cost of personalization is approximately the same for all methods. For each test scenario, 10 queries were issued per user. These queries however are not the same as the previous assessment on the personalization cost.

---

[3] http://lucene.apache.org/

Table 3. Data Retrieval Latency Scenarios

Scenario ID	N. Documents	N. Tags	N. Users	Non-Personalized (ms)	Cosine^{Coef} (ms)
1	500	1500	100	380	1347
2	1000	5000	500	664	1452
3	5000	10000	1000	844	1687

According to Table 3, it is possible to observe that the retrieval latency is relatively low affected as the scenarios scale up. Unsurprisingly, the non-personalized search outperforms our approach in all test scenarios. On the first scenario, the efficiency of the non-personalized method achieves, on average, 380 ms whereas the personalized one achieves 1347 ms. In comparison with the previous assessment on the personalization cost (see subsection 5.1), we notice that the current findings are relatively close to previous result since the cost is 967 ms. The slight difference from previous result (from 967 ms to 910 ms) concerns basically the fact that different queries might have be issued. As a consequence, the result set of some queries might have bigger than the others, thus impacting in the whole retrieval latency.

The difference between the latency of non-personalized method and our approach reduces as the scenarios scale down. On the first scenario, our approach is 71.7% more expensive than the non-personalized method. On the second scenario, such a difference reduces to 54,02% and finally on the third scenario, the difference reduces to 49,9%. Interestingly, this observation demonstrates that the computation of users' preferences is fairly affected as the amount of users and tags evolve.

Another interesting finding can be made on the retrieval latency of each method individually. From the first to the second scenario, the non-personalized approach decreases its efficiency in 42.8% and from the second to the third scenario, the same method decreases its efficiency in 21.4%. This behavior is inverse when comes to the personalized approach. From the first to the second scenario, our approach decreases its efficiency in 7.2% and from the second to the third scenario, it decreases its efficiency in 13.9%. In comparison with the non-personalized method, we can observe that our approach is relatively more efficient as the scenario scales up.

6   Discussion and Limitations

Concerning the role of tags as means of personalizing traditional information retrieval, we evidenced that tags indeed can be used as learning units of user's preference. As results showed, this hypothesis was confirmed when the precision of our solution considerably outperformed the precision of non-personalized search. The immediate benefit of personalized search is the reduction of undesired retrievals at the first positions and thereby not distracting users with unsolicited information. Part of this success relates to the best estimation of coefficients applied to each factor considered in the search. The adoption of coefficients helped us to efficiently determine which tag factors are more representative for an individual over the others. Regarding the applicability of the approach, we are quite positive that existing tag-based systems can utilize and/or adapt our solution to their reality.

The main limitation of the current approach is the lack of tags. In this work we are not addressing this problem since the goal is to emphasize the benefits with the multi-factor approach. A potential solution is seen in the work of [12] that studies tag prediction in social bookmarking environments. Performance is another issue that was not formally evaluated in the current study but we empirically observed that the personalization process is at least 10% more expensive than the basic keyword-based search. However this cost cannot be judged isolated since the personalized outcome can compensate the investment. Further investigation is necessary and planned for future works.

7 Related Work

In recent years many researchers utilize query log and click-through analysis for web search personalization. In [18], the authors combine a topic-sensitive version of PageRank [11] with the history of user clicks data for search result personalization. Joachims et al. [13] study clicks applicability as implicit relevance judgments. They show that users' clicks provide a reasonably accurate evidence of their preferences. [21] explore the use of a less-invasive means of gathering user information for personalized search. In particular, they build user profiles based on activity at the search site itself and study the use of these profiles to provide personalized search results. These studies are relevant to our work in context of predicting user preferences but our approach takes into account user annotations which are called tags as user feedback. Tan et al. [22] propose a language modeling approach for query history mining. Their small-scale study demonstrates significant improvement of personalized web search with a history-based language model over regular search. The user modeling approach described in [19] is based on a decision-theoretic framework to convert implicit feedback into a user profile that is used to re-rank search results.

While user models are usually targeted at search personalization, they could also be applied for personalized information filtering, as was shown in [27] which analyzes click history for the identification of regular users' interests. The work from [24] shows that combining implicit user profiles from several related users has a positive impact on personalization effectiveness. Recently, new approaches for adaptive personalization focus on the user task and the current activity context. There are several approaches trying to predict applicability of personalization while considering the current context of the user's task on query submission [23,7].

Collaborative Filtering (CF) [3] has become a very common technique for providing personalized recommendations, suggesting items based on the similarity between users' preferences. One drawback of traditional CF systems is the need for explicit user feedback, usually in the form of rating a set of items, which might increase users' entry cost to the recommender system. Hence, leveraging implicit user feedback [1], such as views, clicks, or queries, has become more popular in recent CF systems. In this work, we leverage implicit tagging information, which can be viewed as a variant of implicit user feedback. [6] proposes a solution which considers the structure of the user's social network assuming that people which share same social ties have similar interests. In addition to social network, they have another approach similar to our study taking into account user tags to understand user interest. Comparing these two approaches they noted that tagging activity gives efficient information about user preferences for active taggers.

In order to measure relevance between user and search result, [10] considers topic matching instead of tags which we used in our approach. They propose a ranking algorithm which ranks web pages by the term matching between user interest and resource's topic. [9] proposes a (meta-)search engine which queries more than 18 commodity search engines and offers two complementary views on their returned results. One is the classical flat-ranked list, the other consists of a hierarchical organization of these results into folders created on-the-fly at query time and labeled with intelligible sentences that capture the themes of the results contained in them. Users can browse this hierarchy with various goals: knowledge extraction, query refinement and personalization of search results. SnakeT personalizes on-the-fly the original ranked list by filtering out those results that do not belong to the selected folders by users. In [20], there exists a different approach to personalizing search result by building models of user as ontological profiles. They derive implicit interest scores to existing concepts in domain ontology. A different way of personalized search is based on global interests using the Open Directory Project (ODP) categories [14]. In [15], a ranking algorithm is defined similar to previous work using ODP categories for categorizing and personalizing search result. [14] explore ways of incorporating users' interests into the search process to improve the results using an domain ontology. The user profiles are structured as a concept hierarchy of 4,400 ontology classes. The disadvantage of structured user profiles is the need of constant revision of such models and the cost of maintenance.

Focused mostly on tags, [26] proposes an algorithm for personalizing search and navigation based on personalized tag clusters. Slightly similar to our model, they measure the relevance between user and tag cluster and try to understand user interest while we calculate the similarity between user and tags. Tags are used in different manners to find search personalized results answering user needs since tags are chosen by users personally. Similar to our study, in [16], a tag based re-ranking model is presented taking into account tags from *Del.icio.us*. Likewise our model, they compare tags of search results and users to calculate new scores of search results.

8   Conclusions and Future Works

This study introduces a multi-factor tag-based model to personalize search results. We analyze user's tagging activity to learn users' preferences and use this information to personalize the search. We evaluated our approach with other personalization methods and as a result we realized significant improvement of precision. As a future work, we intend to analyze the semantic relationship between tags in order to catch hidden similarities that are not undertaken by this model. In addition, we aim at enhancing the model by considering the tag decay. The goal is to perform a temporal analyzes and filter the results according to the actual users' preferences.

Acknowledgements. The research leading to these results is part of the project "KiWi - Knowledge in a Wiki" and has received funding from the European Community's Seventh Framework Programme (FP7/2007-2013) under grant agreement No. 211932.

This work has been supported by FP7 ICT project M-Eco: Medical Ecosystem Personalized Event-Based Surveillance under grant number 247829. The authors would like to acknowledge GroupLens research at University of Minnesota for providing the MovieLens dataset.

References

1. Au Yeung, C.M., Gibbins, N., Shadbolt, N.: A study of user profile generation from folksonomies. In: Proceedings of the Workshop on Social Web and Knowledge Management (SWKM 2008), Beijing, China, April 21-25, 2007, pp. 1–8 (2008)
2. Baeza-Yates, R., Ribeiro-Neto, B.: Modern Information Retrieval. Addison Wesley (1999)
3. Bender, M., Crecelius, T., Kacimi, M., Michel, S., Neumann, T., Parreira, J.X., Schenkel, R., Weikum, G.: Exploiting social relations for query expansion and result ranking. In: ICDE Workshops, pp. 501–506. IEEE Computer Society (2008)
4. Biancalana, C.: Social tagging for personalized web search. In: AI*IA 2009: Emergent Perspectives in Artificial Intelligence, pp. 232–242 (2009)
5. Boninsegna, M., Rossi, M.: Similarity measures in computer vision. Pattern Recognition Letters 15(12), 1255–1260 (1994)
6. Carmel, D., Zwerdling, N., Guy, I., Ofek-Koifman, S., Har'el, N., Ronen, I., Uziel, E., Yogev, S., Chernov, S.: Personalized social search based on the user's social network. In: CIKM 2009: Proceeding of the 18th ACM Conference on Information and Knowledge Management, pp. 1227–1236. ACM, New York (2009)
7. Dou, Z., Song, R., Wen, J.-R.: A large-scale evaluation and analysis of personalized search strategies. In: WWW 2007: Proceedings of the 16th International Conference on World Wide Web, pp. 581–590. ACM, New York (2007)
8. Durao, F., Dolog, P.: A personalized Tag-Based recommendation in social web systems. In: Proceedings of International Workshop on Adaptation and Personalization for Web 2.0 (AP-WEB 2.0 2009) at UMAP 2009, vol. 485 (2009)
9. Ferragina, P., Gulli, A.: A personalized search engine based on web-snippet hierarchical clustering. Software: Practice and Experience 38(2), 189–225 (2008)
10. Gemmell, J., Shepitsen, A., Mobasher, M., Burke, R.: Personalization in folksonomies based on tag clustering. In: Proceedings of the 6th Workshop on Intelligent Techniques for Web Personalization and Recommender Systems (2008)
11. Haveliwala, T.H.: Topic-sensitive pagerank. In: WWW 2002: Proceedings of the 11th International Conference on World Wide Web, pp. 517–526. ACM, New York (2002)
12. Jäschke, R., Marinho, L., Hotho, A., Schmidt-Thieme, L., Stumme, G.: Tag recommendations in folksonomies, pp. 506–514 (2007)
13. Joachims, T., Granka, L., Pan, B., Hembrooke, H., Gay, G.: Accurately interpreting click-through data as implicit feedback. In: SIGIR 2005: Proceedings of the 28th Annual International ACM SIGIR Conference on Research and Development in Information Retrieval, pp. 154–161. ACM, New York (2005)
14. Liu, F., Yu, C., Member, S., Meng, W.: Personalized web search for improving retrieval effectiveness. IEEE Transactions on Knowledge and Data Engineering 16, 28–40 (2004)
15. Ma, Z., Pant, G., Sheng, O.R.L.: Interest-based personalized search. ACM Trans. Inf. Syst. 25(1), 5 (2007)
16. Noll, M.G., Meinel, C.: Web Search Personalization Via Social Bookmarking and Tagging. In: Aberer, K., Choi, K.-S., Noy, N., Allemang, D., Lee, K.-I., Nixon, L.J.B., Golbeck, J., Mika, P., Maynard, D., Mizoguchi, R., Schreiber, G., Cudré-Mauroux, P. (eds.) ASWC 2007 and ISWC 2007. LNCS, vol. 4825, pp. 367–380. Springer, Heidelberg (2007)

17. Pretschner, A., Gauch, S.: Ontology based personalized search. In: 1999 Proceedings of 11th IEEE International Conference on Tools with Artificial Intelligence, pp. 391–398 (1999)

18. Qiu, F., Cho, J.: Automatic identification of user interest for personalized search. In: WWW 2006: Proceedings of the 15th International Conference on World Wide Web, pp. 727–736. ACM, New York (2006)

19. Shen, X., Tan, B., Zhai, C.: Implicit user modeling for personalized search. In: CIKM 2005: Proceedings of the 14th ACM International Conference on Information and Knowledge Management, pp. 824–831. ACM, New York (2005)

20. Sieg, A., Mobasher, B., Burke, R.: Web search personalization with ontological user profiles. In: CIKM 2007: Proceedings of the Sixteenth ACM Conference on Conference on Information and Knowledge Management, pp. 525–534. ACM, New York (2007)

21. Speretta, M., Gauch, S.: Personalized search based on user search histories. In: IEEE / WIC / ACM International Conference on Web Intelligence, pp. 622–628 (2005)

22. Tan, B., Shen, X., Zhai, C.: Mining long-term search history to improve search accuracy. In: KDD 2006: Proceedings of the 12th ACM SIGKDD International Conference on Knowledge Discovery and Data Mining, pp. 718–723. ACM, New York (2006)

23. Teevan, J., Dumais, S.T., Liebling, D.J.: To personalize or not to personalize: modeling queries with variation in user intent. In: SIGIR 2008: Proceedings of the 31st Annual International ACM SIGIR Conference on Research and Development in Information Retrieval, pp. 163–170. ACM, New York (2008)

24. Teevan, J., Morris, M.R., Bush, S.: Discovering and using groups to improve personalized search. In: WSDM 2009: Proceedings of the Second ACM International Conference on Web Search and Data Mining, pp. 15–24. ACM, New York (2009)

25. Williams, G.: Linear Algebra With Applications. Jones and Bartlett Publishers, Inc., USA (2007)

26. Xu, S., Bao, S., Fei, B., Su, Z., Yu, Y.: Exploring folksonomy for personalized search. In: SIGIR 2008: Proceedings of the 31st Annual International ACM SIGIR Conference on Research and Development in Information Retrieval, pp. 155–162. ACM, New York (2008)

27. Yang, B., Jeh, G.: Retroactive answering of search queries. In: WWW 2006: Proceedings of the 15th International Conference on World Wide Web, pp. 457–466. ACM, New York (2006)

Is Moodle Accessible for Visually Impaired People?

Rocío Calvo, Ana Iglesias, and Lourdes Moreno

Computer Department, UC3M University, Av. Universidad 30, 28911, Leganés, Spain
{mrcalvo,aiglesia,lmoreno}@inf.uc3m.es

Abstract. Most educational centers are currently using e-learning tools to provide the pedagogical resources for the students, especially in higher education. Nevertheless, some students are not able to access to this information because these authoring tools are not as accessible as they should be. The main aim of this paper is to evaluate if one of the most widely e-learning tool used around the world, Moodle, is accessible for visually impaired people. The evaluation shows that the accessibility guidelines provided by the World Wide Web Consortium (W3C) are not accomplished by the tool. Moreover, it shows that people using screen readers are not able to access to the majority of the functionality of Moodle.

Keywords: e-Learning, Moodle, Accessibility, Visual impairments, Screen reader.

1 Introduction

Nowadays, we are involved in a world were technology is essential. In the educational environments, for example, the conventional education is being adapted to new technologies. A new concept, e-learning, emerged as a complementary mechanism to traditional classroom teaching. This learning concept allows students to learn when and where they want regardless of their physical conditions or the technology they use. Students only need an Internet connection to access to learning resources.

Many educational institutions use Learning Content Management Systems (LCMSs) to manage their courses. These e-learning tools are usually Web-based tools which make course management easier for teachers and directors. Oftentimes, the LCMS is even the only tool given students for communicating with peers and teachers or for accessing particular learning resources. Most of teachers who are sensitive to the accessibility barriers in education are focused on creating accessible resources for their students but the main problem is that if the LCMS is not accessible then it does not matter if the pedagogical resources are or not accessible, because the students are not able to access to the information either. That is why these e-learning tools should be accessible and easily to use for everyone. Otherwise students with different functionality or access conditions could not access the learning resources and the educational gaps will become higher, failing one of their current main objective: provide inclusive education and equal access for all.

J. Filipe and J. Cordeiro (Eds.): WEBIST 2011, LNBIP 101, pp. 207–220, 2012.

This paper is focused on identifying the accessibility problems that visually-impaired people face when they interact with LCMSs. Specifically, the paper evaluates the accessibility problems of the widely used authoring tool called Moodle[1].

Most of visually-impaired people use assistive tools for accessing websites and to surf on LCMS's. There are different assistive technologies for each disability [1]; so, each user chooses the best tool to help her/him to access the system according to her/his disabilities. Particularly, visually-impaired people, users with low vision or blindness use screen readers, screen magnificent tools or refreshable Braille displays among others. Each of these tools has different features, for example, the screen readers read text aloud; screen magnificent tools get bigger the information showed in the screen; or refreshable Braille displays convert the web contents to Braille.

The goal of this work is to evaluate the Moodle's accessibility focusing on visual impairments. This paper presents manual evaluations from a user perception and an accessibility expert. This work is part of a complete investigation where automatic and semi-automatic accessibility evaluations are included. This complete investigation gets best results because it uses a combination of manual and automatic evaluation methods [2].

The evaluation presented here is divided into two main parts: a user evaluation and an expert evaluation. Firstly, the user evaluation was carried out by a person with accessibility knowledge and with a low-medium level of screen reader use but without any visual impairment. Because of this, she simulated blindness while she was using two different screen readers for interacting with the system. Next, an expert evaluation was completed in order to analyze Moodle's accessibility in terms of W3C[2] guidelines.

The paper is organized as follows: section 2 presents the state of the art. Then, section 3 describes the evaluation method and main results obtained. Finally, main conclusions and further research are presented in section 4.

2   Previous Work

This section presents the state of the art in e-learning systems, accessibility guidelines and standards, assistive technologies used by people who are visually impaired and previous studies related to accessibility barriers in educational systems.

2.1   E-learning

E-learning has become a new way of learning which could be considered as the evolution of learning distance [3]. The concept of e-learning has many definitions, maybe the easiest could be "Access online to learning resources every moment and everywhere" [4]. The main difference with traditional learning is that the student decides how to study: what, when and where. So, it provides a huge freedom to the user.

There are different e-learning tools which help to organize, store and modify efficiently e-learning courses. These tools are divided into three groups: LMSs

---

[1] Moodle, LCMS Authoring tool. Available in: http://download.moodle.org/windows/ [June 2010].

[2] W3C: The World Wide Web Consortium. Available in: http://www.w3.org/ [June 2010].

(Learning Management Systems), LCMSs (Learning Content Management Systems) and CMSs (Content Management Systems) [5]. Each one has different features: CMSs permit to manage contents; LMSs are focused on administrative and assistive tasks in learning environment; and LCMSs provide authoring tools for learning. Particularly, this paper evaluates Moodle LCMS which is a free and open source tool and is one of the most widely used by learning institutions around the world[3].

2.2   Accessibility Standards

E-learning tool designers should consider different guidelines and standards to design e-learning tools if they want to make these tools accessible for all. There are different institutions like: W3C or IMS[4] which supply guidelines to develop accessible websites or educational resources.

W3C provides guidelines to help designers to create accessible components. For instance, WCAG guidelines [6] for websites content; ATAG guidelines [7] for authoring tools; or UAAG guidelines [8] for user agents. Then, LCMS and every authoring tool should be in accordance to ATAG guidelines. Also, they should fulfilled WCAG guidelines because these authoring tools produce Web pages and Web contents.

Besides, IMS has developed guidelines to create e-learning tools and make accessible its content like IMS Access For All Specification [9] adopted by ISO/IEC SC36. These IMS guidelines are based on six principles: allow the user to customize the website, provide equivalent alternatives to visual and additive content, provide compatibility to assistive tools and provide access to all tasks through keyboard, provide context and information, follow IMS specifications and other relevant specifications, and consider the use of XML.

Moreover, designers should use Universal Design to provide for all. This approach has been adapted to learning by creating Universal Design for Learning (UDL) [10]. In particular, the characteristics of Universal Design have been tailored to e-learning tools like Moodle [11].

2.3   Assistive Technology: Screen Readers

Disabled people use different assistive technologies to access computers and the Internet. This technology helps them to complete tasks such as: sending emails, read the newspaper and so on. There are different assistive technologies which have been adapted to different disabilities. For example, if a person has a paralysis, weakness, or other problems with movement of limbs, s/he can use keyboard with larger, more widely-spaced keys. Besides, if a person has visual impaired problems, s/he can use screen magnificent or screen readers.

Screen readers are used by people who are blind, visually impaired or illiterate or learning disabled people to help them when they are using the computer. These

---

[3] Zacker. Higher-ed LMS market penetration: Moodle vs. Blackboard+WebCT vs. Sakai. Available in: http://www.zacker.org/higher-ed-lms-market-penetration-moodle-vs-blackboard-vs-sakai [July 2011].

[4] IMS. Global Learning Consortium. Available in: http://www.imsglobal.org/ [July 2011].

people are not able to read the screen's text so they need an assistive technology which repeats the text loudly or transforms it to Braille. As there is a huge variety of screen readers, users can choose the best screen reader for their needs. There are screen readers which have been developed to provide better support for different browsers; while others are open-source, free or commercial software and so on.

To carry out this presented work two screen readers have been selected: JAWS[5] and NVDA[6]. JAWS is still the primary screen reader, but its usage is being decreased while the use of NVDA and VoiceOver has been significantly increased.[7]. JAWS is commercial software and it has been improved to read websites in Internet Explorer browser and other user agent like Mozilla Firefox or Safari with a limit support. On the other hand, NVDA is an open source and free software which is able to surf on the Internet in different browsers such as: Mozilla Firefox or Internet Explorer. It is also able to show the text information of the screen reader in audio or Braille in more than twenty different languages, including Spanish.

2.4   LCMS's Accessibility Studies

Accessibility evaluations in e-learning tools can be found in literature. Some of them are centered in e-learning content accessibility. For instance, Fitchen [12] shows that most e-learning content is not accessible for disabled people. Particularly, documents with Flash technology, videoconferences or PowerPoint presentations online are usually inaccessible. Fisseler [13] suggested different solutions for these problems. For example, including alternative texts for images; provide a good structure for the content or a good color contrasts among others.

Other research works evaluate the accessibility features on e-learning tools. For instance, Power [14] evaluates accessibility of three different e-learning tools. The LCMSs evaluated are: Moodle, dotLRN[8] and Blackboard[9]. This study concludes that all of them have serious accessibility problems and none of them are in accordance to WCAG 1.0 accessibility guidelines.

Besides, other evaluations are focused on visual impairments too, as Open University evaluation, which evaluates accessibility of Moodle v1.6 [15] using JAWS 7.0 and Internet Explorer as browser. The evaluation concludes that Moodle is not accessible because there are important accessibility errors of WCAG 1.0. Recently, Buzzi [16] has evaluated accessibility of Moodle for visual impaired people using WCAG 2.0. This work shows that Moodle should improve its accessibility.

Besides, there is a study which evaluates the user experience and the user opinion, while the user fills out an assessment task created with Blackboard LMS [17].This study concludes that visual impairment users have some accessibility or usability errors to complete the online assessment.

---

[5] JAWS. Screen reader. Available in:
  http://www.freedomscientific.com/products/fs/jaws-product-page.asp [June 2010].

[6] NVDA. Screen reader. Available in: http://www.nvda-project.org/ [May 2010].

[7] Screen Reader User Survey #3 Results, Available in:
  http://webaim.org/projects/screenreadersurvey3 [July 2011].

[8] DotLRN. Screen reader Available in: http://www.dotlrn.org/ [May 2010].

[9] Blackboard. Available in: http://www.blackboard.com/ [May 2010].

The evaluation carried out in [18] is one of the last published evaluations related to the accessibility of Moodle. The paper evaluates the accessibility of three LCMSs (Moodle, Sakai and ATutor) from the point of view of four parameters: templates and themes, content editor, Javascript and tables for layout. Finally, it concludes that all LCMSs present accessibility problems according to WCAG 1.0 and ATAG 2.0 guidelines.

To our knowledge, during last years, Moodle's community has been trying to solve the accessibility problems of the tool which have been improved in its last versions. Also, the accessibility and the usability of the screen readers have been improved. So probably the results in previous accessibility studies based on previous versions of the Moodle and screen readers are obsoletes.

On the other hand, preceding accessibility studies evaluated a tiny percent of tasks of the tool and even they did not take into account the administrator profile. Furthermore, an exhaustive expert evaluation based on ATAG guidelines is not found in literature. That is why this paper presents a new accessibility evaluation of Moodle taking into account all these things.

3   Evaluation

The evaluation presented in this paper checks the accessibility of Moodle version 1.9 in the Internet Explorer 6.0 browser and in Windows XP operating system. It is important to emphasize that the version 1.9 is not the last version of Moodle; however, it is the most used nowadays (see Figure 1).

The Moodle's accessibility is evaluated in two different ways. Firstly, a user evaluation is made simulating blindness and using two different screen readers (JAWS version 10 and NVDA version 1010.2) for accessing Moodle. Secondly, it is evaluated by an accessibility expert in accordance to W3C ATAG 2.0 guidelines (because Moodle is an authoring tool) and WCAG 2.0 guidelines (because Moodle is a Web-based system and a web-site). WCAG 2.0 is the current W3C recommendation and it was used in this paper. Although ATAG 2.0 is not a W3C recommendation, it is under development. ATAG 2.0 has been chosen for the evaluation used in this work because is compatible with WCAG 2.0.

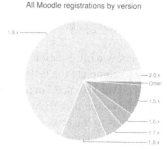

Fig. 1. Moodle Registrations by Version[10]

---

[10] Moodle. Moodle Statistics. Available in: http://moodle.org/stats/ [July 2011].

Both accessibility evaluations have centered in the accessibility evaluation of basic tasks related to the management of á course; so it has been evaluated: the administration of courses and the administration of students (the full list of task are showed in Table 1 and Table 2). However, fall outside the scope of this evaluation, is the multimedia content generated by the editing tools like what-you-see-is-what-you-get (WYSIWYG) HTML and XML editors due to a strong dependence on specific tool integrated in Moodle. It is important to specify that the evaluation carried out of generated web content have been made with the Greenie theme, which does not present accessibility barriers related to the contrast colors and its structure was easier and clearer than the default theme.

The study is centered in the evaluation of tasks that users can execute in the application. In Moodle, administrators have full permissions meanwhile teachers and students have permissions only for subsets of tasks of Moodle. That is why the evaluation are carried out with the administration profile, but the evaluations results can be applied to all the Moodle profiles (students and teachers) too.

3.1   Evaluation Simulating Blindness

This evaluation was carried out by an evaluator with technical knowledge about accessibility but without any visual disability. It is important to emphasize that there are different levels of screen reader use and some full-featured screen readers have a very steep learning curve. This evaluator could simulate a user with low-medium level. She switched off the PC screen in order to simulate blindness. After that, she tried to complete each Moodle task by NVDA and JAWS screen reader. Then, she checked if the task presents accessibility difficulties and if it can be finished by a visual impaired person.

During the evaluation, different accessibility difficulties were frequently found by the user. These difficulties are listed below and Figure 2 shows a graphic of the percentage for each error. This percentage is calculated after counting how many times the error occurs. It is divided by the number of tasks in the application:

- o **E1:** Not all text and combo boxes have associated descriptive texts.
- o **E2:** Pages refresh without asking the user.
- o **E3:** Moodle redirects the user to another page without warning the user.
- o **E4:** The Look & Feel of Moodle changes in some tasks.
- o **E5:** Tables are used for layout.
- o **E6:** Images of text are used to convey information
- o **E7:** It is difficult to know how to complete the task or it is confusing for the user
- o **E8:** There is text in English when the selected language of the tool is Spanish
- o **E9:** There is not a button that allows the user to cancel the operation.
- o **E10:** The table is not well designed so the screen reader is not able to read it well.
- o **E11:** There are not page or table headings.
- o **E12:** There are many rows in the table and it is difficult to read, s/he has to memorize the table structure.

o **E13:** There is a text that only can be modified with a Windows Editor which is not accessible. The Appendix A shows a description about it.

o **E14:** Text description is not correct.

o **E15:** The application does not check the data inserted into. It is not easy for the users to guess what the problem is.

o **E16:** The screen reader does not read the text correctly.

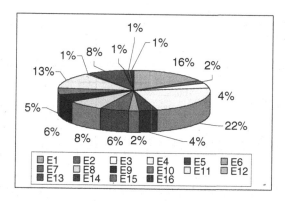

Fig. 2. Error frequency

Table 1 and 2 detail the accessibility difficulties found for each Moodle task. First column in the tables presents which profiles can make the task (A: Administrator; T: Teacher; S: Student). Second and third column present the group's task and the task's name. Fourth column presents the accessibility difficulties found during the evaluation (numbered according previous list).

Finally, last column shows if the task can be completed by the user or not. This column has three different values: *Yes,* if the task can be completed without difficulties; *Yes*,* if the task can be completed but there are accessibility problems that make difficult to complete the task for visual impaired people and *No,* if the task cannot be completed by the user.

After an exhaustive evaluation of Moodle's accessibility by using JAWS and NVDA we can conclude that the accessibility difficulties found with both screen readers are similar. The only difference found are related to the way they read tables. When a cell is empty (has not text), NVDA reads the next column and it says aloud the number's column and its content. It is useful because NVDA shows you where you are in each moment. However, in this situation JAWS does not read in which column or row is the cursor and directly reads the next column. It is confusing for users.

As Table 1 and 2 show, most of tasks are not accessible. However, they can be completed by the user because these accessibility errors are not critical or do not affect to the main purpose of the task. There are accessibility difficulties in the tool. The most frequent errors are E4 and E1. The user can be confused because the appearance of the website is not always the same and because the content is not clear. The least frequent errors are E12, E14, E15 and E16. Although they are important, these errors are insignificant because they appear once in the tool.

Table 1. Accessibility difficulties found for Moodle tasks related with reports, questions, files, groups, events, calendar, forums and profiles

User Profile	Functionality (group)	Task Name	Errors	Can it be completed?
A/T/ S	General	Login user	E1	Yes*
A/T/S	General	Change language Moodle	E1/E2	Yes*
A	Users/ Authentication	Manage authentication	E8 /E10	Yes*
A	Users/ Authentication	Email-based self-registration	E5	Yes*
A	Users/ Authentication	No login	E7	Yes*
A	Users/ Authentication	Manual accounts	E5	Yes*
A	Users/Accounts	Browse list of users	E7/E5/E9/E10	Yes*
A	Users/Accounts	Bulk user actions	E2/E11	Yes*
A	Users/Accounts	Add a new user	E6/E8/E11/E13	Yes*
A	Users/Accounts	Upload users	--	Yes
A	Users/Accounts	Upload user pictures	--	Yes
A	Users/Accounts	User profile fields	E3/E7/E13	Yes*
A	Users/Permissions	Define roles	E7/E8/E13	Yes*
A/T	Users/Permissions	Assign system roles	E1/E9	Yes*
A	Users/Permissions	User policies	E8/E9	Yes*
A/T*	Courses	Add /Edit courses	E4/E13	Yes*
A	Courses	Enrollments	E9/E11	Yes*
A/T/S	Courses	Participants	--	Yes
A/T	Courses	Backup	--	Yes
A/T	Courses	Restore a course	E5/E7/E9/ E10/E11	No
A/T	Courses	Import	E4/E5	Yes*
A/T	Courses	Reset course	E4	Yes*
A	Grades	My preferences grader report	E1/E3/E4/E6/ E7/E11	Yes*
A/T/S	Grades/View	Overview report	E1/E4	No
A/T	Grades/View	Grader report	E1/E4	Yes*
A/T/S	Grades/View	User report	E1/E4/E10	Yes*

Table 2. Accessibility difficulties found for Moodle tasks related with reports, questions, files, groups, events, calendar, forums and profiles (II)

User Profile	Functionality (group)	Task Name	Errors	Can it be completed?
A/T	Grades/Categories and Items	Simple view	E1/E4/E10	Yes*
A/T	Grades/Categories and Items	Full view	E1/E4/E8/E10/ E12	Yes*
A/T	Grades/Scales	View	E1/E4/E10/E13	Yes*
A/T	Grades/Letters	View	E1/E4/E16	Yes*
A/T	Grades/Letters	Edit	E1/E4	Yes*
A/T	Grades/Import	CSV file	E1/E4/E9	Yes*
A/T	Grades/Import	XML file	E1/E4	Yes*
A/T	Grades/Export To	Open doc spreadsheet / Plain text file/Excel spdsht/XML file	E1/E4/E9	Yes*
A/T	Reports	Filter logs	E1/E4	Yes*
A/T	Reports	Activity report	E4/ E14	Yes*
A/T	Reports	Participation report	E4/ E8/E11	Yes*
A/T	Questions	Questions bank	E3/E8/E13	Yes*
A/T	Reports	Live logs from the past hour	E2	No
A/T	Questions	Import	E4/E7	Yes*
A/T	Questions	Export	E4/E9	Yes*
A/T	Files	List of files	E1/E4/E7/E10/ E11	Yes*
A/T	Files	Upload a file	E3/E4/E8/E11	Yes*
A/T	Files	Make a folder	E1/E11/E15	Yes*
A/T	Groups	Create group	E4/E6/E11/E13	Yes*
A/T	Groups	Delete group	E4/E11	Yes*
A/T	Groups	Add/Remove users	E1/E4	Yes*
A/T/S	New event	New event	E11/E13	Yes*
A/T/S	Export calendar	Export calendar	E11	Yes*
A/T	Forums	Add / Edit a new topic	E1/E4/E11/E13	Yes*
A/T	Forums	Delete topic	E4	Yes*
A/T	Forums	Reply	E1/E3/E4/E11	Yes*
A/T/S	Profile	Change password	E4/E8/E11	Yes*
A/T/S	Profile	Edit profile	E4/E8/E11/E13	Yes*

3.2   Expert Evaluation

The evaluation presented in this paper analyses Moodle's concordance with W3C guidelines from the point of view of an expert evaluator. Due to Moodle is an authoring tool, it should be in accordance to ATAG 2.0 guidelines. Moreover, as Moodle generates Web-pages, it should compliance WCAG 2.0 guidelines. However, after the evaluation, the obtained results show that Moodle is not in accordance to ATAG 2.0 and WCAG 2.0 level A at least. These results are showed in Table 3 and Table 4 which show a summary of the Success Criteria failed by Moodle.

With reference to the ATAG 2.0, the first guideline that the tool does not accomplish is the guideline A.1.1 which specifies that the tool should achieve the WCAG 2.0 level A at least. As it will be explained later there are different accessibility barriers for the users. Also, the most important accessibility difficulties found in Moodle are related to the absence of automatic accessibility checks and the absence of accessibility support for authors (ATAG: A.3.6.4/ B.2.1.1/ B.2.2(all its testable success criteria)/ B.2.3(all its testable success criteria)/ B.3.1(all its testable success criteria) /B.3.2(all its testable success criteria) /B.3.3(all its testable success criteria) and B.3.4(all its testable success criteria)).

Table 3. ATAG 2.0 Fails

Principle	Success Criteria		
	Level A	Level AA	Level AAA
A.1	A.1.1.1; A.1.2.1	A.1.1.2	A.1.1.3
A.2	A.2.2.1; A.2.2.2 ; A.2.3.1	--	--
A.3	A.3.1.1; A.3.4.1; A.3.4.2 A.3.7.1; A.3.7.2	A.3.5.1; A.3.6.1; A.3.6.2	A.3.1.4; A.3.1.5; A.3.1.6 A.3.6.3; A.3.6.4
B.1	B.1.1.1	B.1.1.2	B.1.1.3; B.1.2.3
B.2	B.2.1.1; B.2.1.2 ; B.2.2.1 B.2.2.2; B.2.2.3; B.2.2.4 B.2.3.1; B.2.4.1; B.2.4.2 B.2.4.3; B.2.5.1; B.2.5.2	B.2.2.5; B.2.2.6; B.2.2.7 B.2.3.2; B.2.4.4; B.2.5.3 B.2.5.4	B.2.2.8; B.2.3.3; B.2.5.7 B.2.5.8; B.2.5.9
B.3	B.3.1.1; B.3.2.1; B.3.2.2 B.3.3.1; B.3.4.1	B.3.1.2; B.3.2.3; B.3.2.4 B.3.4.2	B.3.1.3; B.3.3.2; B.3.4.3

Besides, the user is not able to change website presentation because there is not any feature that allows the user to complete it (ATAG: A.2.2.1/ A.2.3.1/ A.3.1.1/ A.3.1.6/ A.3.6.3). Furthermore, shortcuts cannot be changed by the user, so sometimes these shortcuts are the same to different features (ATAG: A.3.1.5). Other accessibility difficulty is that there are different situations in which the user cannot change the structure of the Web contents (ATAG: A.3.4.1), there are themes which are not accessible and the tool does not inform the author about it (ATAG: B.2.5 (all its testable success criteria except B.2.5.5 and B.2.5.6)).

Regarding to WCAG 2.0 guidelines, table 4 summarizes which Success Criteria are failed by Moodle. There are WCAG 2.0 Success Criteria that are not implemented successfully so as a result the tool is not accessible because there are important accessibility fails such as: not all text and combo boxes have associated descriptive texts, the tool's "look and feel" is not the same along the website, images of text are used to convey information or there are not headings. Besides, these accessibility problems are worst for blind people. For example, if the tool uses tables for layout, the screen reader identify it as a table and it could be confused for the user because s/he thinks that tables are used to present tabular information. Moreover, if the table markup is used to present tabular information, it is very important to mark up data tables correctly. It should preserve relationships within the information. This information should have data in two dimensions (columns and rows), and the columns and rows must be recognizable in order to perceive the logical relationships. In other case, the user will be lost in the table because the screen reader is not able to read joined or cells without text.

Table 4. WCAG 2.0 Fails

Principle	Success Criteria		
	Level A	Level AA	Level AAA
1. Perceivable	1.4.1	1.4.4; 1.4.5	1.4.8; 1.4.9
2. Operable	2.1.1; 2.2.2; 2.4.2	2.4.5; 2.4.6	2.1.3; 2.4.10
3. Understable	3.1.1; 3.2.1; 3.2.2; 3.3.2	3.1.2; 3.2.3	3.2.5
4. Robust	4.1.2	--	--

4   Recommendations

The evaluation has showed that Moodle is not accessible for people with visual impairments, so it should be necessary to create the tool in an accessible way to solve these found problems.

In this section, we provide a set of useful recommendations to solve the accessibility barriers of Moodle. It is important to notice that if Moodle is not accessible, it does not matter if the content generated could be accessible or not.

o **Separate Content and Structure from the Presentation.** Moodle's developers should separate the content from the presentation. For instance, tables should not be used for layout and presentation elements (color, size, type of font, etc.) or control layout elements (Layout, positioning, layering, and alignment) should be included in a CSS file exclusively. As a result, the user will not have problems to change the appearance of the tool and the screen readers could read aloud the Web pages without accessibility problems.

o **Allow the User to Control the Navigation.** The user should always have the control of the Web page, so the system should not refresh the page. Major changes in the navigation of the Web page can disorient users, if they are made without awareness.

o **Provide Mechanisms to Cancel Actions and go Backwards.** Mechanisms must be available for the users to cancel or allow undoing actions.

o **Show Error Suggestions.** The user should be able to have mistakes when s/he is doing something in the platform. Thus, the user should be informed about his/her mistakes with the aim of avoid and correct them. Also, the tool should be created in usable way to avoid possible mistakes that users could have when they are using the tool. Besides, this issue is important for the user to feel comfortable when s/he is using the tool.

o **Offer Full Keyboard Access.** Users with visual impairments are not able to use the mouse so all the features should be able to be executed using the shortcuts of the keyboard too.

o **Provide Descriptive Headings to Structure the Web Page.** Another important issue is the use of headings in a right way; the webpage should have a structure with headings in a right order. Also, all pages without exception should have headings. It is especially useful for users who use screen readers because headings allow them to navigate Web pages by structure. User can read or jump directly to top level elements (<h1>), next level elements (<h2>), third level elements (<h3>), and so on. Viewing or listening to it, the headings give them a good idea of the contents and structure of the page.

o **Produce Accessible Contents.** Not only the authoring tool user interface should be accessible, the content produced by the system should be accessible too. Because of this, Moodle should provide mechanisms to create accessible content such as: evaluate the content before publish it and allow and guide the user to create accessible content. Some features are easy to change, for instance, guide the user to insert an alternative text of the image; so, if the user has not added this alternative text, then the tool should inform him/her that it is necessary. Also, it is important to make aware the users about the necessity of create accessible content and inform him/her about his/her mistakes.

o **Allow the User to Choose and Save His/Her Preferences.** The user should be able to save his/her preferences related to the layout and presentation elements. As a result, the user will be more familiar with the tool and the user will spent less time executing tasks.

Following these recommendations, the accessibility level of Moodle would be easily increased, avoiding most of accessibility barriers that are currently present in this Moodle version.

5   Conclusions and Further Research

After the results obtained of the user and expert evaluation, some conclusions have been reached.

The user evaluation shows that the difficulties found with both screen readers: JAWS and NVDA are similar. Nevertheless, there is a difference of usability between NVDA and JAWS when they read tables, NVDA reads tables in an easier way. As a result, the user is able to have a better image of the table in his/her mind.

Regarding to the expert evaluation, it demonstrates that Moodle has not a full neither partial Conformance of ATAG 2.0 nor WCAG 2.0. There are many accessibility difficulties which show that the authoring tool and the produced Web pages are not accessible. Many ATAG 2.0 and WCAG 2.0 Success Criteria are not according to accessibility level A at least, mainly because the tool does not provide automatic accessibility checkers and it does not support the user when using the authoring tool. So, it is difficult for the author to create accessible Web contents. Moreover, these accessibility problems become more critical when a person with vision problems try to access to a website.

Besides, as it has been specified the Moodle's Editor is not accessible (See Appendix); however, Moodle have changed its default editor. For the next version the Moodle Editor is TinyMCE[11]. However, we have not evaluated this Editor yet and we cannot assure if it is accessible or not.

To conclude, Moodle, as many LCMSs, is not accessible. Although Moodle's community is trying to solve this problem, there are many changes that should be easily done to be accessible for everybody regardless of their circumstances. Most of teachers and developers are focused on providing accessible resources in order to provide equal opportunities for all the students, but it is important to underline the fact that if the LCMS, is not accessible, the user could not access to it and it will not matter if the educational resources are accessible or not.

---

[11]TinyMCE. HTML Editor. Available in:
http://www.webcourseworks.com/sites/default/files/moodle-tinymce.zip [July 2011]

Currently, we are working to complete the evaluation presented in this paper. A visual-impaired person will evaluate Moodle. Moreover, it could be interesting to consider other impairments to evaluate the tool, such as: deaf, hearing loss or movement disabilities. Furthermore, we are aware that the used technologies are not enough to evaluate the tool. Thus, it should be taken into account other environments and technologies such as: other operating systems, different user agents and versions of them (web browsers and other assistive technologies), etc.

Acknowledgements. The work presented in this paper has been partially founded by MA2VICMR (S2009/TIC-1542), GEMMA (TSI-020302-2010-141) and SAGAS (TSI-020100-2010-184) research projects.

References

1. Cook, A.M., Polgar, J.M.: Assistive Technologies: Principles and Practice, 3rd edn., Saint Louis, MO Mosby (2007)
2. Moreno, L., Iglesias, A., Calvo, R., Delgado, S., Zaragoza, L.: Higher Education Institutions and Learning Management Systems: Adoption and Standardization. In: Disability Standards and Guidelines for Learning Management Systems: Evaluating Accessibility. IGI Global (2010)
3. Caniëls, M.C.J., Smeets-Verstraeten, A.H.J., van den Bosch, H.M.J.: LMS, LCMS, and e-Learning Environments Where Did the Didactics Go? In: The Challenges of Educating People to Lead in a Challenging World, pp. 401–421. Springer, Netherlands (2007)
4. Holmes, B., Gardner, J.: E-learning: concepts and practice, 1st edn. SAGE, London (2006)
5. Harman, K., Koohang, A.: Learning objects: standards, metadata, repositories & LCMS. Informing Science Press (2006)
6. W3C, WAI, Web Content Accessibility Guidelines 2.0, WCAG 2.0 (2008), http://www.w3.org/TR/WCAG10/
7. W3C, WAI, Authoring Tool Accessibility Guidelines 2.0, ATAG 2.0 (2010), http://www.w3.org/TR/2010/WD-ATAG20-20100708/
8. W3C, WAI, User Agent Accessibility Guidelines 1.0, UAAG 1.0 (2002), http://www.w3.org/TR/WAI-USERAGENT
9. IMS Access For All v2.0 Final Specification, http://www.imsglobal.org/accessibility/
10. Universal Desing for learning UDL Guidelines 1.0 (2010), http://www.udlcenter.org/aboutudl/udlguidelines
11. Elias, T.: Universal Instructional Design Principles for Moodle. Canada International Review of Research in Open and Distance Learning 11(2) (May 2010) ISSN: 1492-3831
12. Fichten, C., Asunción, J., Barile, M., Ferraro, V.: Accessibility of e-Learning and Computer and Information Technologies for Students with Visual Impairments in Postsecondary Education. Journal of Visual Impairment & Blindness 103(9), 543–557 (2009)
13. Fisseler, B., Bühler, C.: Accessible E-Learning and Educational Technology - Extending Learning Opportunities for People with Disabilities. In: Proceedings of the International Conference of "Interactive computer aided learning" ICL 2007: EPortofolio and Quality in e-Learning, Villach (Austria), September 26 -28, pp. 1–15 (2007)
14. Power, C., Petrie, H., Sakharov, V., Swallow, D.: Virtual Learning Environments: Another Barrier to Blended and E-Learning. In: Miesenberger, K., Klaus, J., Zagler, W., Karshmer, A. (eds.) ICCHP 2010. LNCS, vol. 6179, pp. 519–526. Springer, Heidelberg (2010)

220   R. Calvo, A. Iglesias, and L. Moreno

15. Moodle. Current status Moodle accesibility,
    `http://70.86.170.226/en/Moodle_Accessibility_Specification#.`
    `Results_from_Initial_OU_Jan.2Feb_2006_Evaluation`
16. Buzzi, M.C., Buzzi, M., Leporini, B.: Accessing e-Learning Systems via Screen Reader: An Example. In: Jacko, J.A. (ed.) HCI International 2009, Part IV. LNCS, vol. 5613, pp. 21–30. Springer, Heidelberg (2009)
17. Babu, R., Singh, R., Ganesh, J.: Understanding Blind Users' Web Accessibility and Usability Problems. Transactions on Human Computer Interaction 2(3), 73 (2010)
18. Iglesias, A., Moreno, L., Martínez, P., Calvo-Martin, R.: Evaluating the accessibility of three open-source learning content management systems: a comparative study. Computer Applications in Engineering Education (June 2011)

Appendix

The default editor of Moodle is a Windows editor (see Figure 3). It allows changing the text format, to include tables, to include bullets, etc. The user evaluation presented in this paper evaluates this editor, because s/he needs it to create content. However, the expert evaluation has not included the study of the editor because Moodle allows the user to change this editor by another one more accessible if s/he wants. The most similar editor is TinyMCE which is the default editor for the next Moodle's version. Also, if the user is not comfortable with this type of html editors, s/he can turn off the editor in Moodle too. Besides, the editor can be adapted for the user necessities because it is possible to change the colour, the font size and other features.

However, even if the user wants to use the editor, it is not accessible mainly because the user cannot access to all tasks using keyboard. In general, this editor has a help feature to inform the user about the shortcuts to access to all features. However, some of these shortcuts are not right because they are the same shortcut to access to different Windows features. For example, Moodle provides the shortcut *ctrl+P* to change width print, it is right because it is an alternative to access to this feature, but there is problem, Windows SO uses this shortcut to show print settings. Thus the user cannot complete the task successfully because s/he cannot use all features.

Also, this editor has combo boxes which have not associated descriptive texts and as a result the screen reader cannot read it right. Another important accessibility problem is that the component uses images to convey information instead of using descriptive text.

Fig. 3. Default HTML editor of Moodle 1.9 Version

Author Index